Supersizing Urban America

Supersizing Urban America

How Inner Cities Got Fast Food with Government Help

Chin Jou

THE UNIVERSITY OF CHICAGO PRESS | CHICAGO AND LONDON

The University of Chicago Press, Chicago 60637
The University of Chicago Press, Ltd., London
© 2017 by The University of Chicago

26 25 24 23 22 21 20 19 18 17   1 2 3 4 5

ISBN-13: 978-0-226-92192-1 (cloth)
ISBN-13: 978-0-226-92194-5 (e-book)
DOI: 10.7208/chicago/9780226921945.001.0001

Library of Congress Cataloging-in-Publication Data

Names: Jou, Chin, 1979– author.
Title: Supersizing urban America : how inner cities got fast food with government help / Chin Jou.
Description: Chicago ; London : The University of Chicago Press, 2017. | Includes bibliographical
    references and index.
Identifiers: LCCN 2016015884 | ISBN 9780226921921 (cloth : alk. paper) | ISBN 9780226921945 (e-book)
Subjects: LCSH: Obesity—Social aspects—United States. | Convenience foods—Social aspects—
    United States. | Convenience foods—Economic aspects—United States. | Fast food restaurants—
    United States—History. | Inner cities—United States. | African Americans—Food. | Nutrition
    policy—United States. | Urban policy—United States—History—20th century.
Classification: LCC RA645.O23 J68 2017 | DDC 362.1963/9800973—dc23 LC record available at https://
    lccn.loc.gov/2016015884

♾ This paper meets the requirements of ANSI/NISO Z39.48-1992 (Permanence of Paper).

CONTENTS

Combating Obesity and Subsidizing Fast Food Expansion

> For more than three decades the fast food industry has used the Small
> Business Administration (SBA) to finance new restaurants . . . A 1981
> study by the General Accounting Office found that the SBA had guar-
> anteed 18,000 franchise loans between 1967 and 1979, subsidizing the
> launch of new Burger Kings and McDonald's, among others . . . In
> 1996, the SBA guaranteed almost $1 billion in loans to new franchises.
> More of these loans went to the fast food industry than to any other
> industry. Almost six hundred new fast food restaurants, represent-
> ing fifty-two different national chains, were launched in 1996 thanks
> to government-backed loans. The chain that benefited the most from
> SBA loans was Subway. Of the 755 new Subways opened that year, 109
> relied upon the U.S. government for financing.[1]

The idea for this book began with this excerpt from Eric Schlosser's *Fast Food Nation* (2001).[2] While rereading the book in 2010,
I was fixated on this one, brief, stunning section. The federal
government helped underwrite the fast food industry? *Really*? Did
Schlosser know more about the history of the SBA and the fast food industry? Could he direct me to more sources? Given that the SBA was incidental to Schlosser's story, it was not surprising when he related that
all he knew on the matter was what he had included in *Fast Food Nation*.

Fast Food Nation did, however, lead me to another source—a 1997

Washington Post opinion piece titled "For Big Franchisers, Money to Go; Is the SBA Dispensing Corporate Welfare?" The essay, written by Scott A. Hodge, then a research scholar at the Heritage Foundation, a conservative think tank in Washington, D.C., argued that SBA loans to franchisees of fast food chains owned by massive corporations, including multinational conglomerates, were not only a perversion of the agency's mission to assist *small* businesses, but also meant that the federal government—and by extension, taxpayers—assumed the financial risks for the continued expansion of mammoth corporations like McDonald's, Burger King, and even General Motors, Ford Motor, and Standard Oil.[3] After reading this 1,777-word piece, I emailed Hodge, who had become the president of another Washington think tank. Hodge politely replied, noting that it had been many years since he investigated the SBA and its little-known gift to corporate franchises. His memory on the issue was understandably fuzzy. And like Schlosser, he had already published what he knew.

No matter. The relative dearth of information on federal sponsorship of the fast food industry simply meant that I had identified a new research project. But unlike Hodge, I was not intent on pursuing the "corporate welfare" angle of SBA largesse for fast food companies, although that was certainly provocative. And in contrast to Schlosser, I was not especially interested in exploring the "dark side" of the fast food industry. He had already nailed that.

Instead, my mind immediately leapt to the history of the American obesity epidemic—a subject I had been studying as a postdoctoral fellow in the Office of History at the National Institutes of Health (NIH) in Bethesda, Maryland. The obesity epidemic had been a particularly hot topic among American biomedical researchers since roughly 2000. According to political scientist J. Eric Oliver, the author of *Fat Politics: The Real Story Behind America's Obesity Epidemic*, this was because the Centers for Disease Control and Prevention (CDC) had been circulating maps showing that obesity was sweeping through the country.[4] These maps made their way to obesity researchers, whose scientific journal articles began routinely describing obesity as an epidemic. Science journalists combing through medical journals would subsequently file thousands of print articles and television news reports heralding the scourge of obesity.[5] By the early 2000s, one had to be living under a proverbial rock not to have gotten the memo that America was in the midst of an obesity epidemic.

While many Americans may have already instinctively regarded traditional fast food fare as fattening, the popular association of fast food with the obesity epidemic in particular seems to have crystallized in the early-to-mid 2000s. In 2002, two New York teenagers sued McDonald's for their obesity in *Pelman v. McDonald's*. Although the lawsuit was widely ridiculed and dismissed by a federal judge in 2003, that such litigation would even be initiated suggested an increasingly common conflation between fast food and obesity. Schlosser's *Fast Food Nation* had also primed Americans to become more critical of fast food more broadly. But perhaps the most salient cultural phenomenon to reinforce popular associations between fast food and obesity in that era was the hit documentary, *Super Size Me*. Released in 2004, *Super Size Me* featured documentary filmmaker Morgan Spurlock consuming a McDonald's diet for one month, which resulted in significant weight gain and a catalogue of other physical, mental, and sexual side effects. The film earned Spurlock the Directing Award at the Sundance Film Festival, was nominated for an Academy Award for Best Documentary, and had grossed $11.5 million domestically within five months of its release. Soon after *Super Size Me* was feted at Sundance, McDonald's retired its "supersize" menu option for fries and sodas; the company maintained that its decision had "nothing to do with [the film] whatsoever."[6]

Today, fast food is synonymous with the obesity epidemic in the public imagination. Just perform a Google Image search for "obesity." You will find photos of hulking flesh, bathroom scales, tape measures around bulging midsections, and fast food—burgers, fries, soda, pizza, and hot dogs.[7] With their ample calories, refined carbohydrates, saturated fat, salt, and sugar (even in "savory" items), fast food also connotes "unhealthy" and "heart attacks." There is even a Las Vegas fast food restaurant predicated on the popular association of fast food with heart attacks: Heart Attack Grill. Its menu includes the Quadruple Bypass Burger freighted with four half-pound beef patties, eight slices of cheese, and plenty of pig fat—twenty strips of bacon and lard liberally smeared on its bun.[8] At nearly 10,000 calories, this caricature of a burger goads its most intrepid, hedonistic (or masochistic) customers, as if to say, "I dare you."[9] More surprisingly, McDonald's, which is considerably less comfortable embracing a reputation as a purveyor of unhealthy foods, was apparently informing its own employees that fast food was unhealthy! An employee resources website called the McResource Line contained a post that read: "While convenient and economical for a busy lifestyle, fast foods are typically high in calories, fat, saturated fat, sugar, and salt and may put people at risk for becoming overweight."[10] This warning about fast food was accompanied, moreover, by a generic photograph of a hamburger and fries—McDonald's signature menu items! Another unexpectedly candid post on the McResource website cautioned employees that large portion sizes at fast food restaurants invited overeating, and that "it is hard to eat a healthy diet when you eat at fast-food restaurants often."[11]

The irony of these messages did not go unnoticed. Company spokespersons quickly distanced McDonald's from the McResource Line site, pointing out that its content was generated by a "third party vendor" (the McDonald's imprimatur on the website evidently notwithstanding). And as soon as media reports of the website's curious existence surfaced, the company promptly removed the site.[12] A similar embarrassment had occurred some two decades earlier, when reports of an internal McDonald's memorandum related to nutrition surfaced. The memo conceded: "We can't really address or defend nutrition. We don't sell nutrition and people don't come to McDonald's for nutrition."[13]

It would seem, then, that the federal government would view McDonald's, Burger King, Wendy's, Kentucky Fried Chicken, Taco Bell,

Pizza Hut, and all the other familiar fast food chains as threats to public health and incompatible with its aim of vanquishing the obesity epidemic. After all, obesity has become the public health crisis du jour, and the federal government has been leading the charge for the last decade.[14] Testifying before a congressional committee in 2003, then–Surgeon General Richard Carmona declared obesity the "fastest-growing cause of disease and death in America."[15] During a speech at the University of South Carolina three years later, Carmona would warn that "obesity is the terror within,"—a threat that "will dwarf 9-11 or any other terrorist attempt."[16]

Numerous other federal entities have joined the Office of the Surgeon General in sounding the alarm on the obesity epidemic. In 2010, the White House announced the creation of a new task force to combat childhood obesity. Headed by First Lady Michelle Obama, the Let's Move initiative allocates $10 billion over ten years for antiobesity programs. Taking an ambitious four-pronged approach to ending childhood obesity "within a generation," the campaign calls for more physical activity, improved access to fresh fruits and vegetables in underserved areas, nutrition information for parents to implement healthy eating habits at home, and healthier school lunches.[17] Readers may already be aware of all this; not since Nancy Reagan's 1980s War on Drugs has a first lady's social cause elicited such extensive media coverage.

Congress is likewise in on the war against obesity. With the goal of slimming down America's schoolchildren, it passed the Healthy, Hunger-Free Kids Act of 2010. The law authorized $4.5 billion for the implementation of new nutrition guidelines for schools nationwide. The new nutrition standards meant that two-percent chocolate milk was out. Skim milk, more fresh fruits and vegetables, and calorie-restricted meals were in, to the exasperation of some schoolchildren.[18]

Congress also funds obesity research by authorizing the annual budget of the NIH, the agency that carries out its own biomedical research and allocates grants to external researchers. (The agency's budget was

$30.3 billion for fiscal year 2015.)[19] To underscore its commitment to mitigating the obesity epidemic, the NIH created an Obesity Research Task Force in 2003. In 2004 and again in 2011, the agency also published a "Strategic Plan for NIH Obesity Research." To help realize its goal of "accelerat[ing] progress in obesity research across the NIH," the agency underwrites research on the molecular mechanisms of weight regulation, the efficacy of potential public policy interventions, and countless other investigations directly or indirectly related to obesity.[20] According to its own estimates, the NIH earmarked $843 million for obesity research in fiscal year 2014—a sum that exceeded its 2014 funding for Alzheimer's ($562 million) and coronary heart disease ($471 million).[21] As much as the federal government has dedicated to obesity research, the United States spends far more treating obesity-related conditions. According to a 2012 report by the Institute of Medicine, obesity costs the United States a hefty $190 billion per year.[22]

Given all these efforts to combat obesity, why does the federal government, via the Small Business Administration, continue to assist the fast food industry's expansion? This is an important, neglected question that should be raised in discussions of how federal policies facilitate what the Duke University public policy school dean Kelly D. Brownell has designated a "toxic food environment," or one in which diet-related diseases flourish with the easy availability of cheap and vigorously marketed foods loaded with fat, sugar, and calories.[23]

But blaming the federal government for helping to create and perpetuate the obesity epidemic that it is now combating, and exposing the inconsistencies of its policies, are not the primary objectives of this book. There are, after all, many instances of competing objectives across different federal agencies, or even within the same federal entity. (The U.S. Department of Agriculture, or USDA, is particularly notorious for instituting food and nutrition programs seemingly at odds with one another.)[24] Rather, this book draws attention to the history of a slice of America's contemporary food environment—that of urban fast food restaurants in predominantly African-American neighborhoods that are now inundated with fast food and marked by high rates of obesity.

◆◆◆

The federal government has shaped the American diet in a number of ways. The work of writer and agricultural reform evangelist Michael Pollan has shown us how farm policies have dramatically changed the way Americans eat since the mid-1970s (and not for the better, in the view of many nutrition experts).[25] The Nixon administration responded to the energy crisis of 1973 and ensuing rising food prices by subsidizing the large-scale production of commodity crops like corn, soy, and wheat. The 1973 Farm Bill encouraged agricultural producers to grow "fencerow to fencerow."[26] Nixon's agriculture secretary Earl Butz was said to have advised farmers to "get big or get out."[27]

This worked. Food prices fell. But what about the unprecedented quantities of commodity crops being produced? They were converted into ingredients like oils, emulsifiers, proteins, and sweeteners like the now-maligned high-fructose corn syrup. These ingredients made their way into sodas and innumerable processed high-calorie foods that, according to author Greg Critser, help make Americans "the fattest people in the world."[28] Compounding this, greater quantities of cheap ingredients meant larger portion sizes of everything from Doritos to Slurpees at the 7-Eleven. So while we now know about the history of government agricultural subsidies that have helped render processed foods made from commodities like corn, soy, and wheat more inexpensive, considerably less attention has been focused on government support of the fast food restaurants that sell items such as beverages sweetened by high-fructose corn syrup, and beef patties made from cattle fattened up with corn in industrial feedlots.[29]

The USDA has also more directly promoted the consumption of foods that nutrition advocates consider unhealthy. In 2010, the *New York Times*'s Michael Moss reported that three years earlier a USDA-funded dairy promotion trade group called Dairy Management Inc. (the group responsible for the iconic "Got Milk?" ads) had been partnering with fast food giants such as Domino's, Pizza Hut, Taco Bell, Wendy's, and Burger King to develop and market recipes stuffed with even more cheese than what these chains' menu offerings already contained. The USDA saw these efforts to promote cheese consumption as necessary to support the U.S. dairy industry, which had accumulated a surplus of whole milk and milk fat when Americans began to eschew full-fat milk for low- and nonfat varieties.[30] So any health benefits American consumers might have gained from replacing whole milk with skim was negated when they bit into fast food pizza that was now topped with more cheese than ever before, and that now increasingly had mozzarella baked *inside* the crust.

Then there is industry lobbying. As the New York University nutrition and food studies professor Marion Nestle has shown in *Food Politics: How the Food Industry Influences Nutrition and Health*, both elected officials and administrators of federal agencies like the USDA, the Food and Drug Administration (FDA), and the Federal Trade Commission (FTC), have often capitulated to the food and beverage industry's mighty lobbying efforts to defeat any measures that might interfere with their ability to market and sell their products.[31] And these products, according to Michael Moss and former FDA commissioner David Kessler, are engineered by food companies to be addictive, with precise formulations of salt, fat, and sugar being central to this enterprise.[32]

The food industry's privileged access to federal policymakers and regulators, as well as the revolving door between government regulators and industry lobbyists, is not new. While agribusiness and other food interests have become more organized, sophisticated, and deep-pocketed in recent years (with help along the way from friendly campaign finance laws and Supreme Court decisions like 2010's *Citizens United v. Federal Election Commission*), they have been flexing their political persuasion muscles for decades. As early as the 1970s, the consumer advocate Ralph Nader's team of muckraking investigators (dubbed

"Nader's Raiders") had published reports indicting the FDA and USDA for failing to ensure the safety of America's food supply. According to Nader's Raiders, improper ties between the two agencies on one hand, and the food industry and agribusiness on the other, were to blame.[33]

The food industry and agribusiness have also had a long history of directly influencing lawmakers. In 1977, South Dakota senator George McGovern was the head of the Senate Select Committee on Nutrition and Human Needs (which existed from 1968 to 1977). McGovern's committee issued a highly publicized report called *Dietary Goals for the United States*. Among its many dietary recommendations, the McGovern Report, as it was known colloquially, encouraged Americans to "reduce consumption of meat."[34] Ranching and beef interests were incensed. They advised McGovern to reconsider disseminating this morsel of dietary advice; if he demurred, they promised political retribution. McGovern was rightly respected for his integrity and circumspection on many other issues, but the cattle industry, which was an especially powerful force in South Dakota politics, triumphed. The following year, McGovern's committee revised *Dietary Goals for the United States* to read, "Choose meats, poultry and fish that will reduce saturated-fat intake."[35]

Cattle interests were a formidable lot, as Oprah Winfrey would learn the hard way some twenty years after McGovern. In 1998, a group of Texas cattle ranchers sued Winfrey for defamation when she proclaimed that she would no longer consume burgers. Howard F. Lyman, a rancher–turned–animal rights activist, had appeared on *The Oprah Winfrey Show* charging that ranchers sometimes fed cattle ground-up livestock—a practice Lyman warned could lead to the spread of mad cow disease. The Texas ranchers sued Winfrey for $12 million in damages, alleging that the popular talk-show host's response to Lyman's revelation ("It has just stopped me cold from eating another burger!") was responsible for a subsequent nosedive in prices for cattle futures.[36] This time, the cattle interests lost. A Texas jury decided that Winfrey did not owe them a cent.

In the 1970s, however, there was another key instance of "the road not taken" in federal nutrition policy during McGovern's tenure in the Senate. Decades before the recent push toward calorie labeling and First Lady Michelle Obama's Let's Move initiative, scattered voices within the federal government raised concerns about the healthfulness of fast food and its role in rising rates of obesity. These concerns, however, were ultimately ephemeral and did not result in any pressure on the industry to change its marketing practices. During nutrition labeling hearings at the Nutrition Subcommittee of the Senate Committee on Agriculture, Nutrition, and Forestry (the successor to the Senate Select Committee on Nutrition and Human Needs) in February 1979, McGovern queried spokespersons from McDonald's, Kentucky Fried Chicken, Pizza Hut, and the National Restaurant Association about the fast food industry's responses—if any—to obesity and hypertension.[37] A representative of the National Restaurant Association responded to McGovern by promising that restaurants would heed customer requests for smaller portion sizes, reduce the amount of salt in their food, and offer more fresh fruits, vegetables, and sugar substitutes. McGovern took industry representatives at their word.

Years later, in January 1991, Representative Mervyn Dymally (D-CA), along with ten congressional cosponsors, authored a bill (H.R. 82) to establish a United States Commission on Obesity. The bill would have charged the Obesity Commission with, among other tasks, "study[ing] the influence of the fast-food industry on obesity and the diet habits of the United States population."[38] Perhaps as a consequence of the influence of the fast food industry on lawmakers in the early 1990s and the relatively low priority accorded to obesity in Washington at the time, Dymally's bill suffered the fate of many legislative initiatives. It was buried in subcommittee (in this case the House Subcommittee on Health and the Environment) and largely forgotten. As obesity became a more salient public health issue and led to concrete policy proposals affecting food and beverage companies, their industry lobbying arms have made use of substantial war chests to defeat any proposals perceived as threatening. In 2009, for example, PepsiCo Incorporated, the Coca-

Cola Company, the American Beverage Association, and a group representing bottlers spent $40 million to dissuade perpetually campaigning
members of Congress from enacting any legislation that might reduce
soda sales.[39] That particular year saw a proposed soda tax intended to
reduce children's sugar consumption and, by extension, childhood obesity rates. The soda tax proposal perished.[40]

This book, then, exists as part of a broader conversation on obesity
and the history of the federal government's relationship to the food industry in the last few decades. There remains an important, relatively
neglected issue within this literature, however. Consider that the media, politicians, and even public health officials often refer to the obesity
epidemic as a blanket phenomenon. The very word *epidemic* suggests
that obesity is extraordinarily widespread. It is true that roughly one-
third of all Americans are clinically obese. (The definition of "clinically
obese" is a body mass index, or weight-to-height ratio, of 30 or over;
whether the BMI should be used as a criterion for health is beyond the
purview of this book.)[41]

But certain groups of Americans are far more acutely affected by the
obesity epidemic than others. In some communities, especially those
that are both predominantly minority *and* low-income, a majority of
residents is overweight (defined as a BMI between 25 and 29.9) or obese.
But other, more privileged enclaves have hardly been touched by this
"epidemic." Comparing the obesity rates of African Americans with
those of whites illustrates some of the racial discrepancies of obesity
in the United States. According to 2012 data from the Department of
Health and Human Service's Office of Minority Health, 25.7 percent of
African-American children between the ages of six and seventeen are
obese, compared to 14.6 percent in their white counterparts.[42] (These
figures are informed by disproportionate rates of poverty among minority children.)[43] Racial disparities in obesity among adult men are less
pronounced, but nevertheless discernible. Among African-American
and white men eighteen years and older, rates of obesity are 31.6 percent
and 27.5 percent, respectively.[44] Disparities among women are the stark-

est.[45] Obesity affects African-American women more than any other demographic in the United States. Their rate of obesity is 41.2 percent, compared to 24.5 percent for white women.[46]

This attention to disproportionate rates of obesity among African-American women and children is not meant to pathologize these groups or to stigmatize large bodies. Scholars such as Julie Guthman, Amy Erdman Farrell, and April Michelle Herndon have justly pointed to the ways in which public health campaigns against obesity can inadvertently supply a health rationale for pathologizing large, nonconforming bodies.[47] This can further stigmatize the obese, reinforcing the notion that they have only themselves to blame for their weight. It is imperative that we condemn all forms of discrimination against obese Americans. And in the same way that stereotypes relating to race, gender, and sexual orientation are rebuked, tired stereotypes representing the obese as lazy and gluttonous should not be tolerated. As various authors and activists within the fat acceptance movement have underscored, it is important to recognize that plenty of overweight people lead active lives, and being slightly overweight may even be associated with a lower risk of death.[48]

At the same time, however, it is difficult to deny that public health authorities are also right that being significantly obese places one at risk of developing conditions such as type 2 diabetes, sleep apnea, heart disease, stroke, osteoarthritis, and some cancers (e.g., cancers of the breast, endometrium, colon, kidney, gallbladder, and liver).[49] These conditions can, of course, adversely affect quality of life and reduce life expectancy.

I also note the socioeconomic and racial dimensions of the obesity epidemic because references to "the obesity epidemic" in the media and public health campaigns often treat obesity as an across-the-board problem. This can obscure the systemic inequalities and historical circumstances that inform why certain groups of people are more likely to be obese than others. Accordingly, a key point to take away from this book is that the current disproportionate consumption of fast food by residents of inner-city African-American communities is not a function of any longstanding cultural preferences for fast food. I propose instead that a confluence of historical developments contributed to the inundation of fast food in urban communities, and that heavy—sometimes insidious—advertising reinforced African Americans' relationship with fast food chains.

In making this claim, I am not suggesting that consumers are devoid of agency. Rather, I am emphasizing that it is necessary to consider how food environments that can constrain consumers' dietary choices came into being, especially if those consumers have limited income, few affordable alternatives for sustenance, and no easy transportation to access healthier food environments. To insist that fast food consumers *choose* to be unhealthy is to presume that all Americans are confronted with the same economic and geographic circumstances. It is no doubt easier, however, for Americans to abstain from fast food if they have means and reside in neighborhoods with few or no fast food outlets, than it would be for car-less, lower-income Americans whose neighborhoods are saturated with fast food. Legal scholar Andrea Freeman gets to the heart of the matter when she points out that "lack of options and resources severely limits the ability to exercise choice."[50]

In underscoring some of the structural explanations as to why certain groups of Americans may be more likely to rely on fast food than others, this book also contests the view that frequent consumers of fast food are lazy, unresourceful, and even immoral. As the food studies scholar Charlotte Biltekoff observes, a number of contemporary healthy eating and cook-from-scratch torchbearers seem to have made moral judgments on those who eat fast food and its similarly stigmatized cousin, processed food.[51] Biltekoff points to bestselling author Barbara Kingsolver and food activist/restauranteur Alice Waters—both of whom are no doubt well-intentioned—as examples. Kingsolver, who in 2007 published a book describing her family's one-year experiment consuming only homegrown and locally produced food, has implied that not cooking (and not consuming locally grown foods) constitutes a neglect of one's civic duty: "Cooking is good citizenship. It's the only way to get serious about putting locally raised foods in your diet, which keeps farmland healthy and grocery money in the neighborhood."[52]

Alice Waters, a matriarch of the contemporary local and organic foods movement and the cofounder of the Berkeley, California, foodie temple Chez Panisse, has been even more direct in her conflation of fast food with moral failure. She has declared that, "when you buy fast food, you get fast food values."[53] Some of these "fast food values," according to Waters, include the ideas that "it doesn't matter where the food actually comes from" and "work is to be avoided at all costs."[54] That such assumptions might be interpreted as elitist and patronizing is obvious, and critics, perhaps none with as much acerbic verve as *The Atlantic's* B. R. Myers, have already taken Waters, foodie culture, and the organic and locavore movements, to task.[55]

More importantly for the purposes of this book, I want to emphasize that the foodie disdain for "fast food values" elides the ways in which historical circumstances, government policies, and targeted, relentless food industry advertising helped create and reinforce fast food consumption in America's low-income urban communities. To this end, the first four chapters explain how predominantly African-American urban communities went from having no fast food chain restaurants to being deluged with them, and how the federal government figured into that transformation. The fifth chapter relates some of the ways that fast food companies appealed to American-American consumers once their restaurants had established a presence in black communities. Each of these five chapters illuminates a particular dimension of the historical context that gave rise to fast food's foothold in urban America. In the last three chapters, I report on how fast food has figured into more contemporary public policies, discuss recent research on links between fast food and obesity, and offer some proposals for what policymakers can do to promote dietary health amid the fast food environment.

CHAPTERS AND CAVEATS

Chapter 1 begins with the urban riots of the mid to late 1960s. From 1965 to 1968, rioters in places such as the Watts section of Los Angeles, Newark, Detroit, Baltimore, Washington, DC, and Chicago demanded government redress of chronic unemployment, poverty, poor housing, police brutality, and racial discrimination. One of the ways the federal government responded to these demands for jobs and economic development in African-American communities was to guarantee loans for black-owned fast food restaurants (and other businesses) in inner cities through the Commerce Department and SBA loan programs. Fast food companies welcomed this development. They had been appealing for government largesse for their minority franchisee recruitment programs as early as 1964. They were also especially keen to open fast food outlets in America's urban centers.

Chapter 2 discusses how the fast food industry—exemplified by the insatiably ambitious McDonald's chief Ray Kroc—looked to expand beyond suburbs and highways as those sites were becoming increasingly saturated with restaurants. McDonald's and other chains sought to establish a presence in small towns and other areas once considered to be risky or only marginally profitable, such as inner cities.[56] By the early 1970s, the major fast food chains had discovered how profitable their urban outlets could be, so they blitzed cities with more of their restaurants. To help underwrite their expansion to African-American neighborhoods, fast food companies recruited minority franchisees who would be eligible for federal assistance through minority entrepreneurship and urban renewal programs.

As chapter 3 explains, this strategy promoted a number of interests: the federal government could claim to promote what Richard Nixon called "black capitalism," the fast food industry could expand into untested markets while transferring the burden of actual financial risk onto the SBA, and African-American entrepreneurs could access start-up capital to open fast food franchises. While gains in SBA-aided minority entrepreneurship were ultimately modest, federal programs were nonetheless part of a remaking of inner cities as fast food havens.

Chapter 4 examines some of the "pushes and pulls" behind the fast food industry's recruitment of minority franchisees. Since the late 1960s, African-American community activists had been calling on businesses to be locally owned, so diversifying was in the interests of fast food companies' public relations and their bottom line. And as some African-American entrepreneurs speculated, fast food companies also looked to them as a way to outsource the everyday risks of opening restaurants in low-income, high-crime neighborhoods. This chapter also considers that there have been limits to fast food companies' efforts to diversify, as they have been dogged by accusations of redlining (confining African-American franchise owners to outlets in low-income black neighborhoods).

Chapter 5 chronicles the fast food industry's robust diversity strategies on the consumer end. In the early 1970s, African Americans were still very much disproportionately represented among America's poor. But the same period also saw the expansion of the black middle class. Madison Avenue and its corporate clients took notice. The fast food industry, along with purveyors of countless other goods and services, vied for shares of the growing black consumer market. Since then, the fast food industry has continued to be unrelenting in its appeals to young urban African Americans—a point this chapter underscores to suggest that it is no accident that this market came to be counted among fast food companies' most reliable consumers.

The remaining three chapters focus on more recent developments. Chapter 6 surveys the various ways in which government policies of the last two decades have intersected with the fast food industry. Many of these policies, particularly those at the federal level, have benefitted fast food companies. Such policies have included allowing the major fast food chains into America's public schools in the mid-1990s and the introduction of legislation to shield fast food companies from lawsuits for obesity in the mid-2000s. Meanwhile, substantive attempts to regulate the industry have been spearheaded by a number of progressive city and state governments. Examples have included San Francisco's attempt to ban toys from fast food children's meals in 2011 and various cities' ongoing efforts to raise the minimum wage for fast food workers.

Chapter 7 unpacks links between fast food and obesity, noting studies that both reinforce associations between BMI and fast food, as well as a few studies challenging conventional wisdom about fast food's role in obesity. Ultimately, however, this chapter emphasizes that while obesity's causes are multifaceted and complex, it is difficult to discount the fact that many urban, low-income African-American neighborhoods are both saturated with fast food and disproportionately affected by the obesity epidemic. This book concludes by outlining possible ways to mitigate this problem through policy interventions designed to facilitate healthy eating among residents in underserved areas.

Before moving on to these chapters, a few caveats are in order. While chapter 3 discusses the minority enterprise assistance and recruitment efforts of two federal agencies—the SBA and the Commerce Department's Office of Minority Business Enterprise (OMBE)—it is impossible to determine the total number of black-owned fast food franchises that have resulted from these agencies' minority outreach efforts. Historian Jonathan J. Bean notes that the SBA "began informally collecting racial statistics on borrowers as early as 1964" in order to provide the agency with a "crude measure of civil rights compliance and [highlight] the importance of reaching out to the minority community."[57] The SBA's willingness to share such informal statistics is another matter. The agency reports that documents identifying borrowers' race and other personal information are classified, and that records of loan guarantees are destroyed after borrowers fulfill their loan obligations.[58] The figures that this book cites are therefore limited.

Similarly, various figures and information on fast food companies' internal operations are notoriously difficult to access given that I am an independent investigator, and this book is not commissioned by any fast food interest. As a McDonald's representative informed me in a commendably expeditious, but fruitless, reply to one of my inquiries: "[T]he information you are specifically requesting is considered proprietary business information. I'm sorry I cannot answer your specific questions."[59] To fill these voids, I have tried my best to cull information from other sources, such as franchising industry publications, contemporaneous periodicals, memoirs from fast food industry figures, and publicly accessible records of the SBA and Commerce Department.

Finally, a note on the geographical and chronological scope of this book. The focus here is not on individual U.S. cities per se, but on American cities more broadly. While every city has dealt with a unique set of historical circumstances, this book is concerned with these cities' general commonalities and shared histories, such as having been sites of urban rioting. Urban riots also inform the chronology of this book, which starts roughly in the mid-1960s because that period witnessed the beginnings of a wave of urban unrest, prompting federal officials to consider African-American economic development in riot-torn cities. For a variety of reasons that will be described in the next chapter, inner-city fast food franchises were seen as one of the potential antidotes to more unrest.

ONE

Solving Urban Challenges Through Fast Food

In 2009, the Subway sandwich chain received 142 loan guarantees worth nearly $27.7 million from the federal government's Small Business Administration. Subway is just one fast food company (even if it is the fast food chain with the most franchises worldwide). Meanwhile, in that same year, all the combined grocery stores in the United States appear to have received a total of seven SBA loan guarantees worth $4.1 million.[1] Such disparities in federal loan support can help shed light on the question of why there are so many fast food restaurants relative to grocery stores in America's inner cities.[2]

There are, of course, other relevant considerations. Perhaps the most obvious explanation as to why fast food restaurants tend to outnumber grocery stores in America's inner cities is that fast food is generally more profitable than the grocery business. Recent media reports indicate that margins for individual fast food franchisees are in the neighborhood of 4 to 6 percent, while those for grocery stores are "razor thin," averaging just 1.3 percent after taxes.[3] Grocery stores also often occupy more square feet than fast food outlets. In city centers where space is limited, prospective grocers may be stymied by fewer real estate options, zoning restrictions, lack of available parking for customers, and costly leases.

And then there are fears of crime in urban areas. Despite reduced levels of violent crime in a number of America's major cities in recent years, grocery entrepreneurs may still be reluctant to open stores in inner cities because of concerns about robberies and vandalism. Mitigating these concerns requires considerable outlays, including installing security equipment and taking out insurance premiums that are especially costly for entrepreneurs doing business in "risky" areas. Of course, such costs of doing business in urban areas also apply to the fast food industry. But perhaps higher fast food margins make up for these expenses, whereas thinner grocery margins are insufficient to offset these costs.[4]

Fast food's profitability relative to grocery retailing may not entirely account for its prevalence on inner-city blocks, however. There are other structural contributing factors. Consider, for instance, that national fast food companies often rely on individual franchisees to distribute their products. This means that individual fast food outlets representing regional and national chains have been able to qualify for federal loan guarantee programs for "small businesses." This contrasts with leading national grocery retailers, many of which are owned and operated by corporations rather than individual franchisees. Such an ownership structure often precludes grocery retailers from receiving the same government small business loan guarantees that are available to the fast food industry.

More specifically, the SBA, which guarantees loans of up to $3.75 million that individual businesses can borrow from commercial banks, imposes eligibility criteria on qualifying businesses' participation in its 7(a) Loan Program.[5] To participate in the 7(a) Loan Program, the agency's "primary program for helping start-up and existing small businesses," qualifying businesses have to fit the definition of "small."[6] According to current SBA regulations, this means that the annual gross receipts of qualifying grocery stores and supermarkets may not exceed $30 million, and that fast food and "limited service" restaurants cannot gross more than $10 million.[7] These regulations favor national fast food companies over supermarket chains because many individual fast food restaurants are owned by franchisees and gross less than $10 million, while the majority of individual supermarkets representing national chains are owned by companies, conglomerates, and private equity firms that gross in excess of $30 million.

The Subway sandwich chain exemplifies how the fast food franchising model has been ideal for participation in the SBA's 7(a) Loan Program. With over 44,000 outlets as of 2016, Subway has more restaurant locations than any other fast food company in the world.[8] All of its restaurants are franchised, with its U.S. locations pulling in an average of $452,000 in sales as of 2010.[9] Not coincidentally, Subway has been far and away the leading recipient of SBA loan guarantees in recent years.

Over at McDonald's, the company reports that "more than 80%" of its outlets are currently owned and operated by franchisees.[10] According to the fast food industry trade publication QSR (quick service restaurants), the average U.S. McDonald's restaurant took in annual sales of $2.4 million in 2010.[11] At Kentucky Fried Chicken (part of the Yum! Brands conglomerate), 13,489 of the company's 18,198 locations were individually owned and operated as of 2013, with the average U.S. outlet (both franchised and corporate-owned) raking in $933,000 in annual sales in 2010.[12] Similarly, two of the other major fast food chains, Burger King (part of the global private equity firm 3G Capital as of 2010) and Wendy's, have announced plans to transfer 100 percent and 85 percent of restaurant ownership to franchisees, respectively.[13] Like the other fast food chains, industry figures from 2010 showed that Burger King and Wendy's franchisees registered annual sales under the SBA eligibility threshold of $10 million ($1.2 million and $1.4 million, respectively).[14]

Unlike the fast food industry, most of the country's leading grocery retailers are not franchised and, given their billion-dollar gross sales, ineligible for SBA 7(a) loan guarantees.[15] Led by Walmart, which grossed $422 billion worldwide in 2010, these companies include Target, Costco, Publix, Aldis, Trader Joe's, Whole Foods, and a handful of other supermarket chains.[16] While a few national and regional grocery chains, such as IGA, Piggly Wiggly, Giant Eagle, Save-A-Lot, and ShopRite, are franchised, these stores account for a relatively small segment of the grocery sector. (Queries to two of the nation's large supermarket chains,

Kroger and Safeway, regarding whether they are franchised to individual owners, have gone unanswered.)[17]

There was the curious case of one franchised supermarket chain in the 1960s, however. In 1967, a Baltimore-based, black-owned company called the Jet Food Corporation announced plans to open a chain of franchised supermarkets in inner-city African-American communities; the company eventually opened supermarkets to considerable fanfare in Baltimore and Cleveland.[18] According to Jet Food Corporation president Herman T. Smith, the company was founded with three objectives in mind: to ensure that profits remained in black communities, to create jobs, and to provide inner-city African-American consumers with access to high-quality, affordable groceries.[19] It is uncertain whether the supermarket chain received federal assistance. One article in the November 30, 1967, issue of the African-American magazine *Jet* reported that "the Jet Food Corp. boasts that it was opened without the assistance of federal or foundations [sic] funds." But that same article also noted that SBA head Robert C. Moot helped cut the ribbon for the grand opening of the Baltimore Jet Food supermarket in 1967, which implies some involvement between the agency and Jet Food.[20] Similarly, historian Robert E. Weems, Jr., refers to "a cooperative effort by the Small Business Administration, the Commerce Department's Affirmative Action program, and the Jet Food Corporation"; what this "cooperative effort" entailed is unclear.[21] One fact that *can* be ascertained about the Jet Food Corporation is that between the years 1970 and 2010, there is no record of the company having any SBA 7(a) loan to franchised businesses.[22]

Jet Food Corporation's absence in SBA 7(a) loan records is not unusual among grocery operators. Today, only a fraction of franchised grocers participates in SBA loan assistance programs. A look at relatively recent SBA 7(a) loan guarantees illustrates just how few franchised grocery stores receive SBA assistance relative to fast food chains. Franchisees of only four grocery chains—Big M Supermarkets, IGA, Piggly Wiggly, and Save-A-Lot—received SBA loan guarantees in 2009.[23] Big M obtained one loan guarantee, while the other chains each collected two. The seven

SBA loan guarantees totaled roughly $4.1 million. Meanwhile, as pointed out at the beginning of this chapter, the Subway sandwich chain alone received 152 SBA loan guarantees amounting to $27.7 million in 2009. Subway was the single largest beneficiary of SBA loan guarantees to franchise businesses in 2009, and the fast food industry was better represented than any other franchise sector among loan guarantee recipients. That year, 668 fast food outlets representing 132 chains obtained SBA loan guarantees totaling $170 million.[24] (See appendix, table 1.)

Over the past four decades, such SBA support has contributed to the proliferation of fast food and the expansion of individual chains like Mc-Donald's in years past, and Subway in more recent years.[25] Even though the agency's loan guarantees have ostensibly been made to individual fast food franchisees, ultimately that support has also helped subsidize the mammoth fast food corporations under which those franchisees have been operating. New franchisees, after all, generate additional franchising and leasing fees paid to corporate headquarters. Exposing how SBA 7(a) loan programs favor fast food franchises over supermarket chains demonstrates how federal policies can help shape the development of food landscapes throughout the country. So how did the U.S. federal government get involved in fast food, particularly fast food in urban African-American communities, in the first place?

◆◆◆

The federal government has had a history of involvement in African-American economic development that predates the arrival of fast food in America's inner cities in the late 1960s. That involvement, however, had been relatively superficial and ephemeral. One can make the case that the federal government first intervened in African Americans' economic and business interests when the U.S. Bureau of Refugees, Freedmen and Abandoned Lands, or Freedmen's Bureau, was created under the aegis of the War Department near the end of the Civil War in 1865. The agency, which had been established to transition African Americans from slavery to freedom, included the facilitation of freedpeople's labor contracts with former masters or landowners. But the Freedmen's Bureau was hardly a successful and unequivocal advocate of African Americans, as the agency often negotiated labor contracts that were unfavorable and constricting to former slaves.[26] Moreover, the bureau was effectively defunct by the early 1870s, and an official federal bureaucratic arm focusing exclusively on promoting black businesses would not materialize until 1927. That year, the Coolidge administration created a Division of Negro Affairs within the U.S. Department of Commerce.[27]

The Division of Negro Affairs was established to serve as a resource for African-American entrepreneurs and those seeking information on how to market to African-American consumers, though not necessarily in that order. The division's information guide on *The Negro in Business* (1936) noted that the publication would be handy to a variety of people, including "persons interested in exploring the Negro market for increased sales."[28] The division also collected information about existing black businesses and disseminated that information to government agencies, as well as "students, publicists, educational institutions and libraries, Negro banks and insurance companies, distributors and manufacturers, newspapers and advertising agencies and chambers of commerce and trade associations."[29]

But while the Division of Negro Affairs was intended to promote African-American businesses, it did not provide entrepreneurs with direct financial assistance. Although the division sponsored "business clinics" to help African-American entrepreneurs develop business plans, it offered little in the way of practical support.[30] As Weems points out, during World War II "most African American businesses were able to help themselves and the war effort only by obtaining subcontracts from larger white firms that had secured prime government contracts." By the Eisenhower administration, the federal government's commitment to the Division of Negro Affairs had become so tenuous that it eventually abolished the office, citing budget imperatives and a need to streamline the federal bureaucracy by eliminating "unessential" programs and offices. The Eisenhower administration's designation of the

Division of Negro Affairs as "unessential," Weems speculates, was likely informed by "racial considerations."[31]

It was not until the mid-1960s that the federal government began to consider more substantive support for black businesses. As part of its civil rights and antipoverty platforms, the Lyndon Johnson administration saw a need for the federal government to promote African-American entrepreneurship and job creation. Given the context of the Cold War, federal responses to African Americans' economic and social circumstances were, of course, also informed by geopolitical concerns. Both Johnson and his successor Richard Nixon believed that African Americans might be ripe for Communist recruitment as long as economic prosperity and racial equality eluded them. During his 1960 presidential bid, Nixon declared that "every act of [racial] discrimination was like handing a gun to the Communist."[32] He and Johnson also recognized that the continued marginalization of African Americans only bolstered Soviet propaganda on the failure and farce of American democracy.[33]

As part of its efforts to identify barriers to African-American economic development, the Johnson administration collected data on lending to minorities by federal agencies. Its findings led to the creation of programs designed to improve African-American entrepreneurs' access to credit so that they could be better positioned to launch small businesses. In 1964, Vice President Hubert Humphrey, a Minnesotan who had first gained national attention sixteen years earlier for having delivered a rousing speech supporting civil rights during the 1948 Democratic National Convention, ordered the SBA to investigate its history of loans to minority businesses. In accordance with Humphrey's request, the SBA's review found that only seventeen loans had been made to African Americans in the agency's ten-year-plus history.[34] The newly established Equal Opportunity Loan program (EOL) sought to rectify that.

Born out of Title IV of the Economic Opportunity Act of 1964, the EOL was part of Johnson's War on Poverty. It provided loans of up to $25,000 for low-income would-be small business owners and for proprietors of

existing small businesses located in communities with high unemployment. By requiring less collateral than what was typically necessary for
conventional loans with commercial banks, the loans were intended to
help borrowers who might otherwise have had difficulty obtaining access to credit. The EOL program was not explicitly a minority assistance
initiative, and indeed, it ultimately counted more white beneficiaries
than African Americans.[35] But Johnson, Humphrey, and congressional
backers like Jacob Javits, the liberal Republican senator from New York,
had intended for African Americans to be the primary beneficiaries of
the program.[36]

Other initiatives to promote African-American enterprise during this
period included a SBA loan program established in 1964 called "6-by-6."
Applicants approved for participation in the program received managerial training and individual loans of up to $6,000, which would have
to be repaid in six years. Eligibility for 6-by-6 loans was not restricted
to African Americans, but Weems notes that "black entrepreneurs were
given special consideration"—an observation consistent with the establishment of the program in cities with considerable African-American
populations (Washington, D.C.; Camden, New Jersey; Philadelphia; New
York City; Houston; and San Francisco).[37]

At the Commerce Department, officials identified corporate franchisors as potential partners in facilitating African-American enterprise.
The undersecretary, Franklin Delano Roosevelt Jr. (the namesake son of
the former president), headed the department's Task Force for Equal
Opportunity in Business.[38] Roosevelt's task force began compiling information on corporate franchisors that "pledged to enter into franchise
agreement on a nondiscriminatory basis and without regard to race,
color, or national origins." The task force's compilation led to the publication of the Franchise Company Data Book beginning in 1965. In 1965, this
Commerce Department tally of companies amenable to minority franchisees numbered only 18. Two years later, that figure had risen to 267.[39]
Between those two years, rioting in U.S. cities brought urban African
Americans' economic doldrums to the fore, and African-American eco-

nomic development had come to assume even greater urgency among policymakers.

◆◆◆

The riots conjured up images of urban war zones—plumes of smoke from smoldering storefronts, looting, and confrontations between young black men and white police in full riot gear.[40] But even such dramatic imagery failed to capture the full extent of the chaos and carnage of the riots, which took place in predominantly African-American communities from the mid to late 1960s.[41] There were some three hundred riots between 1965 and 1968; the notorious "long hot summer" of 1967 alone saw 176 riots.[42] An estimated 200 Americans, including riot participants, bystanders, firefighters, and police, died in some of the more catastrophic riots, which typically began in the summer months and lasted for a period of a few days in each city. In August 1965, in the Watts district of South Los Angeles, there were 34 fatalities. The Newark and Detroit riots, which took place in mid to late July 1967, left 26 and 43 dead, respectively. Approximately 600 businesses were destroyed by looting and arson in Watts, and 1,000 and 2,500 in Newark and Detroit, respectively.[43] Following the assassination of Martin Luther King, Jr., on April 4, 1968, riots erupted again in Washington, Baltimore, Chicago, and other cities. As one observer remarked, "it was Detroit and Newark that blew the lid clear off . . . America stood at the edge of a volcano."[44]

The events that ignited the Watts, Newark, and Detroit riots could be traced to outrage over the treatment of African Americans by police. Police brutality and charges of racism were among a host of grievances and frustrations that brought rioters to the streets. Despair was also high on the list. Many African Americans had been left behind by America's vaunted postwar prosperity, and they lived in communities increasingly beset by concentrated poverty, blight, neglect, crime, poor housing, and failing schools.[45] Perhaps most devastatingly, Watts, Newark, Detroit, and other combustible cities had been rife with unemployment, a perennial problem exacerbated by the decline of manufacturing

in the second half of the twentieth century.[46] Even as national unemployment rates fell from 7 percent to 4 percent between 1960 and 1965,
rates of joblessness in Watts had only declined by 1 percentage point
(from 11 percent to 10 percent) during the same period.[47] This sharp economic inequality persisted in spite of civil rights victories like the Civil
Rights Act of 1964 and the Voting Rights Act a year later.[48] As the *Washington Post* reported in 1968, "the average Negro family in America is
earning only 59 per cent as much as the average white family."[49] Meanwhile, the black unemployment rate was a full 5 points higher than for
whites—8.8 percent compared to 3.8 percent, in 1968. Employed African Americans, moreover, were disproportionately working in lower-
paying, unskilled jobs.[50]

Such economic frustrations informed the urban riots of the mid to
late 1960s. A majority of African Americans were still denied full participation in what the historian Lizabeth Cohen calls the "consumer's
republic."[51] While federal civil rights legislation might have addressed
African Americans' physical access to the consumer marketplace, it
did not guarantee economic justice.[52] Being able to walk into stores
was one matter; possessing the wherewithal to buy merchandise from
those stores was quite another.[53] During the mayhem of the riots, some
decided to grab armfuls of merchandise like clothing, electronics, and
food. And if such looters were opportunists, as some historians have
asserted, some of that opportunism was nevertheless likely informed by
economic frustrations.[54] Some riot participants may have also plundered
and vandalized stores to retaliate against what they perceived as discrimination, price gouging, and the sale of inferior goods and services
by white business proprietors, although rioters ultimately destroyed
some black-owned businesses as well (despite attempts to spare those
businesses in initial stages of the disorders).[55]

◆◆◆

The riots had social and political consequences beyond the neighborhoods in which they were staged. Among whites who viewed televi-

sion coverage of Watts, Newark, and Detroit from the safety of their living rooms, the riots reinforced racial anxieties, which the Republican Party would subsequently harness into electoral support. Although some whites might have been sympathetic to the social and economic plights of urban African Americans, many also felt threatened by the riots and any assertions of black power. Whites fled cities for suburbs and small towns, if they had not already done so in previous decades. And even though most whites did not live in the vicinity of the sites of urban unrest, many expressed a desire for the swift restoration of "law and order"—a racially coded phrase that politicians like presidential candidate Richard Nixon and then–California governor Ronald Reagan would use in their later appeals to white voters.[56]

Immediately following the riots, the Johnson White House too was concerned about restoring "law and order," but the administration was also earnestly seeking answers and possible antidotes to the causes of urban unrest—antidotes that would eventually include a role for the fast food industry. Following the Watts riots, Johnson promised federal aid to the area, and dispatched a SBA representative and other federal officials to South Los Angeles to investigate and find ways to "eliminate the deep-seated causes of riots."[57] This fact-finding mission led SBA chief Eugene P. Foley to write the memo "Possible Steps to Be Taken in the Los Angeles Riot Area," which was passed on to Johnson's senior domestic policy aide Joseph Califano, Jr. In accordance with Foley's recommendations in the memo, the Johnson administration opened two Small Business Development Centers offering information, advice, and training to would-be entrepreneurs—the first in riot-stricken Watts, and the second in similarly distressed East Los Angeles.[58] The thinking was that getting businesses off the ground in these communities was essential for generating jobs.

After five additional canvassing trips to African-American neighborhoods in Oakland, California, in 1965 and 1966, Foley found himself "convinced that the single most important element in relieving tensions in urban ghettos is the provision of satisfactory long-term jobs for ghetto residents."[59] Even before the riots, Foley had been concerned about poverty in urban African-American communities; he had helped to establish loan programs like EOL and 6-by-6 as ways to alleviate that poverty by creating jobs. After Watts and his visits to Oakland, Foley was convinced that such programs were needed more than ever. He reported that "representatives of all parts of that [Oakland] community, from militant young Negro leaders to conservative businessmen," all agreed that "jobs for the presently unemployed are the key to solving the problems of Oakland's ghetto." In a memo to the White House, Foley soberly concluded that "the consequent unemployment of human resources is leading to hopelessness, anti-social anger, and violence."[60] Foley would outline a policy response in his book *The Achieving Ghetto*, in which he advocated a domestic "Marshall Plan" to revitalize economically depressed post-riot communities such as the ones he had toured in Watts and Oakland.[61]

Commerce Department investigations conducted in the aftermath of the riots reinforced Foley's call for jobs and federal support to improve African Americans' economic conditions. In a 1968 memo titled "Employment and Urban Areas," Commerce Department official John Flory wrote that "the primary conclusion of the study is that *the creation of open and increased job opportunities may be the most critical need of our major cities over the coming decade*" (original emphasis).[62] That same year, a Commerce Department report, *A National Strategy for Developing Minority Business Opportunities*, argued that "recognizing and enforcing the civil rights of minority Americans will not, in itself, break the cycle of despair described as urban poverty."[63]

Such Commerce Department conclusions were echoed by another government-sponsored inquiry, the *Report of the National Advisory Commission on Civil Disorders*, or the Kerner Report. While the Detroit riots were taking place, Johnson had established the National Advisory Commission on Civil Disorders, known colloquially as the Kerner Commission (named after its chair, Illinois governor Otto Kerner, Jr.). In 1968, the Kerner Commission released a report recounting the riots, analyzing its causes, and proposing ways to forestall future unrest. The widely distributed report emphasized the role of high unemployment and poverty in causing the riots, and recommended job training programs, welfare relief programs, improvements in housing, and minority entrepreneurship in African-American neighborhoods.[64]

The publication of the Kerner Report and additional riots triggered by the assassination of Martin Luther King, Jr., on April 4, 1968, also made urban unrest more salient to policymakers in Washington. Maine senator Edmund Muskie, the Democratic vice-presidential nominee in 1968 and a member of the Banking and Currency Subcommittee on Housing and Urban Affairs, wrote to an official at the Economic Development Administration (EDA) in which he conveyed his "deep interest and concern with the causes, impact and implications of the urban riots."[65] Whether they were addressing African Americans' economic frustrations or assuaging whites' anxieties about "law and order" (or both), politicians like Muskie could not afford to ignore America's urban tinderboxes.

After federal inquiries into the riots, Washington responded with promises of aid to what policymakers called "ghettos," and programs to revitalize communities affected by rioting. As historian Jonathan J. Bean has chronicled, the federal government was "stingy" about compensating riot victims, with the Small Business Administration offering "little financial or moral solace" to business owners affected by the riots.[66] (The SBA did, however, repeal its policy of barring liquor stores and bars from loan assistance—a move intended to build up black-owned businesses after the riots, but one that led to opposition from members of Congress who believed that the federal government should not be supporting businesses selling alcohol.)[67] But if policymakers were parsimonious with direct relief funds, they were more likely to underwrite broader community initiatives in America's troubled urban centers.[68] In 1968, Johnson appealed to Congress for a $350 million jobs package meant to create 100,000 jobs in the nation's fifty largest cities.[69]

Federal agencies like the Department of Commerce, the Department of Housing and Urban Development (HUD), and the SBA were also charged with developing programs to build up America's cities. At the SBA, administrator Robert C. Moot declared that the agency "has cast itself for a major role in bringing new economic life and hope to the nation's ghettos." According to Moot, this meant strengthening existing businesses and creating new ones, as well as promoting local (i.e. African-American) ownership of businesses to "reverse the flow of profits and capital out of the ghetto"; this could be ownership by individuals or collectives. To help realize these goals, Moot reported that his agency had established management skills training programs with existing and aspiring "ghetto businessmen" participating as management interns while earning trainee salaries financed by the SBA.[70]

Notably, the SBA and other federal agencies' post-riot job training and entrepreneurship programs included partnerships with the franchised fast food companies that have helped make fast food chain restaurants conspicuous features of the urban food landscape.[71] That federal agencies saw franchised businesses as potential agents of economic revitalization in blighted urban communities was also evident in events such as a three-day conference on urban renewal featuring the business community, as well as government officials representing the Commerce Department and the SBA. That conference, held in New York City from June 3–5, 1968, and called "Managing for a Better America: Mobilization for Urban Action Programs: An Urgent Call for the Immediate Mobilization of Management in the Attack on Urban Despair and Decay," included a formal discussion of "Developments in Franchising" (during a session called "Creating and Implementing New Business Ventures for Ghetto Entrepreneurs").[72] As published proceedings of the conference recounted, "Franchising as a possible solution to the ghetto entrepreneur's difficulties got considerable attention at the conference."[73]

Speakers on the "Developments in Franchising Panel" included SBA administrator Robert C. Moot and Robert M. Rosenberg, the president of Dunkin' Donuts of America, Inc.[74] Extolling the federal government's efforts to promote black-owned small businesses (and franchises in particular), Rosenberg asserted that by owning a small business, "the minority entrepreneur" could become "integrated into American society" by undergoing "a radical change—a change in values, a change in the educational opportunities he set up for himself and his family, and in the responsibility he showed for his community."[75] The implication was that fostering such community paragons would form a bulwark against future urban unrest. There is no reason to doubt that Rosenberg earnestly believed this, but his participation at the Managing for a Better America business and government conference also had the potential to enhance his company's bottom line. With the help of loan guarantees from the SBA, Dunkin' Donuts could open new franchises. And that's exactly what happened. Records show that just two years after the conference, the Massachusetts-based donut chain received eleven SBA loan guarantees worth $414,700 (in 1970 dollars).[76]

Government officials and industry executives at the Managing for a Better America conference promoted franchises such as those from Dunkin' Donuts as the most promising vehicle for creating a black entrepreneurial class. Their pitches for the suitability of franchises in urban communities included paternalistic explanations for why owning a franchise offered the "ghetto businessman" his best chances for success. Published proceedings of the conference underscored that owning a small business had become more "complicated" than in previous years, and that the contemporary business proprietor had to possess "fairly sophisticated knowledge" about merchandising, marketing, public relations, and "a hundred other intangible skills."[77] That the challenges of running a business might be insurmountable was evidenced by a 90 percent small business failure rate, according to the conference summary.

Industry and government officials expressed particular pessimism about fledgling urban African-American entrepreneurs' ability to meet these challenges. The conference statement declared that "the small business route to membership in our society may not be workable in the ghettos, where there is a shortage of the kind of training and experience necessary for business success." But franchising offered a "solution"; franchise owners could benefit from parent companies' support "in virtually every area—personnel, advertising, marketing, merchandising, finance, quality control, etc."[78] In short, the SBA, the Commerce Department, and the International Franchise Association seemed to believe that minority entrepreneurs required special assistance to navigate the complexities of owning a business, and franchisors (the companies that granted franchises) could provide that crucial assistance.

If franchises were seen as urban minority entrepreneurs' golden ticket, the fast food outlet was the default option for franchised businesses. While other business sectors, such as gas stations and car dealerships, also adopted the franchise business model, the fast food sector had begun to embrace franchising like no other. And as the next chapter details, by the late 1960s many national fast food chains were keen to expand into city centers as their traditional markets became increasingly saturated, and they recruited African-American franchisees to help them reach urban consumers. That way, they could outsource the everyday challenges associated with operating stores in "risky" areas. But there was another reason why policymakers might have seen fast food outlets as an antidote to the urban unrest of the mid to late 1960s: those restaurants could be a source of jobs, especially for idle, restless youth who might otherwise be drawn to more sinister pursuits.

Given recent media reports of fast food workers' wage strikes, it may take some imagination to recognize that historically, fast food work has been imagined as a rite of passage of sorts, a means of acquiring discipline and work experience, and even a first step on the path to upward mobility, especially in lower-income communities.[79] Although an estimated 68 percent of fast food workers today are adult primary wage earners rather than teenagers seeking supplemental income, for decades the fast food industry has idealized its minimum-wage, entry-level positions as opportunities for teenagers looking to save for college or earn spare cash.[80] Fast food franchise boosters have also maintained these fast food jobs can be especially beneficial in inner-city communities. Some two decades after the 1960s riots, the executive vice president of the International Franchise Association still rhapsodized in a *Washington Post* opinion piece: "As more and more franchises are opening in inner-city neighborhoods, more and more jobs are provided for the disadvantaged youth looking for a start on the ladder to a decent life."[81]

Such romanticized representations of fast food work have, of course, been promulgated to justify the modest wages paid to entry-level employees. That the average fast food employee remains at the job only for six months also points to relative job dissatisfaction in entry-level fast food work, and even the working conditions and pay of salaried managers are often not vast improvements over entry-level positions.[82] Nevertheless, one could make the case—albeit a stretched case—that the fast food industry has been an especially fertile source of jobs (especially in inner-city communities where few alternative employment options exist), and that for some, entry-level fast food positions have led to career advancement. It has been estimated that one in eight people in the American labor force has worked at McDonald's restaurants alone at some point in their life.[83]

African Americans have had an even greater association with fast food work. Unsurprisingly, McDonald's has promoted this association in its advertising. A 1984 ad that appeared in *Ebony* magazine featured an African-American McDonald's employee in uniform, along with an oversized headline that read, "Who's the largest employer of Black youth in America?"[84] But perhaps the most memorable McDonald's advertising campaign to represent the burger chain as a benevolent employer and force for good in the African-American community was a series of commercials that aired from 1990 to 1992. The "Calvin" campaign had been created by Burrell Communications, the black advertising agency McDonald's first began partnering with in the 1970s. Set in an inner-city neighborhood that evokes a much more benign version of Spike Lee's Brooklyn in *Do the Right Thing*, these earnest commercials featured a fresh-faced teenager named Calvin. Calvin gets a part-time job at Mc-

Donald's, and gains newfound purpose and self-confidence. His job also comes with the respect of smitten teenage girls, elderly gossips, and a trio of unemployed young men hanging out on a brownstone stoop who secretly admire Calvin despite needling him. Eventually Calvin is promoted to the McDonald's "management team," and the last commercial in the series hints that ownership of a McDonald's franchise might even be in the young man's future.

The Calvin ads have been criticized and parodied. In 2014, journalist Gene Demby commented that "the Calvin spot doesn't even pretend to be about food," and is a case of McDonald's lecturing to inner-city black youth: *"Get off those streets and get you a damn job!"*[85] Comedian Dave Chappelle parodied the Calvin series on his eponymous sketch comedy show in 2004. But in Chappelle's parody, Calvin's job at WacArnold's is a source of genuine scorn among Calvin's peers. An elderly neighbor who had previously applauded Calvin for working at WacArnold's even ends up dying of high cholesterol—a consequence of the deceased's habit of consuming "too much WacArnold's."

As trenchant as such critiques and satire of the Calvin ads are, sociologist Katherine S. Newman's award-winning ethnography of fast food work in 1990s Harlem appears to lend some credence to the narrative put forth by McDonald's. Newman observes:

> The fast food industry is actually very good about internal promotion. Workplace management is nearly always recruited from the ranks of entry-level workers. Carefully planned training programs make it possible for employees to move up, to acquire transferrable skills, and to at least take a shot at entrepreneurial ownership. McDonald's, for example, is proud of the fact that half of its board of directors started out as crew members. One couldn't say as much for the rest of the nation's Fortune 500 firms.[86]

And while Newman was critical of the low wages fast food workers received, and lamented the challenges of adults who "remain[ed] in jobs designed for teenagers and tr[ied] to manage adult responsibilities on hopelessly inadequate wages," her ethnography also revealed that fast food employees acquired a sense of confidence and pride about their work ethic and being "gainfully employed."[87] Despite the lack of social cachet associated with entry-level fast food employment, workers came to identify themselves as productive members of society distinguished from others in their communities who were unemployed or involved in illicit activities.[88] In practical terms, fast food jobs injected a measure of structure into workers' daily lives, gave them experience that could be applied to their subsequent endeavors, and showed them models of success in the coworkers who were promoted or had graduated to more high-status ventures.[89]

◆◆◆

Fast food has also provided opportunities for fast food workers' employers—the franchise owners—to accumulate considerable wealth. According to one news source, McDonald's franchises have been responsible for making millionaires out of hundreds of African-American entrepreneurs.[90] Roland L. Jones, who was the owner of three urban McDonald's franchises and the company's director of urban operations in the mid-1970s, boasts that the Golden Arches "has made more African American millionaires than everyone else."[91] Jones had helped found the National Black McDonald's Operators Association (NBMOA) in 1972, which was formed to support African-American franchisees.[92] The group currently reports a membership of 300 franchise owners representing 1,300 McDonald's outlets; given that the average U.S. McDonald's location generated annual sales of nearly $2.4 million, many of the NBMOA's current members are likely millionaires.[93]

While some of these franchisees are second- and third-generation owners born into relative privilege, the fast food industry also counts African-American rags-to-riches stories, like that of Detroit businessman La-Van Hawkins.[94] In the late 1990s, Hawkins had amassed over 150 fast food franchises and had plans to open an additional 125 Burger King outlets.[95] Hawkins had risen from a childhood in Chicago's notoriously tough Cabrini-Green housing project, involvement in a street gang, and scrubbing toilets at McDonald's after dropping out of high school to become a fast food mogul.[96] Before Hawkins ran into legal trouble in the mid-2000s and was sentenced to prison for various white collar crimes, he exemplified how fast food could offer opportunities to inner-city minority entrepreneurs from disadvantaged backgrounds.[97]

The thriving Hawkins of the 1990s, whose Pizza Huts, Burger Kings, and drive-thru Checkers restaurants in Atlanta, Baltimore, Chicago, Detroit, and Washington also provided thousands of jobs in African-American communities, was perhaps what fast food industry boosters and federal officials envisaged when they saw fast food as one of the potential antidotes to future urban unrest. Although the 1960s riots did not directly *cause* the proliferation of fast food in America's inner cities, policymakers' concerns in the aftermath of the riots helped inform the development of fast food–friendly policies that the industry, of course, welcomed.

Even before the riots, fast food companies had been keen to avail themselves to federal largesse. As early as March 1964, A. L. Tunick, a businessman who had founded the fast food chain Chicken Delight in 1952, had approached the Commerce Department about establishing a Task Force for Equal Opportunity in Business, through which companies like Chicken Delight could receive federal assistance in their efforts to recruit minority franchisees.[98] After the riots, the Johnson and Nixon administrations gave such initiatives greater urgency and invested federal funds to promote minority enterprise. And as the next chapter explains, this dovetailed with another key development in the late 1960s: the fast food industry's own plans to expand into America's cities as suburban and highway locations became increasingly saturated with fast food franchises. In short, the 1960s urban riots and federal policymakers' ensuing desperation to avert future unrest could not have come at a better time for fast food.

TWO

Searching for New Urban Markets

In the 1988 comedy film *Coming to America*, an African prince named Akeem and his royal attendant Semmi are shown cleaning windows and mopping floors at an inner-city fast food restaurant. Despite having been raised as pampered royalty, Akeem cheerfully performs this manual labor. Not long before, he had refused an arranged marriage and journeyed from his father's kingdom of Zamunda to the United States, with Semmi in tow. Akeem and Semmi had decided to move to Queens, New York, figuring that a place with such a name would be particularly auspicious for scouting a regal bride.

While attending a community charity event, Akeem had seen and become besotted with Lisa, the daughter of a fast food restaurant owner. Akeem had to devise a way to see Lisa again. He and Semmi would obtain entry-level jobs at Lisa's father's burger joint, a McDonald's knockoff called McDowell's. (That the owner of McDowell's mimics McDonald's and is being pursued by the well-known burger chain for copyright infringement is a source of humor throughout the film.) The earnest and likeable Akeem ultimately wins Lisa's affections, and by the end of the movie, they are lavishly wed in Zamunda. But before the film's fairy tale ending, there are numerous scenes depicting everyday life in Akeem and Semmi's African-American neighborhood in Queens. The emblem of urban black life—the gossip-trading barber shop—makes a number of appearances. And of course, McDowell's, the fast food outlet, is also featured prominently.

The centrality of McDowell's to *Coming to America* illustrates the extent to which fast food has become a defining feature of inner cities in the public imagination.[1] That the McDowell's restaurant was located in the New York borough of Queens turned out to be apt given the history of fast food and African Americans in the nation's largest city. The first McDonald's franchise in New York City proper opened in 1972, at 215 West 125th Street. This was the address of a lot next to a symbol of black New York—the Apollo Theater in Harlem.[2] But the McDowell's in *Coming to America* could have also been set in Chicago, Detroit, Washington, Philadelphia, Baltimore, Cleveland, Gary (Indiana), New Orleans, Atlanta, Birmingham, Memphis, or any number of U.S. cities with significant African-American populations. As noted in the introduction to this book, many urban black communities have had more than their fair share of fast food restaurants. Roughly one-fourth of all hamburgers in the United States are sold to inner-city consumers.

For an increasing number of middle-class and affluent, health- and status-conscious Americans, fast food restaurants are the dining spots of last resort. But not so in low-income inner-city communities. (The same could be said of rural areas, especially those in the South and Midwest, where fast food restaurants are most frequented.) The appeal of a Burger King or KFC in blighted neighborhoods is understandable. In many instances, fast food restaurants have been sanctuaries in otherwise desolate communities lacking commercial and social spaces. With their hard plastic seating and soft menu items requiring little chewing and few utensils, McDonald's and other chains were designed to maximize traffic and get customers in and out as quickly as possible.[3] Even the primary colors that screamed at patrons as they entered McDonald's restaurants were meant to discourage dawdling diners, surmises journalist and cultural critic Martin Plimmer. In the British daily *The Independent* in 1998, Plimmer wrote:

> Getting the Hell out of there is the point. The interior colours have been chosen carefully with this end in mind. From the scarlet and

yellow of the logo to the maroon of the uniform: everything clashes. It's designed to stop people feeling so comfortable they might want to stay.[4]

Indeed, many of McDonald's customers have not wanted to stay. The average visit to the fast food chain lasts less than twenty minutes.[5] The extent to which this owes to McDonald's interior design and color scheme is anyone's guess. But what Plimmer described has changed somewhat in recent years, as some McDonald's outlets have been renovated to conjure up the relaxing atmosphere of Starbucks stores, with neutral colors, flat-screen televisions, more inviting chairs, and a coffeehouse ambience.[6] But in the impoverished urban areas where fast food has been most popular, patrons have always been more likely to linger, even in the days of hard plastic chairs and primary colors.

Urban fast food restaurants have often been housed in pleasant, clean, and air-conditioned (or heated) spaces that are safer than the streets, and more capacious and comfortable than one's own home.[7] Few know this better than Roland L. Jones. Jones, a former director of urban operations at McDonald's, had also operated three inner-city McDonald's franchises from the 1970s to the 1990s. In a 2006 autobiography, Jones explained why the typical McDonald's outlet in urban African-American communities might be bustling: "Black families didn't have the leisure to dine out together, and McDonald's often served as a baby sitter, a place where inner-city children could safely go for a meal when their elders were at work."[8] McDonald's and other fast food restaurants have also become social gathering places where one might catch a glimpse of retirees playing cards, friends engaged in lengthy conversations, and patrons tapping and touch-screening away at their electronic devices while munching on french fries and McNuggets.[9]

In 2014, a McDonald's franchise in the Flushing neighborhood in Queens even had to call the police multiple times in order to expel a group of retirees with a penchant for lingering at the restaurant. (A McDonald's spokeswoman told the *New York Times* that the chain did not have a policy prohibiting customers from lingering, but that some franchises displayed signs suggesting that customers should occupy tables for no more than half an hour.)[10] In Flushing, a fraternity of elderly Korean immigrants would arrive at their neighborhood McDonald's outlet as early as dawn, and spend their days at the restaurant gossiping, discussing politics with one another, and killing time; they often did not leave until dark.[11]

This McDonald's outlet, at the corner of Northern and Parsons Boulevards, became a de facto senior's center, acquiring a reputation for being the antithesis of "fast" food. The retirees' protracted daily gatherings became a problem for the Flushing McDonald's. The men's orders were sparse (a coffee here, a single packet of fries there), and they occupied seats intended for more efficient, paying customers.[12] These loungers illustrated *New York Times* reporter Sarah Maslin Nir's observation that McDonald's had been "adopted by a cost-conscious set as a coffeehouse for the people, a sort of everyman's Starbucks."[13] (The Korean retirees and the Flushing McDonald's franchise they patronized eventually reached a détente when both parties agreed that the men could remain at the restaurant for as long as they wished, provided that they were not commandeering tables during peak service hours between 11 AM and 3 PM.)[14]

Some urban fast food restaurants, such as one McDonald's outlet in New York's Times Square, have also acquired reputations as havens for drug addicts. Some locals have apparently christened the Times Square McDonald's on Eighth Avenue between 34th and 35th Streets as "zombie McDonald's" or "junkie McDonald's." Located a stone's throw from a methadone clinic, a needle exchange site, and two substance abuse outpatient facilities, this particular McDonald's is the go-to haunt for addicts to doze off after taking methadone. Others might retreat to the restaurant's bathroom to sell, buy, and use drugs. In a post–Rudolph Giuliani New York in which formerly dodgy parts of the city have been scrubbed clean for tourists and gentrifiers alike, this McDonald's is, as the *New York Times* observes, "a throwback to a seedier era in New York."[15]

Of course, addicts comprise a minority of everyday urban fast food denizens. Teenagers are actually among the most reliable contingent of fast food regulars. Dollar menus are within many teens' modest price points, after all. But beyond their affordability, fast food restaurants have also held a degree of social cachet among poor and working-class youth. As a seventeen-year-old in Chicago told the *Wall Street Journal* in 1990, eating fast food demonstrated that one had "some juicy cash flow going." According to this teenager, fast food could communicate a powerful message to one's peers: "I can afford McDonald's. You can't— you've got to wait till the end of the month, for a welfare check."[16]

For young people beginning to assert their independence from parents and other authority figures, eating and hanging out at neighborhood fast food joints has also offered temporary emancipation from the parental yoke, as well as respite from the monotony of bland homemade meals. One nineteen-year-old Chicagoan, identified by the *Wall Street Journal* as a gang member, related, "Everyone is tired of their mother's food—rice and beans over and over. I wanted to live the life of a man. Fast food gets you status and respect."[17] While this particular teen had been interviewed in 1990, indications are that fast food remains popular among urban youth. A 2006 *New York Times* article on the success of the McDonald's dollar menu included interviews with high school–aged regulars of the burger chain. As he was about to place his customary order of two McChicken sandwiches (off the dollar menu), fries, and a McFlurry shake, a fifteen-year-old named Shamell Jackson said, "When I was younger, my mom never used to let me come here. She thought it was nasty. But I've got my own money now." Many other New York City teens seemed to share Jackson's taste for McDonald's. The register line in which he stood was, according to the *Times*, "15 deep and filled with teenagers."[18]

Fast food outlets have also tended to attract lots of foot traffic in low-income inner-city communities because there are few alternative dining options. One high school senior from Newark pointed to such constraints in 1990: "Sometimes my friends say, 'Let's just walk someplace,' but in this neighborhood the closest—and the only—thing are fast food restaurants."[19] A 1997 *Washington Post* investigation found that although the District of Columbia boasted "670 sit-down, family restaurants," there was not a single full-service eating establishment in Ward 7, a 5.7-square-mile area of predominantly low-income African-American residents. Rather, Ward 7 was "a culinary wasteland of carryouts and at least 15 fast-food joints, or 'limited-service' restaurants, such as McDonald's and Wendy's."[20] Proprietors of full-service eateries have been deterred from doing business in Ward 7 and places like it across the country on the assumption that residents of these communities would not be able to afford higher-priced menu items. They have also feared that their restaurants would be vulnerable to robberies and vandalism. This "inner-city premium" has similarly been a concern of fast food companies, but one fast food has sought to circumvent by recruiting African-American franchisees.

Fast food has also been popular in urban areas for the same reason it has been popular elsewhere. Ready-made burgers, fries, pizza, tacos, and fried chicken are convenient. From the moment one steps into a fast food restaurant, it may only take a few minutes to be presented with a complete meal. Cooking, in contrast, is more burdensome, particularly for low-income people without cars. There's the usual washing, chopping, and prepping of food after a taxing workday. But cooking meals from scratch also requires access to raw ingredients. While not all inner-city neighborhoods are "food deserts" or "food swamps" bereft of supermarkets and fresh food, seldom are they affordable green-market utopias, either.[21] As early as the mid-1960s—just a few years before fast food companies began their urban expansion—journalists had been noting substandard yet pricey groceries in low-income inner-city neighborhoods. Some inner-city neighborhoods were lucky to have supermarkets representing national or regional chains, but these supermarket chains often stocked their urban stores with inferior products at inflated prices. Perhaps fast food companies sensed an opportunity.

Consumers lacking access to high-quality and affordable raw materials for cooking still needed to be fed, after all.

A 1964 magazine investigation of how one unnamed large supermarket chain operated its stores in both poor and upscale neighborhoods in Washington provides a sense of available grocery options in inner-city neighborhoods at the dawn of the fast food invasion.[22] James F. Ridgeway, the author of the *New Republic* article "Segregated Food at the Supermarket," reported that "in the numerous small stores of the [supermarket] chain, located in run-down sections of the city, whether white or Negro," items such as "wilted" lettuce, "bruised" apples, "shriveled" green peppers, and "brown around the edges" meat were the norm.[23] Ridgeway noted that customers from poorer neighborhoods suspected (but had no definitive proof) that the browned meat being sold in their local supermarkets were "leftover, shipped from chic stores which must stock meat to meet the demands of well-heeled customers." And while the condition of perishable items was decidedly lower grade than that found in the supermarket's outpost in the affluent Georgetown neighborhood, the same items were actually priced higher in poorer neighborhoods than in Georgetown.[24]

Similarly, at the supermarket chain's low-income locations the least expensive brands of packaged foods were often missing from store shelves, and many items even lacked any indication of how much they cost. Customers would have to ask supermarket staff for prices on such items. What these customers might discover was that, as with produce and meat, many packaged food items for sale in supermarkets located in poor neighborhoods were more expensive than in wealthier communities. Then as well as now, some supermarket chains manage to get away with such inventory and pricing inconsistencies because their competition in low-income areas—if any exists at all—usually consist of bodegas with even poorer selections and higher prices.[25]

Supermarkets are also able to take advantage of residents of deprived areas because those residents are more likely to be "captive" customers without cars to transport them to other neighborhoods. This also helps to explain the appeal of fast food in low-income communities. For car-less urbanites, grocery trips involve walking or taking the bus or subway, or a combination of both. Because of this, the trunk full of groceries those with cars take for granted are simply out of the question for inner-city pedestrian shoppers. Instead, they are limited to buying only the groceries they can carry, which likely means having to make multiple grocery runs a week. With all this legwork involved in cooking from scratch, it's no wonder that consumers—especially those with pleading, young mouths to feed—might be tempted to order a Domino's pizza or a bucket of the Colonel's chicken for dinner.

Aside from the convenience factor, fast food outlets also draw inner-city customers (and customers in general) because their menu offerings are appetizing and satisfying to many palates. According to researchers who locate the origins of the obesity epidemic in evolutionary adaptation, we are biologically programmed to favor energy-dense foods—in other words, foods high in calories, fat, and sugar.[26] Because our ancestors existed in a state of feast or famine, when nutrient sources became available it made sense for them to gorge on those foods that would most efficiently fatten and cushion their bodies through leaner times. Energy-dense foods also helped sustain our forebears as they hunted bison, ran away from mastodons and other predators, wandered for miles foraging for edible parts of nature, and carried out other physically demanding everyday tasks.[27] But while most of us no longer have such strenuous calorie-burning activities built into our daily lives, we've nonetheless inherited our ancestors' life-saving predilection for fattening foods. And the food industry has been remarkably adept at catering to (and reinforcing) our still-hearty appetites. As recent books like Michael Moss's *Salt Sugar Fat* and David Kessler's *The End of Overeating* have argued, fast food restaurants and food manufacturers have expertly engineered their products to exploit our biological urges to consume liberal quantities of fat, sugar, and salt.[28] A quarter pounder with cheese, fries, and a full-calorie soft drink (or any other McDonald's "extra value meal" option, for that matter) hit all the right evolutionary notes.

◆◆◆

But despite its current popularity, there was a time not too long ago when fast food was entirely absent from the diets of inner-city African Americans. McDonald's and most of the major fast food chains only opened in urban areas starting in the late 1960s and early 1970s.[29] Brady Keys, a former pro-football player and African-American fast food franchising pioneer, recalls that before the emergence of fast food, African Americans consumed more meals at home; there was simply "no opportunity to eat anywhere else [relatively cheaply]." According to Keys, meal standbys in African-American households consisted of "beans, rice, [and] greens" in the pre–fast food era.[30]

Going farther back, to the turn of the twentieth century, U.S. government-sponsored dietary surveys revealed that "beef, pork, pork sausage, fish, milk, flour, bread, beans, potatoes, sweet potatoes, and cabbage" appeared regularly in the diets of poor and working-class African Americans in Philadelphia in 1892 and in Washington in 1905. The surveys also found that African Americans in these cities supplemented such staples with ham, chicken, cornmeal, hominy, and peanuts. (Poor and working-class whites ate many of the items from the first list, but the surveys indicated that foods from the second list were "used less often, if at all," by whites.)[31]

Among African Americans in the Deep South at roughly the same period, "hog and hominy" ruled, as historian Frederick Douglass Opie has documented.[32] A survey of black sharecroppers in Tuskegee, Alabama, in 1895 found that salt pork, cornmeal molasses, wheat flour, and lard were dietary mainstays. These core foods were supplemented by sweet potatoes, turnips, and collard greens; there were also occasional protein sources such as fresh pork and chicken, as well as opossum and rabbit from hunting excursions.[33] Some African-American sharecroppers in the South planted gardens with leafy vegetables, tubers, and legumes, or they may have obtained such items from local famers and roadside produce stands.[34] A survey of African-American households in eastern Virginia in 1897 reported that dietary staples included pork shoulder, salt pork, beef, cornmeal, wheat flour, bread, rice, lard, sugar, sweet potatoes, cabbage, mustard greens, and fresh fish as well as salted dried herring.[35]

Traditional southern African-American cuisine is often associated with dishes such as fried chicken, greens rendered in pork fat, macaroni and cheese, mashed potatoes, sweet potatoes, cornbread, chitterlings (small intestines of the pig), and other "soul food" favorites.[36] But these items were not fast food. They were usually made from scratch and took time to prepare. And collard greens were still vegetables and recognizable as such, even if they were slow-cooked with pork fat. The same could be said about black-eyed peas with ham hocks, candied yams, fried okra, and other homemade vegetable dishes made more flavorful by the addition of salt, sugar, and fat.

One U.S. Department of Agriculture dietary survey in 1939 compared the diets of African-American and white households. In cases where households spent roughly the same money on food, African Americans seemed to take greater advantage of the summertime bounty of fresh fruits and vegetables, as their diets contained more vitamins, minerals, and proteins than those of their white counterparts during the summer months.[37]

African Americans who migrated from the South to the urban North in the first half of the twentieth century, and to New York City in particular, also had access to a variety of inexpensive ethnic street foods. As Opie points out, early twentieth-century New York tenement house communities hosted African Americans, immigrants from southern and eastern Europe, and Caribbean immigrants. This meant that African Americans could purchase such portable meals and snacks as pepper-onion sausage sandwiches from Italian street vendors, knishes (dough filled with potatoes and onion) and *arbes* (seasoned chickpeas sold in paper bags) from Jewish vendors, and various meat-filled pastries like *alcapurrias* from Puerto Rican purveyors. African-American street vendors, meanwhile, could be found offering oysters, fried fish, and soft-shelled crab.[38] The historian of American foodways Harvey Levenstein notes that African Americans in the urban North also consumed "breakfast cereals, sweet snacks, and other nutritionally deficient foods." In households headed by women who worked long hours as domestics and laundresses, women "had little time for their own kitchens," and thus relied on convenience foods to feed their families.[39] As for what African Americans drank every day before the arrival of fast food chains, Opie quotes a woman born in 1935 who recalled, "We didn't have a whole lot of sodas, we drank water or milk."[40]

While soul food and other traditional African-American cuisines have endured to varying degrees, dietary surveys of the last few decades have revealed that the everyday diets of African Americans of all incomes have changed considerably since the arrival of the major fast food chains. As Brady Keys noted, the availability of fast food "dramatically changed" what many African Americans ate.[41] A 1996 analysis of dietary surveys affirmed this anecdotal observation. University of North Carolina at Chapel Hill nutrition researchers Barry M. Popkin and Anna Maria Siega-Riz found that starting in the mid-1960s, traditional African-American staples like greens, black-eyed peas, and sweet potatoes increasingly gave way to typical fast food fare—pizza, tacos, and heavy pasta dishes.[42] African Americans were, in 1965, consuming dietitians' recommended quantities of fat, fiber, fruits, and vegetables at twice the rate of whites. But by 1996, a near-reversal had taken place. Dietary surveys indicated that 28 percent of African Americans, and only 16 percent of whites, now consumed unhealthy diets.[43]

How did this diet revolution happen? How did fast food franchises come to dominate much of the food landscape in urban African-American communities? These questions are at the heart of what follows. The story begins with the introduction of fast food chains in American food culture more broadly.

◆◆◆

Many of today's household names in fast food got started in the mid-twentieth century, but fast food in the broadest sense of the concept goes back to Antiquity. Ancient Rome had booths serving no-frills fare, including what the contemporary world might recognize as pizza.[44] Meanwhile, proto-franchising has been around since at least the Middle Ages. One could say that the idea of franchising was developed by the leading profit-making entity at the time, the Catholic Church. The medieval Church, whose immense power extended beyond the spiritual realm and into political and economic life, functioned as an Internal Revenue Service of sorts. It required people to pay taxes, usually tithes, or 10 percent of their wealth or crops. But the Church needed help with the onerous task of tax collection, particularly in far-flung places. So clerical leaders devised a solution: they would outsource tax collection to relatively high-ranking individuals (parish priests, for instance) who would be permitted to receive a cut of the duties they managed to wrangle from taxpayers.[45] So in a way, these medieval tax collectors were self-employed contractors, or franchisees. They were free to conduct their own business but were still working on behalf of a larger enterprise. (The word franchise is thought to have derived from *affranchir*—French for "to free.")[46]

In the United States, the advent of fast food franchises can be traced to the rise of Singer sewing machines. Although nearly synonymous with the fast food industry today, franchising as a modern American business model began not with the fast food industry, but with these sewing machines in the mid-nineteenth century. Starting in 1851, Isaac Singer, the founder of the Singer Sewing Machine Company, gave independent salespeople territorial rights to sell Singer products in exchange for a fee (what would be considered a franchising fee today).[47]

Other industries followed, particularly during the heady turn of the twentieth century. General Motors began issuing licensing rights for its cars in 1898. The Boston-based drugstore chain Rexall began franchising in 1902. Scores of other businesses in industries as diverse as soft drink bottling, oil and gas, general merchandising, and grocery retailing did the same in the first decades of the twentieth century.[48] The service sector also began to adopt franchising, with A&W root beer stands popping up nationally in 1925, Howard Johnson's restaurants in 1936, Arthur Murray dance studios in 1938, Baskin-Robbins ice cream parlors in 1940, and Duraclean carpet-cleaning services in 1943.[49] But franchising really took off about a century after it began, when the fast food industry embraced its distribution-savvy business model in the mid-twentieth century.

Fast food first flourished along America's interstates and in suburbs in the 1950s and 1960s. This was facilitated by the Federal-Aid Highway Act (also known as the National Interstate and Defense Highways Act) of 1956, legislation that paved the way for the construction of 41,000 miles of interstate highways. About two decades before that, brothers Richard and Maurice McDonald had opened their first eponymous drive-in in San Bernadino, California, in 1937; in the years that followed, the McDonalds would build additional restaurants in southern California.[50] The brothers were content with being comfortably, but not spectacularly, rich. They had amassed eight burger outlets and had no designs of prolific expansion.

Everything changed when Ray Kroc crossed paths with the McDonalds.[51] Kroc, who had been a traveling multi-mixer milkshake machine salesman, first became aware of the McDonald brothers when they ordered eight of his mixers. This sizeable order caught Kroc's attention; most restaurants only purchased one or two of his mixers. Curious about the McDonald brothers' successful business, Kroc decided to learn more about their restaurants. He took note of how the McDonald's menu featured only four items—hamburgers, cheeseburgers, fries, and milkshakes—and how this pared-down menu represented McDonald's overall streamlined operations.

Ever the business opportunist, Kroc saw untapped potential in the burger outlets. He had visions of hamburger grandeur that extended far beyond the McDonald brothers' relatively modest empire. So in 1955, he began his takeover of McDonald's. That year, Kroc acquired his own McDonald's franchise in Des Plaines, Illinois, not far from his hometown in the Chicago suburb of Oak Park. By 1961, he had bought the rights to the burger chain from the McDonald brothers for $2.7 million. Kroc's ambitions for McDonald's would, of course, be realized in the ensuing decades as the chain ballooned into the burger behemoth known worldwide today. Other fast food giants were born around the same era that Kroc assumed the reins at McDonald's: Kentucky Fried Chicken in 1952, Burger King in 1953, Pizza Hut in 1958, Subway in 1965, and Wendy's, a relative newcomer in 1969.

◆◆◆

During the 1950s and 1960s, interstates and suburbs were these fast food chains' bread and butter, and they kept building new franchises in these locations. McDonald's method of identifying new suburban stores was outlined by Ray Kroc in his 1977 autobiography, *Grinding It Out*:

> Back in the days when we first got a company airplane, we used to spot good locations for McDonald's stores by flying over a community and looking for schools and church steeples. After we got a general picture from the air, we'd follow up with a site survey.[52]

Pretty soon McDonald's planes would be taking more time circling the skies in search of new burger outposts, as there would be few communities with schools and churches that remained untouched by the Golden Arches. By the early 1970s, suburbs were, in the words of Brady Keys, already "saturated with franchises."[53] "Market saturation" was indeed an industry buzz phrase at the time. In a 1974 interview with *Black Enterprise* magazine, Norman Axelrod, McDonald's vice president for public information, likewise noted that suburban locations were "pretty well saturated."[54] Starting in the 1980s, McDonald's began scouting promising new franchise sites with a cartographic computer software program called Quintillion, which provided census, demographic, and marking data, as well as satellite images and forecasts of where new neighborhoods would develop and where school districts were likely to open.[55] Journalist Jacob Ward remarked that this commercial use of geographic information systems was the reason why "there's always a McDonald's where you'd expect one," as the burger chain "looked down from the heavens and dropped new franchises wherever it saw the right combination of kids, interstates, and suburbs."[56]

Returning to the 1970s, the saturation of suburbs was one among a number of developments that compounded fast food's growing pains. Fast food commerce along the interstates was becoming unpredictable by the early to mid 1970s; this was partly a function of turns in international politics.[57] The Nixon administration had provided arms to Israel during the Yom Kippur War, and the Organization of the Petroleum Exporting Countries (OPEC) retaliated by imposing an oil embargo on the United States. Between October 1973 and March 1974, oil prices soared. American motorists responded by logging fewer highway miles and making fewer visits to interstate fast food outlets. Arab petroleum producers eventually resumed oil sales to the United States, but gas prices remained higher than they had been before the embargo. This did not, of course, bode well for highway fast food outlets. The fast food industry decided to turn its attention to opening new restaurants in "walking" communities.[58] This meant cities.

Even before fast food companies conceived of urban expansion as a way to, in the words of Roland L. Jones, "placate jittery stockholders," industry watchers had already anticipated the limitations of suburb and highway locations.[59] In 1972, the business information provider Dun & Bradstreet declared that the fast food industry had "already run into the twin specters of market saturation and dwindling site locations."[60] The Fourteen Research Corporation, an equity research firm McDonald's hired to assess its growth prospects, arrived at the same conclusion in 1974.[61] Fourteen Research noted that McDonald's national advertising campaigns were already exposing a large segment of American consumers—and not just suburbanites—to the fast food chain. This exposure to McDonald's, the research firm pointed out, likely meant that the chain already had built-in demand for Big Macs and other highly promoted items—demand that was being unmet in places without McDonald's restaurants. Kroc and McDonald's executives subsequently decided to go ahead and expand beyond suburbs and highways. They would target places that, in Kroc's words, held "primary concentrations of a population."[62] And where were there more concentrations of people than in cities?

McDonald's would not be the first "quick service" (industry parlance for "fast food") purveyor of meals in American cities. Since the 1910s, Philadelphia and New York City had been home to Horn & Hardart automats.[63] At Horn & Hardart, customers deposited tokens into machines that dispensed an array of foods and beverages including, at various times, coffee, pie and cake slices, pudding, sandwiches, salads, rolls, baked beans, mashed potatoes, creamed spinach, macaroni and cheese, Salisbury steak, fish cakes, pot pies, and beef stew.[64] After picking up their desired items, customers could enjoy their snacks and meals in Horn & Hardart's simple dining area.

Horn & Hardart automats were not the only option for diners looking for quick and relatively cheap eats. Many cities also had dime stores and pharmacies with soda fountains and lunch counters. At the Chicago-based Walgreen's, as well as in other chain or local drug stores, patrons could find soda water, ice cream, root beer floats, sandwiches, soups, and desserts on the menu. There were even burger restaurants, such as White Castle. Known for its wafer-thin beef patties, White Castle was founded in Wichita, Kansas, in 1921; by 1930, it had expanded eastward and opened its first New York City location. Still, cities were by no means saturated with quick-service restaurants. They remained relatively untouched by the major chains. This would change starting in the late 1960s and early 1970s.

But before McDonald's and company joined Horn & Hardart, Walgreen's, and White Castle in establishing urban locations, they had to come to terms with the expenses and idiosyncrasies particular to running restaurants in cities. The cost of leasing or purchasing spaces in which to house urban outlets was typically higher than in suburbs. And unlike suburban fast food restaurants that routinely attracted patrons who would be willing to drive several miles just to satisfy a burger craving, market analysts cautioned that urban franchises could only really count on customers who lived or worked within a few city blocks.[65] Moreover, while suburban outlets might have enjoyed steady flows of customer traffic throughout the day, their counterparts in downtown locations might experience heavy traffic at lunchtime but sparse turnout the rest of the day. On weekends, urban franchises, especially those in office districts, could be virtually dormant—so quiet, in fact, that it made no sense to even remain open on Saturdays and Sundays.

Yet urban fast food outlets could also be highly profitable. In the case of McDonald's, franchises located in major metropolitan areas would later become among the chain's most lucrative.[66] There were, after all, significant advantages to urban locations. Fast food companies could build more compact restaurants in cities. They could save money by dispensing with parking lots for many of their urban stores, since city dwellers usually walked rather than drove for their burger fix. But most importantly, as Roland L. Jones pointed out, "Whether inner-city communities were rich, poor, or in-between, residential or commercial, their populations were large and concentrated."[67] This was crucial for sales volume. In fact, sales volumes in urban outlets—particularly those in the densest districts—often beat those of suburban franchises even though they had fewer operating hours.[68] In 1974, McDonald's projected that a new outlet near Penn Station and Madison Square Garden in Manhattan would yield sales three-and-a-half times that of the average McDonald's franchise.[69]

Promises of such urban cash cows were irresistible to McDonald's and other major chains. By the early to mid 1970s, they had become the new kids on the city block. As one McDonald's vice-president told *Business Week* in 1974, urban areas represented "a new market for us."[70] And they went after this new market hungrily. Between 1972 and 1974, Ray Kroc's expanded his Golden Arches empire with ninety new urban outlets. The chain launched a particularly aggressive blitz on Manhattan, opening sixteen restaurants on the 13.4-mile-long island alone during this period.[71] Not to be excluded from the urban fast food gold rush, Kentucky Fried Chicken also decided to aggressively invest in the urban market. In the mid-1970s, the company determined that one-fifth of all its restaurants would be located in U.S. cities.[72]

This foray into urban markets would help fuel continued growth for KFC, McDonald's, and their competitors. The proliferation of fast food was especially stupendous from the 1970s to the 1990s. Between 1972 and 1997, the per capita number of fast food restaurants in the United States doubled.[73] These restaurants fueled and created consumer demand. Americans' fast food expenditures surged from about $6 billion in the early 1970s to $110 billion thirty years later. Around this time, fast food also made up a significantly larger share of consumers' total restaurant receipts—from 14.3 percent in 1967 to 35.5 percent by 1999.[74]

But while fast food franchises multiplied and flourished from the 1970s to the 1990s, they were unable to steamroll their way through every urban community. McDonald's, for one, has had to contend with various groups objecting to the Golden Arches being erected in their neighborhoods. These groups have been concerned that McDonald's would introduce unwanted traffic—both vehicular and human—on nearby streets, and that the restaurants would, in the words of some territorial urbanites, "change the character of the neighborhood."[75] Such opponents of McDonald's and other fast food restaurants have been surprisingly diverse. It hasn't just been elites with historical preservationist bents that have objected to the impending arrival of fast food franchises near their stomping grounds. Working-class African Americans have also protested the opening of new burger outlets in their inner-city neighborhoods. But class (and perhaps race) has been critical to the outcome of battles between expansionist fast food chains and their neighborhood antagonists.

Consider, for instance, a standoff between McDonald's and residents of a tony, mostly white New York neighborhood, versus one between the burger chain and a working-class African-American community in Boston. In 1974, McDonald's had been eyeing the gilded Upper East Side of Manhattan as part of its urban expansion program. It had planned to open a store at the corner of 66th Street and Lexington Avenue, taking over a lot formerly occupied by a funeral parlor. This was to be a "classy" franchise without the usual bright colors and kitschy McDonald's architecture. The façade of this Lexington Avenue outlet would be made to resemble a "tasteful" townhouse-like structure characteristic of some Upper East Side residences.[76] But none of this was enough to mollify a contingent of neighborhood anti-McDonald's activists who believed the chain's presence would threaten the exclusivity of their Manhattan enclave.

In what became known in the press as the "Battle of Lexington," the Upper East Siders waged a formidable campaign against the proposed McDonald's. They circulated petitions and gathered 11,000 residents' signatures, including those with such bold-faced names as *Rockefeller*, as well as others representing New York's power elite in the literary and financial worlds.[77] Being a highly literate bunch, the Upper East Siders also deluged McDonald's corporate headquarters with letters, including missives promising reprisals should the chain follow through with their proposed restaurant. Among these letters, the acclaimed author and longtime Upper East Side denizen Theodore H. White rather cryptically warned McDonald's chairman Ray Kroc, "The enmity of this community is not a matter to invite lightly."[78]

But the activists' most effective artillery against McDonald's was financial. Through their connections in the financial services sector, they were able to boot McDonald's Corporation from a brokerage firm's list

of recommended investments.[79] Then the Upper East Side activists delivered their final strike. In the summer of 1974, they managed to get
the influential financial newspaper *Barron's* to publish a piece charging
that McDonald's Corporation had previously intentionally overstated
its earnings to inflate its stock value.[80] This exposé sent the burger giant's stock plunging by $357 million.[81] That did it. McDonald's corporate
headquarters threw up the white flag on the Upper East Side.[82]

From 1988 to 1990, a contingent of working-class African American
community activists also took on McDonald's when the chain moved
forward with plans to open a franchise in the Roxbury section of Boston. As soon as Boston's Zoning Board of Appeals approved McDonald's
request to build a restaurant in Roxbury in 1988, some forty residents
protested the decision in front of Boston City Hall.[83] They maintained
that the proposed McDonald's would introduce more traffic, trash, drug
trafficking, and unhealthy diets to their community. And they rejected
McDonald's claim that an outlet in Roxbury would serve as an economic
boon to the community by creating jobs. As one anti-McDonald's activist told the *Boston Globe*, "I agree that McDonald's can provide spending money or supplemental income, but no one can raise a family from
wages earned by flipping burgers."[84] The efforts of these demonstrators
were ultimately futile, however. The Roxbury McDonald's opened for
business in September 1990.

That the Roxbury activists possessed little of their Upper East Side
counterparts' resources undoubtedly contributed to the difference in
outcomes in Boston and New York, respectively. The relative ease with
which McDonald's was able to proceed with its expansion in Roxbury
is emblematic of the fast food industry's aggressive and effective in-
cursion in inner-city minority communities. Along with downtown office buildings and commercial business districts, fast food companies'
pursuit of the urban market also meant going after African-American
inner-city communities. It was no coincidence that Harlem was the site
of the first McDonald's franchise in New York City. No business hop-

ing to capture a substantial segment of the urban market could afford to overlook African-American consumers. African Americans were overwhelmingly urban when the fast food industry first set its sights on cities in the late 1960s and early 1970s. In 1970, more than 80 percent of African Americans lived in cities, according to the U.S. Census. Similarly in 1976, the minority marketing research firm D. Parke Gibson International estimated that three-fifths of urban African Americans lived in cities' central districts.[85]

Not only were African Americans overwhelmingly urban by the 1970s (a consequence of both the Great Migration and white flight from cities), they also constituted a sizeable proportion of the total population of many of America's largest metropolitan areas in the Northeast and Midwest.[86] Some cities, like Washington and Newark, were majority-black. In Washington, dubbed "Chocolate City," African Americans made up 71 percent of the population in 1970.[87] In Newark, the figure stood at 54 percent in 1970, followed closely by Baltimore (46 percent), Detroit (44 percent), Cleveland (41 percent), and Chicago (33 percent).[88] No wonder, then, that in late twentieth-century America, the term "urban" had come to connote "black." (Consider, for instance, the name of the prominent civil rights organization, the National Urban League.)

So the fast food industry began its inner-city offensive. As Brady Keys, who became Kentucky Fried Chicken's first African-American franchisee when he opened a Detroit location in 1971, observed, "All the franchise companies want to go into the inner city now."[89] McDonald's led the charge, opening franchises not just in Harlem, but also in places like Chicago's South Side (1969) and Cleveland's Hough neighborhood (1969). Incidentally, some of these outlets shared street space with barber shops, that other iconic business of urban black communities. In 1969, Herman Petty had been a barber shop owner when he became McDonald's first African-American franchisee in Chicago. His restaurant was located on the city's South Side, at 6550 South Stony Island Avenue, near his existing barber shop.[90] (*Coming to America* got some things right.) But Herman Petty was just the beginning. To help subsidize their expansion into black neighborhoods, fast food companies would seek to enlist additional African-American franchisees who might be eligible for federal assistance through minority entrepreneurship and urban renewal programs.

THREE

Creating Fast Food Cities with Government Help

In 1978, Robert L. Alexander, thirty-two, opened a Hardee's hamburger franchise in Washington, D.C.[1] Alexander had a lengthy list of accomplishments before becoming a fast food entrepreneur. He was a combat veteran of the Vietnam War and had earned a doctoral degree from Rutgers University.[2] Leading up to his venture into fast food, Alexander had been a political appointee in the Gerald Ford administration. An African American, he served as a minority recruiter for the Central Intelligence Agency (CIA). But by the end of 1977, Ford had lost the presidency, and so went Alexander's CIA position.[3] Even before the Ford administration had been swept out of office, Alexander had contemplated opening a Hardee's outlet in a predominantly African-American neighborhood in Northeast Washington. With the loss of his job at the CIA, Alexander redoubled his efforts to become a fast food franchisee.

Given his military, educational, and professional credentials, franchise ownership seemed like a relatively attainable goal for Alexander. But realizing this goal proved challenging, especially when it came to securing financing for the restaurant. "It took me two years and I went to more than fifty lending institutions before anyone would give me any money," Alexander recounted.[4] A wearied but persistent Alexander then sought assistance from a nonprofit minority entrepreneurship advocacy group called the Greater Washington Business Center. With the advocacy group's help, Alexander obtained training in "professional marketing" and assembled a dossier of supporting materials, including a petition with 518 signatures from District of Columbia residents and community leaders. Individual case workers at the Greater Washington Business Center also exerted what the *Washington Post* described as "strong moral and personal pressure" on banks to lend to Alexander.[5] Only then did he finally obtain a loan of roughly $500,000 from Washington Federal Savings Bank.[6]

The Greater Washington Business Center was able to help Alexander and other minority entrepreneurs secure bank loans in part by familiarizing them with SBA loan guarantee programs and assisting them with loan applications.[7] At the time, the SBA's loan guarantees promised to pay lending institutions up to 90 percent of borrowers' loans should those borrowers default. Without that government-backed guarantee, banks like Washington Federal Savings would have been much more reluctant to loan Robert L. Alexander half a million dollars.

As Chapter 1 emphasized, urban riots of the mid to late 1960s gave more urgency to the task of promoting economic development and minority entrepreneurship at the federal level. After the riots, policymakers in the Johnson administration saw urban centers as social tinderboxes. Agencies like the SBA were tasked with revitalizing urban communities and raising the number of black-owned businesses. Meanwhile, starting in the late 1960s, the fast food industry would draw on SBA and Commerce Department minority entrepreneurship programs to help underwrite its expansion into America's cities.

◆◆◆

The SBA had good reason to boost the number of African-American businesses in urban communities. In fifteen urban African-American neighborhoods around the country where rioting occurred from 1965 to 1967, only about a quarter of all businesses were black owned.[8] As a 1969 Commerce Department internal staff report noted, "some 15 per cent of our population [primarily racial minorities] live in communities owned largely by outsiders."[9] If relatively few businesses in

African-American communities were black owned, overall figures for black-owned businesses were even more sobering. Before a gathering of African-American church conference attendees on May 2, 1968, Vice President Hubert Humphrey lamented, "Count 40 white Americans. One is a proprietor. To find one black proprietor, count one thousand. And with rare exceptions, he is in a marginal business."[10] While Humphrey exaggerated these statistics for dramatic effect, the dearth of business opportunities for African Americans was undeniable. In 1969, the nation's 22 million African Americans made up roughly 11 percent of the total population, but they owned just 163,000 businesses, or 2.2 percent of all U.S. businesses.[11]

Black-owned businesses operating as franchises, both in the fast food industry and in other sectors, were also scarce in the years immediately preceding and following the riots. It was likely that the number of African Americans who owned nationally franchised fast food outlets in the 1960s could be counted on one hand. Brady Keys was one of the country's first African-American franchisees, and he did not obtain his first franchise from an established chain—a Kentucky Fried Chicken outlet in Detroit—until 1971. (Keys had, however, started his own fast food franchise, All-Pro Fried Chicken, in 1967.)[12]

The few African-American businesses that did exist were likely to be economically "marginal," as Humphrey related in his 1968 address to black church leaders. The gross sales of black-owned businesses in 1969 represented only 0.3 percent of the nation's total.[13] As of 1971, only one-third of all minority businesses counted gross receipts of at least $50,000, while half of all white businesses did. The average equity of minority businesses was $14,000 (and only $3,700 in the case of median equity), compared to $25,000 for whites. Minority enterprises also employed comparatively few people. As of 1971, only 5.1 percent employed 10 or more workers; for white-owned businesses, the figure was 20 percent.[14]

The dearth of black-owned businesses owed to limited access to seed and maintenance capital as well as the view that, in writer and civil rights activist Theodore L. Cross's words, "the ghetto borrower is risky, unpredictable, and unreliable."[15] Even if lenders ignored these racial stereotypes, prospective African-American franchisees' relative lack of collateral also frustrated their ability to secure loans. While black-owned banks were, in theory, alternatives for African-American lenders, these banks tended to possess fewer assets and were few in number. According to published proceedings from a business conference on revitalizing post-riot cities, there were only a total of twenty-three black-owned banks in the United States as of 1968.[16]

African-American entrepreneurs interested in opening fast food franchises faced another hurdle: obtaining approval for new outlets from corporate franchisors (i.e., fast food companies' national or regional offices). Robert M. Beavers, the African-American McDonald's executive charged with minority franchise recruitment in the late 1960s and 1970s, recalled that in his day, the company's regional licensing gatekeepers—almost all of whom were white—"automatically" rejected prospective black franchisees. McDonald's historian John F. Love, who interviewed Beavers, writes that this was because regional licensers frequently discriminated against African Americans who "did not fit their notions about how a licensee should look, talk, and dress, and about the amount of formal education he should have."[17] The irony was, of course, that some would-be African-American franchisees like Robert L. Alexander possessed educational credentials that exceeded those of typical fast food franchisees, and the same could be said for the few African Americans in fast food management and executive positions in the 1960s and 1970s. As Roland L. Jones recalled of his experience as a McDonald's management trainee in 1965: "I was definitely overqualified for a trainee, and I later learned that all the black managers in Washington [D.C.] were college-educated while most of the white managers were high school graduates."[18]

◆◆◆

The federal government attempted to address some of these barriers to African-American business ownership through programs within the

SBA and the Commerce Department. Created in 1953 to "aid, counsel, assist and protect" small businesses, the SBA (successor to the Commerce Department's Office of Small Business) has been the largest guarantor of business loans in the United States; by its own count, it has participated in over 20 million loan transactions. The agency has gone about its mission by advising businesses and guaranteeing up to 90 percent of borrowers' loans with commercial banks. In some cases, the agency has also made direct loans to businesses, although it has been much more likely to provide loan guarantees.[19] Borrowers who have secured SBA loan guarantees have typically been able to obtain credit under relatively favorable terms, including lower interest rates, longer repayment periods, and lower equity requirements than what would be required in conventional loan agreements.[20]

For an entrepreneur looking to open a fast food franchise with SBA support, the process would begin with the prospective franchisee approaching a lending institution (most likely a community or national bank) for an SBA-backed loan application. After the fast food hopeful completed and submitted the loan forms, the bank evaluated the loan request and performed a credit analysis. If it judged both to be satisfactory, the lender passed the credit forms on to the closest SBA district office for further vetting. Together, the lender and the SBA would consider the loan applicant's collateral, business experience, likelihood of repayment, and the applicant's own investment in the desired business.[21] The bank would disburse the loan after the would-be franchisee obtained approval from the bank and the SBA, and the borrower would repay the loan directly to the bank.

For borrowers, SBA support greased the wheels of credit access, as lenders would be more likely to approve loans knowing that defaulted loans would be bailed out by the federal agency. (This was the case with the Greater Washington Business Center's clients in the late 1960s.) Having the SBA as a guarantor also allowed borrowers to earmark 100 percent of their annual profits toward loan repayment. (Whether borrowers would have chosen to direct all their profits toward loan repayment is another matter.) Entrepreneurs without SBA backing, in contrast, typically would have had to demonstrate that their annual loan repayments would not exceed two-thirds of their annual business income.[22]

The SBA loan guarantee program did not specifically target urban minority communities when the agency was first created. But when the Equal Opportunity Loan (EOL) program became part of the SBA in 1966, the SBA was charged with an additional task of assisting small business in economically depressed urban and rural communities across America.[23] (As noted in chapter 1, the EOL was created as part of Lyndon Johnson's War on Poverty in 1964; after the urban riots of the mid to late 1960s, the imperative to promote business in African-American communities gained even greater urgency.) The EOL program and the SBA regarded franchises representing national chains as "small businesses," which rendered individually owned McDonald's, Burger Kings, Kentucky Fried Chickens, and their ilk eligible for federal largesse intended to assist communities with high unemployment.[24] Franchisees of these and other chains availed themselves to this opportunity. By 1979, the EOL program had disbursed about $25 million in 1,560 individual loans to entrepreneurs opening franchises.[25]

Fast food chains also tapped into a number of other special SBA programs designated for minority communities and other populations with high unemployment. McDonalds, for example, used the SBA's Section 502 Local Development Company (LDC) loan program to open new black-owned outlets in Philadelphia. Under the 502 LDC program (which existed until 1995), the agency guaranteed loans made by municipal governments and community development organizations. In 1979, the local development organization Greater Philadelphia Enterprise Development Corporation (GPEDC), the SBA, and the McDonald's Corporation announced a partnership whereby prospective African-American entrepreneurs who wanted to own McDonald's franchises could apply for GPEDC loans under more favorable lending conditions than those at private banks, and those loans would be backed by the SBA.[26]

Fast food companies also relied on the SBA's various other minority entrepreneurship initiatives, like Project OWN, which was launched in 1968 and intended for entrepreneurs in all business sectors. That ambitious initiative, which disbursed $40 million in 1968, was designed to provide seed money to 10,000 new minority-owned businesses by 1969, and 20,000 new businesses by 1970.[27] It was part of a package of SBA programs created in response to congressional authorization of a budget increase (to $2.65 billion) for the agency, with the proviso that the SBA dedicate half of its loan budget to disadvantaged communities in inner cities and rural areas.[28]

Fast food chains interested in establishing a presence in inner-city markets could also take advantage of the SBA's programs for group-owned enterprises, like Minority Enterprise Small Business Investment Companies (MESBICs).[29] Created in 1972, MESBICs were modeled after the SBA's Small Business Investment Companies (SBICs), a venture capital initiative begun in 1958. The SBICs were structured so that the SBA provided loans and loan guarantees at reduced interest rates to investment management firms that would then pool those and other funds to invest in small businesses.[30] Even though these investment funds were made possible and licensed by the SBA, the agency had a largely hands-off approach, emphasizing that SBICs were "privately owned, privately controlled."[31]

In the early 1970s, the SBA began promoting MESBICs as a way to spur minority enterprise and assist "socially and economically disadvantaged Americans."[32] The idea was to incentivize venture capital firms and other corporations to invest in black-owned small businesses.[33] Private sector sources were to commit a minimum of $150,000, which they could then leverage by selling the Small Business Administration up to three dollars in debentures for every dollar raised.[34] Critics of MESBICs pointed out that already-moneyed venture capital firms seemed to benefit more from this arrangement than fledgling minority entrepreneurs. But this federal subsidy would be relatively limited—the Nixon administration pledged to support only forty-one MESBICs at the program's start.[35]

Some fast food chains eyed MESBICs as a way to multiply in African-American communities by recruiting minority franchisees. Like the SBA conventional loan guarantee program, MESBIC rules treated fast food franchises as small businesses eligible for program funds.[36] To take advantage of this additional opportunity for government-backed expansion, fast food companies resourcefully sought out potential investors with whom they could pair franchisees for the MESBIC program. As E. Patric Jones, the president of an investment group called Urban Fund of Illinois and Combined Opportunities, told *Black Enterprise* magazine: "We are into the fast foods because that's where the franchises have been aggressive about approaching us." Fast food's courtship of Jones's investment group paid off. Between 1971 and 1985, the Urban Fund of Illinois and Combined Opportunities teamed up with thirty-two fast food franchisees for MESBIC program funds, investing $3.5 million, which would be leveraged into more than $10 million with debenture sales to the SBA.[37]

Some fast food companies, like Burger King, were even able to access MESBIC funds for their franchises without outside investors. They discovered a way to bypass that process altogether by establishing their own investment corporations in order to obtain MESBIC funds. In an August 29, 1980, inquiry on MESBICs, an officer from the Minority Business Development Agency (until 1979 called the Office of Minority Business Enterprise) related: "Burger King has a MESBIC of its own which has been quite involved in providing financial assistance to Burger King's franchisees."[38] Not only was this *not* against SBA rules, it was encouraged!

The MESBICs did not endure, however. An analysis by Timothy Bates, an economist evaluating the SBA's commitment to minority programs, found that by the 1980s, the SBA had begun to "renege upon its matching commitments, providing insufficient funding for the program, at times attempting to reallocate MESBIC funding to other programs, or attempting to eliminate the program altogether." Moreover, the SBA rarely appealed to Congress for additional funds to honor its MESBICs' existing matching commitments. From 1985 to 1987, the Reagan administration even sought to end the MESBIC program—a move as part of the administration's plans to abolish the SBA altogether.[39] The SBA as a whole survived due to continuing congressional support, but its MESBIC program was eventually axed by Newt Gingrich's 104th Congress in 1995.

◆◆◆

Under the administration of Richard Nixon (1969–74), the federal government continued to underwrite fast food via SBA loan guarantees and aforementioned programs to promote businesses in struggling communities. In 1969, Nixon, a self-styled exponent of "black capitalism," also created the Office of Minority Business Enterprise (OMBE), a Commerce Department entity offering technical and managerial training to minority entrepreneurs, including fast food franchisees. But Nixon also had more longstanding, direct associations with fast food.

Nixon had been singing the praises of the humble hamburger as a symbol of hardworking, ordinary Americans since at least 1960. During Nixon's run for the White House that year, he depicted his rival John F. Kennedy as an out-of-touch son of privilege while affirming his own unpretentious, hamburger-eating ways. He also recounted how the salt-of-the-earth neighbors of his childhood had similarly simple tastes, choosing hamburger rather than more expensive cuts of beef when they shopped at his parents' grocery store in southern California.[40]

Nixon's most well publicized association with fast food, however, occurred later, when McDonald's chairman Ray Kroc opened his checkbook to Nixon's subsequent presidential campaigns in 1968 and 1972. In 1968, Kroc donated a modest $1,000 to Nixon's bid for the White House; notably, it was the first time the burger entrepreneur had ever given to a political campaign.[41] Four years later, Kroc became one of Nixon's most generous donors, contributing $250,000 to the thirty-seventh president's reelection campaign. (Sources vary on the exact amount of Kroc's contribution; in his 1977 autobiography, Kroc placed the figure at a quarter of a million.)[42]

Kroc insisted that the hefty donation had been made as a fluke, not as part of any calculated effort to extract political favors from Nixon, or as an indication of any staunch political partisanship. According to the McDonald's chairman, he had only planned to donate $25,000, but he "let [himself] be talked into [the much larger sum] by Nixon's fund raiser [and former Commerce Secretary], Maurice Stans."[43] Kroc maintained that he was not even much of a political stalwart, and that his "motive was not so much pro-Nixon as it was anti–George McGovern." (He believed the latter would usher America into a socialist dystopia.) As an example of how partisan politics were putatively absent from his management of McDonald's, Kroc pointed to Fred Turner, his right-hand man at the burger chain (and Kroc's successor as chairman of the company). According to Kroc, Turner was a McGovern supporter.[44]

The actual motivations behind Kroc's donation to Nixon's 1972 campaign and the precise nature of his personal politics may be difficult to pinpoint. That said, any casual reader of his autobiography, which was full of veneration for "free enterprise," could infer that he leaned to the right. And Kroc may not have been entirely forthright when he claimed that his campaign contributions were made without any expectation of how they might affect his fast food empire. A journalist once quoted Kroc relating that he viewed his donations as purchasing "some insurance in the free enterprise system, in which I strongly believe."[45] Nonetheless, Kroc may very well have been, as he claimed, tolerant of those with differing political views. In addition to the McGovern supporter Fred Turner, Kroc's third wife and the love of his life, Joan (a large chunk of his autobiography was an account of his tireless courtship of her), was a generous contributor to Democratic politicians and progressive causes. The minister, civil rights activist, and politician Jesse Jackson, as well as National Public Radio (a media organization some conservatives consider left-leaning), were among the recipients of Mrs. Kroc's beneficence.

Regardless of precisely what prompted Kroc's campaign contributions to Nixon, and whether those contributions were responsible for Nixon's policy positions, the thirty-seventh president did seem to be favorably inclined both to Kroc the man and the hamburger empire Kroc built. After the McDonald's chairman's 1972 donation, the White House invited Kroc to a black-tie dinner for a few of Nixon's largest donors—a group that included Texas billionaire H. Ross Perot, who would run for president as a third-party candidate in 1992 and 1996. According to accounts of conversations between Nixon and Kroc, the president asked the McDonald's chairman, "What is it now, eight or nine billion [burgers sold]?" Kroc replied, "Mr. President, it's twelve billion," to which an admiring Nixon congratulated, "My goodness, isn't that wonderful?"[46]

A fancy dinner at the White House and a fawning president were not the only "thank you" gifts Kroc received. Kroc's autobiography included the following defensive recollection: "The worst thing about the donation was the subsequent implication by some sons of bitches that I had made it in order to get favorable treatment from the federal price commission in regard to the price of our Quarter Pounder."[47] (The price commission to which Kroc referred had been created as part of the Economic Stabilization Act of 1970.) In 1971 (before Kroc's infamous campaign contribution), McDonald's had come under the price commission's scrutiny for adding a few cents to the price of its Quarter Pounders.[48] The commission deemed this price hike illegal. McDonald's protested. Kroc then pledged $250,000 to Nixon's campaign. The commission subsequently decided to let the new prices on Quarter Pounders stand. While Nixon's opposition to government price controls could be traced back to the 1940s when a wartime stint working for the Office of Price Administration (OPA) left him hostile to the directives of the OPA, more than one commentator pointed to a link between Kroc's contribution and the auspicious turn of events for McDonald's.[49]

The so-called McDonald's bill and McDonald's veto raised even more eyebrows. In 1972, Congress deliberated on raising the minimum wage, a move that Nixon and congressional advocates of business sought to contain by proposing what labor interests derided as the "McDonald's bill." The bill would have allowed sixteen- and seventeen-year-olds to be paid at 80 percent of the minimum wage.[50] This age cohort disproportionately staffed McDonald's outlets, and the company employed an estimated 150,000 youth nationwide around this period.[51]

Not unlike the fast food industry's opposition to raising the minimum wage today, Nixon, Kroc, and supporters of the 1972 youth exemption bill argued that a wholesale minimum wage increase would result in employers hiring fewer workers and raising prices for consumers. The youth exemption ultimately passed the House but died in the Senate. And when the minimum wage bill (without exemptions for teenagers) reached the Oval Office, Nixon vetoed it, dismissing the bill as "inflationary."[52] (The price of consumer products had indeed been rising, but workers' existing wages failed to keep pace with the 5 to 6 percent inflation during this period.)[53]

Whether Kroc's campaign contribution was directly responsible for Nixon's veto is unclear. A number of Nixon advisers left the White House to work for his infamous Committee for the Re-Election of the President (CRP, or "CREEP," as Nixon's detractors called it), and they were replaced by a coterie of probusiness advisers who would steer the Nixon administration toward a host of policies that were decidedly favorable to big business.[54] At the time of Nixon's veto, however, the link between Kroc's donation and the White House stance on the minimum wage bill seemed clear to Nixon critics and some in the popular media; they christened this instance of executive privilege the "McDonald's veto."[55] (The bill overcame Nixon's veto, and the minimum wage rose from $1.60 to $2.00 per hour in 1974.)

After the McDonald's veto, Nixon continued to sing McDonald's praises. A letter he addressed to the McDonald's chairman in 1974 has been on proud display at the Ray A. Kroc museum in Oak Brook, Illinois.

In the letter, the hamburger-lover-in-chief rhapsodized that a recent outing to a California McDonald's outlet had convinced him that the chain epitomized "fast service, cheerful hospitality—and probably one of the best food buys in America."[56]

◆◆◆

There was more to Nixon and fast food than his special relationship with McDonald's. He also saw franchise ownership—both in fast food and in other types of franchising—as a means of achieving what he called "black capitalism." In 1969, Maurice Stans, Nixon's loyal Commerce Secretary who would later become finance chair of the CRP, urged Ray Kroc and Ford Motor Company chief Henry Ford II to recruit African-American franchisees.[57] Like the Johnson administration, the Nixon White House's domestic policy plans regarding African Americans were informed by the urban unrest of the mid to late 1960s. As scholars such as Dean Kotlowski and John David Skrentny point out, Nixon, like Johnson, saw programs for black economic development as "crisis management tools" intended to "allay urban unrest."[58] Nixon's strategy for urban African-American communities also mirrored his approach in foreign policy—to co-opt erstwhile hostile constituents. As historian Robert E. Weems, Jr., observes, "Just as Nixon and Kissinger linked the concessions associated with détente to Soviet and Chinese behavioral modification, black capitalism offered U.S. black militants a monetary incentive to repudiate notions of 'Burn, Baby, Burn.'"[59] Nixon biographer Stephen E. Ambrose put it this way: "Nixon advocated bringing the Chinese into the family of nations, once the Chinese had learned how to behave; Nixon advocated bringing blacks into the body politic, once they learned how to behave."[60]

When Nixon pitched black capitalism before African-American audiences, he was not quite as paternalistic as what Ambrose described, of course. Vice President Hubert Humphrey, Nixon's Democratic rival in the 1968 presidential election, had been an advocate for civil rights since the 1948 Democratic National Convention. Humphrey vowed to promote

African-American economic development during the 1968 campaign, and Nixon found himself advocating something similar. Throughout his campaign, Nixon pledged to create programs to help African Americans, boasting that once his programs were implemented, "ghettos will gradually disappear."[61] He also vowed to integrate African Americans into broader economic life, and to ensure that they did not live as "a colony in a nation."[62] During his acceptance speech at the Republican National Convention in August 1968, Nixon reaffirmed his support for black capitalism and federal programs, declaring that he would help African Americans get an "equal chance" at the American dream.[63]

Accompanying this rhetoric, Nixon proposed job training programs, business and home loan assistance for African Americans, and tax incentives for companies willing to do business in poor inner-city communities.[64] In a radio address called "Bridges to Human Dignity" on April 25, 1968, the Republican presidential hopeful declared that "by providing technical assistance and loan guarantees, by opening new capital sources, we can help Negroes to start new businesses in the ghetto and to expand existing ones."[65] In a 1970 position paper, as he was already contemplating reelection strategies, Nixon continued trumpeting the importance of minority enterprise:

> What we need is to get private enterprise into the ghetto, and get the people of the ghetto into private enterprises—not only as workers, but as managers and owners. Then they will have the freedom of choice they do not have today; then the economic iron curtain which surrounds the black ghettos of this country will finally be breached.[66]

Nixon made such paeans to black capitalism because he thought he could win at least 20 percent of African-American votes in 1972.[67] According to historian Dean J. Kotlowski, Nixon and his advisers believed that minority enterprise was the "best political theme" for appealing to the increasing demographic of middle-class African Americans, which he estimated might account for one-fifth of the African-American electorate.[68] Harry S. Dent, Sr., known for helping to orchestrate Nixon's Southern strategy targeting conservative white Southerners, also saw the possibility of simultaneously pulling in African-American votes by championing black capitalism.[69] In a December 22, 1969, memo to Nixon advisors Bryce Harlow and John Ehrlichman, Dent wrote: "Every-thing we can do, to increase minority business holdings, minority home ownership, and more jobs for minorities, will in the long run mean more to the minorities and help increase our political favor."[70]

This was a period in which Nixon reassured white voters of his commitment to upholding "law and order" in the aftermath of urban riots, and when he actively sought the support of whites disaffected by perceptions that affirmative action, busing, and social welfare spending privileged African Americans at the expense of whites. But his advocacy of black capitalism was seen as comparatively anodyne—a win-win strategy that would not cost white votes.[71] As Ehrlichman wrote in an internal reelection memo dated September 2, 1971, endorsing African-American economic development could "put the Administration in a good light with Blacks without carrying a severe negative impact on the majority [white] community, as is often the case with civil rights issues."[72]

Nixon was careful to couch black capitalism not as a government handout, but as self-help that would pay dividends.[73] Maurice Stans explained that his boss believed that by cultivating African Americans as capitalists, "they [then] become employers, taxpayers, and we shift the burden in the economy for a lot of these people away from welfare and being taxpayers."[74] Kotlowski similarly points out that black capitalism "advanced Republican ideals of self-reliance, private enterprise, and individualism."[75] This reframing of African-American economic development as self-help exemplified what historian Bruce J. Schulman has observed of a strategy Nixon and his advisers employed: to co-opt traditionally liberal programs while simultaneously weakening those programs by reconstituting them within conservative frameworks.[76]

Nixon's support of black capitalism made for a curious alliance with

black power advocates like the Congress of Racial Equality (CORE) leaders Floyd McKissick and Roy Innis.[77] (Nixon, however, feared backlash
from white voters, and did not publicize his meetings with McKissick
and Innis.)[78] In declaring his support for Nixon, McKissick even derided
social welfare programs in language that reactionary whites might have
used. "Handouts are demeaning," McKissick asserted. "They do violence
to a man, strip him of dignity, and breed in him a hatred of the system."[79]
But as Nixon pointed out—perhaps with a hint of disingenuousness, as
his detractors might argue—the tenets of the black power movement
and his own advocacy of black capitalism were in some ways doctrinally
similar. While on the campaign trail in 1968, Nixon noted that while
"black extremists are guaranteed headlines when they shout 'burn' or
'get a gun,' much of the black militant talk these days is actually in terms
far closer to the doctrines of free enterprise than to the welfarist 30s."[80]
Nixon called for a "new approach" to tackle black poverty that would be
directed toward "black ownership, black pride, black jobs, black opportunity and, yes, black power, in the best, the constructive sense of that
often misapplied term."[81] This "misapplication" included the notion that
black power advocates sought racial separation and government free-
bies without having to work. Rather, according to Nixon, "what most of
the militants are asking for is not separation, but to be included in—not
as supplicants—but as owners, as entrepreneurs—to have a share of the
wealth, and a piece of the action."[82]

For the most part, however, Nixon was coolly received by the black
community. African-American voters, the black press, and respected
civil rights groups like the Southern Christian Leadership Conference
(SCLC) regarded Nixon's advocacy of black capitalism as inadequate to
address social and economic inequality.[83] Andrew F. Brimmer, an economist and the first African American to serve on the Federal Reserve Board
of Governors, blasted black capitalism in urban African-American communities as "one of the worst digressions that has attracted attention
and pulled substantial numbers of people off course." Brimmer opposed
black capitalism on both pragmatic and more ideological grounds. In

practical terms, self-employed African Americans operating businesses in the "ghetto" would earn considerably less than if they held salaried positions in corporations or were employed in skilled wage labor, Brimmer pointed out. The prominent economist also predicted that an exclusive focus on black capitalism would perpetuate the economic and social isolation of African Americans, confining them to the limited black economy rather than ensuring their "full participation in the national economy with its much broader range of opportunities."[84]

There were other reasons some African Americans might not have regarded black capitalism as a panacea and Nixon as their savior. While Nixon's civil rights record included a number of creditable measures, by the late 1960s, African-American support for Republicans had already been eroding for about three decades. During his tenure as vice president during the Eisenhower administration, Nixon served as chairman of the President's Committee on Government Contracts (PCGC). As chairman of the PCGC, he pushed for antidiscrimination provisions in federal government contracts, and urged businesses to comply.[85] Once he assumed the presidency, Nixon oversaw the expansion of the Voting Rights Act, enactment of affirmative action programs with goals and the timetables, passage of the Equal Employment Act of 1972, and an infusion of aid to historically black colleges.[86] A majority of African-American voters, however, had been voting Democratic in presidential elections since parting with the GOP in 1936. It was unlikely that they would shift party allegiances for Nixon in 1968 and 1972.

That Nixon expressed a personal opposition to busing (though he did enforce busing in school desegregation decrees), made oblique racial appeals to white voters, and had a penchant for racist epithets toward African Americans, Jews, and white ethnics (which may or may not have been widely known in the late 1960s and early 1970s) probably did not help.[87] There was a time, however, when Nixon earnestly believed he had a shot at winning a majority of African-American votes. His assumption may not have been so farfetched. In his 1960 bid for the presidency against John F. Kennedy, Nixon had the support of prominent African Americans like Martin Luther King, Sr. (the father of the civil rights leader), and major league baseball pioneer Jackie Robinson, among others. Nixon only lost considerable African-American backing about one month before the general election, after he had failed to offer moral support to Martin Luther King, Jr. when the civil rights leader's involvement in an Atlanta sit-in resulted in his being sentenced to prison in Georgia.[88] While Kennedy expressed solidarity with King and offered to assist with the civil rights leader's release from jail, Nixon did nothing. By Election Day on November 8, Kennedy reaped the electoral rewards of his gestures to King, winning 68 percent of African-American votes to Nixon's 32 percent.[89]

Notwithstanding his lack of African-American electoral support since November 1960, Nixon did honor his pledge to promote black capitalism by establishing the Office of Minority Business Enterprise (OMBE) within the Commerce Department when he signed Executive Order 11458 on March 5, 1969. The OMBE, which *Time* magazine somewhat simplistically described in 1969 as being the "primary financier, cheerleader, and quarterback of black capitalism," was not an entirely new agency.[90] (It replaced the Equal Opportunity Loan Program, and whether it was an effective and adequately funded agency is another matter that will be discussed later in this chapter.) The OMBE was not a source of direct loans or a facilitator of minority set-asides for government contracts, as *Time*'s characterization of it might have suggested. Any funds that flowed from the agency to minority entrepreneurs and local business development organizations were intended for "technical and managerial" training.[91] The SBA, which was an agency separate from the Commerce Department, was still the government agency responsible for loan guarantees, direct loans, and set-asides.

A White House fact sheet clarifying the role of the OMBE, as well as the office's director, John L. Jenkins, reiterated the point that the OMBE was "not an agency that fund[ed] businesses."[92] Rather, it was a "coordinating agency" linking sundry minority enterprise stakeholders—individual (or group) entrepreneurs, existing businesses, trade associations, investment organizations, foundations, schools, and local, state, and federal governments—and providing technical and managerial assistance, and training, to these groups.[93] The agency was also responsible for compiling data and other information that it believed would be "helpful to persons and organizations throughout the nation in undertaking or promoting the establishment and successful operation of minority business enterprises."[94]

While the Nixon administration and the OMBE touted these functions as critical to the development of minority enterprise, Nixon's commitment to black capitalism had flagged by the early 1970s, and was constrained by a struggling economy. In 1969, his administration froze the OMBE budget as part of its efforts to reduce federal spending during stagflation.[95] (Executive belt-tightening also extended to the SBA. The agency saw its budget shrink from $554 million in 1968 to $263 million in 1969.)[96] Total federal funds disbursed for minority enterprise (including grants, loans, loan guarantees, and purchases from all agencies) were somewhat respectable—$200 million in 1969, $315 million in 1970, and $630 million in 1971—but OMBE's share of that amount was smaller than what one might have expected for an agency with "minority enterprise" in its name.[97]

Both Stans and Jenkins appealed for more funding from the Office of Management and Budget (OMB), which controlled the purse strings for executive agencies. In a July 21, 1971, memo to Nixon, Stans noted that while he had requested a budget of $188 million for the OMBE in fiscal year 1972, the OMB allocated only $65 million to the agency for the following two years. The OMB's allowance, Stans lamented to the president, was "inadequate to achieve the program goals," and "fail[ed] to meet the proposals of your Advisory Council on Minority Business Enterprise."[98]

Perhaps grasping that Nixon was particularly sensitive to political barometers and criticisms, Stans reminded him that "our efforts to date have been haunted by the criticism that there is no evidence of a commitment by this Administration to a substantial effort to promote minority enterprise"; he added that both the Advisory Council on Minority Business Enterprise and the Congressional Black Caucus were among those who made these criticisms.[99] Nixon's response was not to channel more money to the OMBE from Management and Budget, but to ask Congress for an additional $100 million on October 13, 1971, just three months after submitting to Congress an OMBE budget wish list of $325 million for fiscal years 1971 to 1973.[100]

That Nixon went to bat for OMBE, but relatively lackadaisically and short of his loftier promotion of black capitalism on the campaign trail, reflected his philosophy about the agency's purpose. Nevertheless, he acknowledged a role for government in assisting minority enterprise, which he articulated in a message to Congress on July 20, 1971:

> The gross disparity in business ownership demands corrective government action, in ways that the government can legitimately and effectively help. Government can, and must, assist disadvantaged persons who wish to establish or expand a business in gaining access to the tools needed for success. Assistance in obtaining financing, trade credit, markets, skilled manpower, legal and other professional aid, training and similar business needs must be provided if minority businessmen are to have an equal chance to compete in our economy.

Nixon's call for government redress of racial inequality in business ownership was blunted, however, by his emphasis in the same speech that "ultimate control and responsibility for the program [OMBE] must rest in the local community." Sounding as if he had ripped a page from contemporary Republican stump speeches' formulaic juxtaposition of an inefficient and out-of-touch Washington with the inherent virtuousness of local communities, Nixon asserted that "any attempt to directly operate a minority business program by means of a long pipeline from Washington would introduce needless red tape, would be divorced from the realities of local situations and needs, and would lead to frustration and failure."[101]

Nixon also preferred that the private sector, rather than the federal government, assume primary responsibility for advancing minority enterprise. Presuming that the private sector was interested in developing black business (whether this presumption was disingenuous or not is unclear), Nixon asserted that the private sector possessed "the bulk of the resources and skills necessary for business," and that it "control[led] the bulk of the capital, management services and technical assistance resources, to commit the necessary recourses to make the minority business enterprise program successful."[102]

This idealizing of private enterprise may have been just another excuse for Nixon's aversion to expanding the federal bureaucracy, but the thirty-seventh president was by no means a small-government Republican. He threw his support behind regulatory agencies such as the Environmental Protection Agency, the Occupational Health and Safety Administration, and the National Transportation Safety Board. The Nixon White House also expanded the Food Stamp Program and even proposed the ultimate entitlement program—the Family Assistance Plan, which would have provided poor families with a minimum income guarantee. A Democratic-controlled Congress may have certainly pushed Nixon to the left on these matters, but the point is that Nixon's reluctance to commit ample federal resources to the Office of Minority Business Enterprise was not a given. Perhaps Nixon was concerned about alienating white voters in advance of his reelection bid, fearing that he would be perceived as diverting government resources to a program intended exclusively for African Americans and other minorities (even if that program had been originally pitched as an initiative that would make taxpayers out of its beneficiaries).

With what limited funding it did have, the OMBE agenda included securing partnerships between minority entrepreneurs and corporate franchisors—including those representing the fast food industry. The agency even had an official "franchising program" meant to "develop business opportunities for minorities in the franchising field," to quote Jenkins in 1973.[103] Soon after the agency was established in 1969, the

OMBE developed a program called "25 x 25 x 2," in hopes of yielding 10,000 new minority franchisees.[104] Under the program, the OMBE convened eight groups of twenty-five franchisors to its Washington office and invited them to sign pledges to register twenty-five new minority franchisees each year for two years.[105] Franchisors had an incentive to participate because their prospective franchisees would be eligible for Commerce Department training programs and SBA loan guarantees—valuable assistance to which corporate franchisors did not have to contribute. As of December 3, 1969, the agency amassed 734 franchise pledges representing seventy-two franchisors.[106] These pledges ostensibly resulted in significant gains, with the number of minority-owned franchises multiplying from 405 in 1969 to 1,184 just two years later. But an information officer from the OMBE conceded that these figures, which were supplied by corporate franchisors, had not been substantiated by the agency. There was also "no way of knowing" how many of the 1,184 minority-owned franchises resulted directly from OMBE assistance.[107]

◆◆◆

In promoting the idea of African Americans as fast food franchise owners, the OMBE and the Commerce Department paraded Brady Keys, a former National Football League player who had become a fast food entrepreneur, as a success story; the Nixon administration similarly saw Keys as an opportunity to showcase its putative responsiveness to calls for African-American economic development.[108] Keys enjoyed remarkable ease of access to Commerce Department officials, and he was able to convince them to finance his motley of fast food franchises. Archived Commerce Department documents indicate, for instance, that on December 16, 1970, Keys had written the agency requesting a meeting with OMBE officials. Just three holiday-packed weeks later on January 7, 1971, Keys had a meeting with representatives from the OMBE's "business opportunities" division, where he "discussed his proposal for a minority franchise institute." Following that presentation, Keys had one-on-one meetings with Commerce Department gatekeeper Jay I. Leanse and Maurice Stans. In these meetings, the charismatic businessman requested "long term financing"—"$2 to 3 million"—to open fast food franchises.[109] Keys recounted his pitch in *Black Enterprise* magazine in 1974:

> I told [Stans] I needed some money to make it—a lot of money, to buy land, to build buildings. And I told him that if I fail, your whole damn minority concept fails, because I'm the only one that's succeeding. So they decided to loan me a lot of money.[110]

Keys was not exaggerating. The Commerce Department did loan him "a lot of money." By his own count, between 1969 and 1973 Keys received $9 million in loans from the Commerce Department's minority enterprise programs, chiefly within the Economic Development Administration (EDA).[111] This was a reasonable estimate given that, in 1971 the EDA loaned Keys's All-Pro Enterprises $2,366,650 to help underwrite nineteen new fast food restaurants. Just two years later, the EDA issued another loan to Keys's company, this time for $5,528,350. According to Keys, the second check would be used to help his "mini-conglomerate," All-Pro Enterprises, open fifty inner-city fast food outlets and generate 1,325 jobs in Cleveland, Chicago, New York City, and Washington—cities that had been sites of urban unrest and that had continued to struggle with high rates of joblessness.[112]

Soon after he received his second round of Commerce Department largesse, Keys became the face of the Nixon administration's minority enterprise public relations campaign. In 1973, not long after the ink had dried on Stans's approval of Keys's $5.5 million loan, Nixon appointed the fast food mogul to his Advisory Council on Minority Business Enterprise and to the President's Council for Equal Opportunity for the International Franchise.[113] As Keys's commissioned biography highlighted, his appointment to the latter post made him the "first Black man to serve as a board member of that association."[114] After being lionized as a star defensive back while playing on high school football teams in Texas and California, and subsequently at Colorado State and for the Pittsburgh Steelers, Minnesota Vikings, and St. Louis Cardinals, Keys had grown accustomed to being in the limelight. He seemed delighted to oblige when Nixon sought his participation in the political pageantry of White House minority enterprise and "equal opportunity" franchise councils.

The idea of promoting black enterprise with successful former athletes like Keys made sense because of their visibility and influence, especially among African-American youth. As Abraham S. Venable, who had been appointed director of the OMBE in 1970, observed in an undated memo: "The Negro athlete is a symbol of achievement, success, and leadership, and in many instances, can and does control the destiny of millions of young Negro Americans." Venable had also been concerned about African-American athletes' economic well-being since careers in professional sports tended to be relatively short. He urged the NFL to create an "executive counseling service" for African-American players to learn about business and employment opportunities after retirement. In conversations with Buddy Young, a former professional football player and the first African-American executive in the NFL, Venable suggested that the league direct players to franchising, noting that "the franchise industry represents a tremendous possibility for Negro players to become business operators."[115]

The federal government also provided direct aid to former African-American athletes going into business. Brady Keys was not the only black athlete to transition from sports to fast food, and to rely on federal assistance to do so. In her study of African-American Republicans in the 1960s and 1970s, historian Leah Wright notes that former professional and college athletes were "among the prime beneficiaries" of the Nixon administration's efforts to bolster black capitalism; over one thousand "athlete-entrepreneurs" received some form of government support in the Nixon years.[116] The household names among them included the NBA superstar Wilt Chamberlain, who used federal funds to launch a franchise of eponymous diners, as well as Cleveland Browns running back Jim Brown, who established the Black Economic Union, an organization that invested in black-owned businesses.[117] Notably, Chamberlain publicly supported Nixon's presidential campaigns and advised the Republican candidate on matters related to African Americans during the 1968 campaign.[118] Brown, meanwhile, was known to have visited Nixon in the Oval Office in 1972.[119] Engagement with high-profile African Americans like Brown and Chamberlain, and appointing some of them to be "ambassadors" to the black community, were part of Nixon's strategy of appealing to African-American voters in his 1972 reelection campaign.[120]

Chamberlain and Keys were just two of numerous African-American professional athletes (or retired athletes) who became entrepreneurs of fast food. For example, former NBA star-turned-Milwaukee Bucks general manager Wayne Embry was a contemporary of Chamberlain and Keys, and also one of the first African-American McDonald's franchise owners in the Midwest.[121] Among household names in sports, the baseball hall of famer Hank Aaron has, at various times, owned 13 Church's Chicken franchises, 7 Arby's outlets, 5 Popeyes Louisiana Kitchen restaurants, and 1 Krispy Kreme Doughnuts store.[122] And as of 2013, the retired basketball superstar Shaquille O'Neal owned 155 franchises of the Five Guys burger chain.[123] A growing roster of other African-American professional athletes—both active and retired—have also become owners of an array of fast food franchises, including Dunkin' Donuts, Papa John's, Bojangles, Buffalo Wild Wings, Wendy's, and Cold Stone Creamery.[124]

◆◆◆

Given the existence of federal minority entrepreneurship programs that have been used to open fast food franchises since the late 1960s, just how many loan transactions for black-owned inner-city fast food franchises have federal agencies—and the Small Business Administration in particular—facilitated? In 2000, media estimates of the percentage of SBA loan guarantees going to African Americans placed the number around 15 percent, a figure roughly 2 percentage points higher than the proportion of African Americans in the total U.S. population at the time.[125] It may be impossible to corroborate this figure, however. According to author Jonathan J. Bean's history of the SBA, the agency kept unofficial records on borrowers' racial backgrounds going back to 1964; these records were meant to shed light on the agency's progress regarding civil rights compliance and minority outreach.[126] But the SBA has not been keen to publicize these figures. The agency maintains that it classifies records identifying borrowers' race and other personal information. Records of individual loans are also unavailable to the public, and are destroyed five years after having been paid.[127]

When assessing the results of minority enterprise programs since the late 1960s, it is worth noting that federal loans and loan guarantees to minority entrepreneurs fell short of Nixon's promises even during the heyday of "black capitalism." Nixon pledged 40 percent of the SBA's loan budget to minority business in 1969, but by the end of that year, only 15 percent of the SBA's loan funds had gone to minority borrowers.[128] And while SBA loans and loan guarantees to minority borrowers outpaced the agency's aggregate (not racially based) loan programs from 1968 to 1970, minority lending declined relative to the SBA aggregate between 1970 and 1972.[129] In 1970, 23 percent ($160.4 million out of a total of $709.6 million) of total SBA loan transactions went to minority borrowers, but that declined to 19 percent a year later ($213 million out of a total of $1.1 billion).[130] By 1976, that number would dip even further, to 13 percent.[131]

Moreover, some of the fast food restaurants receiving federal funds in the 1970s, ostensibly to promote "minority enterprise," were actually partly under the ownership and control of whites. The decade saw schemes in which whites installed black figurehead partners in order to tap into government programs intended for African-American entrepreneurs.[132] Roland L. Jones described how these "salt-and-pepper" or "zebra operations" functioned:

The black partner in these arrangements would be the owner-operator and the visible face in his store, without having to come up with the full cost of the franchise. The white partners would bring business savvy to the table; provide a substantial part of the capital for the turnkey operation, including training, labor, and adequate working capital; and share the profits, but they would stay in the background.[133]

The first black-owned McDonald's franchise in Chicago, which opened in 1969, was a salt-and-pepper operation. Jones suggests that Herman Petty, the African-American partner of that franchise, may have been short-changed by the arrangement. According to Jones, whose knowledge of McDonald's operations derived both from his role as an executive in the company and as the owner of three McDonald's franchises, Petty's white partners deducted "higher than normal" administrative and accounting charges from his profits. That Petty's white partners would charge administrative fees at all was suspicious, Jones said, because they "did nothing to manage [the restaurant]," and were in effect double-dipping in the franchise's money pot.[134]

Administrative deficiencies and lack of oversight at the SBA and the OMBE during the Nixon administration may have contributed to the failure of these agencies to prevent and rectify such potentially exploitative arrangements. And not only were these agencies criticized for being ineffective, the Senate Banking Subcommittee also investigated them for malfeasance in connection with the Watergate scandal. A handful of small business owners and SBA whistleblowers in California had accused Nixon's 1972 campaign operatives, the CRP, of extortion.

The office of U.S. Senator Alan Cranston, a California Democrat, received complaints that White House staff and CRP figures coerced small business owners who had received SBA funding or government contracts set aside for minority entrepreneurs to contribute roughly $1,000 each to Nixon's reelection campaign; business owners who refused would risk losing their SBA financing or government contracts.[135] The OMBE was also implicated in the kickback scandal, with applicants for the agency's support alleging that OMBE officials also pressured them to make illicit payoffs as a condition for securing or maintaining government assistance.[136] Cranston, who led the Senate investigation, reported that "apparently a quota had been set up where the Administration wanted a million dollars out of minority business[es] doing business with the government."[137]

The OMBE of the 1970s also suffered from general administrative mismanagement. This was manifest in the higher-than-average failure rates among black-owned franchises that were supposed to be under the agency's tutelage. While some of these franchises might have been more vulnerable anyway given their owners' insufficient reserves to cushion against losses, business historian Robert Yancy asserts that the OMBE deserved some blame for failing to ensure the success of minority franchisees. The agency could have exercised more oversight over corporate franchisors to make certain that they offered adequate support to sustain struggling franchisees. Similarly, OMBE officials could have been more aggressive in certifying that corporate franchisors fulfilled their pledges to recruit more African-American franchisees from the outset.[138] In the circle of blame, such shortcomings could be—and were—ascribed to inadequate funding for minority enterprise in the early 1970s.[139]

Such failings aside, the SBA under the Nixon administration deserves some credit. It sponsored minority loan transactions at a rate that was, at the very least, greater than the percentage of minorities in the overall population, especially when one considers the *number* (not dollar amount) of minority loans the agency backed relative to the aggregate.[140] In fiscal year 1970, for instance, 6,262 out of a total of 15,102 loans (41 percent) went to minorities; a year later, the figure was 7,776 out of 21,494 loans (36 percent).[141]

Actual gains in minority enterprise (and franchising in particular) during the Nixon years, however, followed the same pattern as the budgets earmarked for minority businesses—respectable, but with important caveats. First, consider the laudable developments in minority entrepreneurship during the Nixon administration. As Brady Keys underscored in his loan application to the Economic Development Administration in 1973, the fast food industry had been flourishing in recent years, and black-owned franchises like his own Kentucky Fried Chicken, Burger King, and All-Pro Chicken outlets had been part of the growth in the industry.[142] The number of franchises run by minorities had indeed risen measurably, from 405 in 1969, to 1,659 in 1972, to a total of 2,453 in 1974.[143] While some minority entrepreneurs owned multiple franchises, Commerce Department data showed that the number of individual minority franchisees also rose from 743 in 1970 to 1,170 the following year, representing an increase of 57 percent.[144]

This trajectory was reflected in the number of black-owned McDonald's franchises from 1969 to the mid-1970s. McDonald's counted only 1 African-American franchisee in 1969. But by 1975 that number had risen to 89 minority franchisees representing 116 outlets, and all of these outlets were located in urban areas.[145] (A majority of McDonald's minority franchisees in 1975 would have been African American.) Rates of minority franchising continued to rise into the 1980s. Between 1975 and 1986, the number of total minority franchisees grew from 3,413 to 10,142.[146] McDonald's was one of the leading companies with minority franchisees. National news reports of the mid-1980s estimated that between 9 and 16 percent of the burger chain's franchises were owned by African Americans.[147]

Gains in minority franchising from the late 1960s to the 1980s should be qualified, however. Minority fast food entrepreneurship was part of the mushrooming of the fast food industry as a whole; between 1976 and 1986, the number of fast food restaurants in the United States tripled.[148] And in spite of McDonald's relatively high minority franchise ownership, as of 1993 minorities owned only about 5 percent of U.S. franchises across all sectors.[149] (African Americans alone made up roughly 12 percent of the total U.S. population at the time.)

Notably, during this period African-American entrepreneurs were more likely to be in fast food than any other industry employing the franchise model. Of *Black Enterprise* magazine's top ten companies with the greatest number of African-American franchisees in 1988, seven were purveyors of fast food.[150] McDonald's and the smaller chain Popeyes, which had an astounding black franchise ownership rate of 21 percent, were industry leaders in minority franchising.[151] Other fast food chains trailed. The 1988 *Black Enterprise* survey found that at Burger King, 3.9 percent of franchisees were minorities, owning 174 outlets out of a total of 4,491.[152] The black ownership rate at KFC was 3.8 percent, followed closely by Subway at 3.7 percent, and Church's Chicken lagging behind its two larger fried chicken competitors at 1.5 percent.[153] The majority of these black-owned McDonald's, Burger King, KFC, Subway, Wendy's, and Church's Chicken outlets were concentrated in inner-cities, a phenomenon that prompted charges of corporate franchisors' redlining of their African-American franchisees—an issue examined in greater depth in the next chapter.

By the 1990s, African Americans' share of minority-owned franchises had declined, giving way to a larger proportion of Asian-owned outlets—a trend that began in the 1970s and one that would accelerate in the two successive decades. (This was partly a function of the Immigration and Nationality Act of 1965, which allowed for more immigrants to the United States from non-European countries.)[154] In 1979, for example, African Americans comprised 43.4 percent of the nation's minority-owned 4,758 franchise outlets (including fast food restaurants, convenience stores, and automotive services and products), followed by Hispanics with 34.4 percent, Asians with 19.8 percent, and the remaining 2.4 percent owned by Native Americans.[155] By 1993, African Americans and Asians both owned about 36 percent of 10,142 minority franchises (35.6 percent and 35.7 percent respectively), with Hispanics at 27.7 percent, and Native Americans with 1.0 percent.[156] But while African Americans accounted for a declining share of minority-owned franchises, this did not mean that there were fewer fast food franchises in urban black neighborhoods. These franchises were just owned by members of other racial and ethnic groups.

Most recently, in the mid to late 2000s, the International Franchise Association and the Commerce Department's Minority Business Development Agency (formerly the OMBE) reported that minorities were more likely to own franchises than nonfranchised businesses, as well as more likely to own fast food franchises than other types of franchised businesses.[157] As of 2007, minority entrepreneurs owned 14.2 percent of nonfranchised businesses, 20.5 percent of franchised businesses, and 21.2 percent of all fast food franchises.[158] Of the 20.5 percent of minority-owned franchises, Asians accounted for 10.4 percent, Hispanics for 5.2 percent, and African Americans for 4.9 percent.[159] Figures for the percentage of minority-owned fast food restaurants are more imprecise. McDonald's, for example, boasts that 45 percent of its franchisees are minorities and women, but does not break down the proportions of women and racial minorities, respectively, within this figure.[160] (It is also unclear whether franchisees are double-counted in the "women" and "minority" categories.)

◆◆◆

Even though long-term gains in minority enterprise (particularly among African Americans) have been relatively modest, federal agencies have indeed provided funding opportunities that helped underwrite the expansion of fast food in America's inner cities. In his 1986 commissioned history of McDonald's, John F. Love was surprisingly candid about federal financing of McDonald's minority-owned franchises. "Working through the Small Business Administration and the Office of Minority Business Enterprise, McDonald's helped black businessmen secure SBA-guaranteed loans to raise most of the capital needed to open a McDonald's," Love explained.[161]

After the Johnson and Nixon administrations (and after Love's history of McDonald's), the SBA and OMBE have continued to help facilitate the growth of the fast food sector (and not just those owned by racial minorities). This has been accomplished through conventional SBA loan guarantees to fast food franchisees (regardless of race), as well as through the franchise coordination and training assistance programs of the Commerce Department's Minority Business Development Agency (the current name for the OMBE).[162] In 1990, for example, the Minority Business Development Agency (MBDA) began teaming up with the International Franchise Association.[163] As a promotional magazine article reported, this partnership sought to raise the number of minority franchisees by "disseminating information to prospective minority entrepreneurs regarding franchise opportunities, as well as providing screening, preparatory business training and assistance in arranging financing through its 105 Minority Business Development Companies (MBDC) across the country."[164] The International Franchise Association's participation in this initiative was a no-brainer. By partnering with the MBDA, the fast food industry and other sectors employing the franchise model could enhance their public relations by claiming to be agents of diversity in business ownership.

Perhaps even more appealing for fast food companies, federal financing of their urban expansion could also be immensely lucrative. The potential profits to be reaped from opening new fast food franchises, and the broader question of what other forces prompted the fast food industry to seek out African-American franchisees in urban areas, are explored in the next chapter.

FOUR

Diversifying out of Necessity

I n his 1977 autobiography *Grinding It Out: The Making of McDonald's*, McDonald's chairman Ray Kroc touted the diversity of his company's employees and owner-operators:

> McDonald's is vastly different now from the company it was back in the early days, and that's good. We responded to the social changes of the late sixties by increasing minority hiring, and organizing a program to bring in qualified black and women operators.[1]

Kroc's quote suggested that "social changes of the late sixties"— most likely a reference to the civil rights and second-wave feminist movements—spurred McDonald's to diversify its workforce and franchise ownership. The implication was that McDonald's was socially adaptable and altruistic, a company that merrily changed with the times.

Kroc was right about McDonald's being adaptable. It is likely that the Golden Arches would not have flourished as it did in subsequent decades had it *not* adapted by diversifying. One could also plausibly assert that McDonald's self-congratulatory plaudits of its diversity are relatively well-deserved. As noted in the previous chapter, today some 45 percent of the company's franchisees are minorities and women, and its president and chief executive officer from July 2012 to March 2015 was Donald "Don" Thompson, an African-American electrical engineer turned corporate executive.[2]

What Kroc's quote elides, however, was that starting in the late 1960s diversity was very much in the interests of McDonald's and other fast food companies. The fast food industry stood to profit from becoming more diverse. They could win public relations "diversity points," and enlisting African-American franchisees dovetailed with fast food companies' plans to expand into urban markets. As McDonald's Roland L. Jones stated, "It wasn't altruism that integrated the company. It was a hard-nosed business decision."[3]

◆◆◆

Recruiting new franchise owners (regardless of their race and ethnicity) has generated substantial income for McDonald's and other fast food corporations. Fast food companies have charged their franchisees fortunes for opening and maintaining outlets. In 1955, McDonald's one-time franchise licensing fee was a relatively modest $950. By 1969, when McDonald's recruited its first African-American franchisee in Chicago, the company had raised the licensing fee to $10,000. The licensing fee, combined with outfitting a new restaurant with equipment, supplies, and furniture purchased from company suppliers, put the total startup cost at around $53,000 in 1969.[4] About a decade later, in 1978, *Black Enterprise* magazine estimated that "the start-up cash required for fast food restaurants was, on average, $165 thousand."[5] In the mid-1980s, the total start-up cost of a McDonald's had risen to $400,000.[6] McDonald's was among the industry's priciest chains, but the franchisee of the typical fast food chain also had to amass a considerable sum just to open for business at that time. In 1988, the International Franchise Association Educational Foundation found that the median cost of opening a restaurant franchise was $250,000.[7]

In more recent years, franchising start-up costs have only escalated, with Subway sandwich shops on the low end, and McDonald's, Wendy's, and Taco Bell on the high end. In 2014, a franchise from Subway—the world's leading fast food chain with more than 44,000 outlets compared to McDonald's 36,000-plus locations (as of 2016)—could be obtained for $116,000 to $262,850, a sum that generally included licensing, leasing, and three-months' initial operating costs.[8] Franchisees of McDonald's, Wendy's, and Taco Bell respectively, are currently required to possess between $750,000 (McDonald's and Taco Bell) and $2 million (Wendy's) in liquid assets.[9] Requiring such hefty bank accounts seems understandable given that a McDonald's franchise in 2012 cost between $955,708 and $2.3 million (including a relatively incidental $45,000 franchise fee); precise costs depend on an outlet's size, location, and other considerations, such landscaping and parking lot needs.[10] And that is just the range to *open* a McDonald's.

Operating a McDonald's or other fast food franchise incurs even more expenses to be paid to corporate headquarters. In the late 1960s, McDonald's franchisees were required to fork over royalties of 2.8 percent of gross sales, in addition to 8 percent of gross volume to cover rent on twenty-year leases.[11] Today, it is typical for fast food companies to charge franchisees annual royalties of 3 to 5 percent of gross sales; McDonald's "service fee" was 5 percent of gross (as of 2014).[12] Subway, perhaps to compensate for its lower start-up costs, charges its franchisees an annual royalty of 8 percent of gross sales.[13] Some chains also impose an additional charge called an "advertising assessment" to ostensibly support national advertising campaigns; this fee usually ranges from 1 to 4.5 percent of total sales.[14] Corporate franchisors also rely on another continuing revenue stream from franchisees—supply sales and replacement equipment. Franchisees of Burger King, for example, procure bags of frozen french fries, plastic utensils, and paper cups stamped with the Burger King logo from one of a number of the company's supply distribution centers.[15]

For many franchisees, the greatest recurring expense has been paying their rent or lease, often to the corporate franchisor that owns the building or land (or both) that their restaurant occupies.[16] As many observers have pointed out, McDonald's Corporation in particular has been as involved in real estate as in hamburgers.[17] And McDonald's is not alone in its real estate ventures. In the 1970s, when the major fast food chains began to make significant inroads into America's inner cities, it was estimated that some 73 percent of corporate franchisors leased or rented buildings and land to their franchisees.[18] In the case of McDonald's, by 1986 the company owned the property occupied by 60 percent of its outlets, and leased the remainder.[19] (The company was more likely to own suburban properties and lease urban ones.)[20] Burger King had a slightly different real estate model, one that may help to explain why it required potential franchisees to post a net worth of at least $1.5 million, including $500,000 in liquid assets.[21] In the 1980s, the company maintained a real-estate division that identified potential franchise sites from which franchisees could choose. Burger King would then facilitate the construction of individual outlets, but franchisees were responsible for all building costs.[22] As all these costs associated with opening and operating fast food franchises demonstrate, corporate headquarters at Burger King, McDonald's, Subway, and other chains had a lot to gain by signing up new franchisees.

To generate additional profits from new franchises, fast food companies made efforts to enlist more franchisees. When they sought to expand to inner-city areas and discovered federal minority entrepreneurship programs, fast food chains were especially keen to enroll prospective African-American franchisees. By the mid-1970s, fast food franchisors were actively recruiting African-American entrepreneurs and encouraging them to explore sources of federal funding for the start-up capital they would need to open franchises.

One of the ways the fast food industry reached out to African Americans was by placing advertisements in magazines catering to the entrepreneurial set, most notably *Black Enterprise*. Founded in 1970, *Black Enterprise* currently describes itself as "the premier business, investing, and wealth-building resource for African Americans"; the magazine reports a readership of 4 million.[23] *Black Enterprise* was a favorite for McDonald's minority franchisee recruitment efforts. One ad appearing in the April 1978 issue of *Black Enterprise* presented a photograph of an African American named Harry Cromwell, described in the ad as the

"Director of Operations for McDonald's in New York and Connecticut." Cromwell was shown jogging, perhaps to evoke fitness and discipline as well as middle-class leisure afforded by a career at McDonald's. His image was accompanied by the caption, "The McDonald's Executive: 7 Special Ingredients"—"motivated, bright, ambitious, responsible, involved, energetic, decisive."[24] An address where perspective McDonald's executives could send their résumés appeared at the bottom of the ad.

Advertising in black business media like *Black Enterprise* also seemed to yield McDonald's and other chains well-placed articles promising lucrative opportunities in the fast food business. One article in the May 1974 issue of the magazine assured readers that while the $140,000 start-up costs for a McDonald's franchise "may sound steep," they could be recouped relatively quickly. "The average [McDonald's] store sold enough Big Macs and French fries to register a gross of $621,000[,] netting the franchise a pre-tax profit ranging from $50,000 to $75,000," the article pitched.[25] Such promises of ringing cash registers were accompanied by testimonials, most notably those of Brady Keys.[26]

Magazines celebrated Keys as a prolific fast food franchisee whose combination of industriousness and fidelity to the franchise formula could serve as a model for African-American entrepreneurs. In 1984, Keys's self-described "miniconglomerate," the Keys Group Company, owned six Burger King outlets in Michigan and seven Kentucky Fried Chickens in Georgia, as well as franchises from a multitude of smaller restaurant chains, including A&W Root Beer and Bonanza Steak House.[27] In magazine interviews, Keys touted the familiar refrain of fast food franchisors' courtship of prospective franchisees. He promulgated the idea that franchising "gives the person the opportunity to be in business *for* himself but not *by* himself"—a description conjuring up historian Daniel Boorstin's characterization of the franchise owner as a "semi-independent businessman."[28] In a 1974 interview with *Black Enterprise*, Keys elaborated:

That's the only way I recommend blacks go into business—via the franchise route. I'd add only joint ventures and spin-offs . . . You need management talent. Blacks don't generally have it, we don't have the experience, but the franchisers do. You've got to go with the people who've got it.[29]

As Keys's promotion of franchising suggested, recruitment of African-American franchisees included assurances that lack of business experience need not deter would-be franchisees. Corporate franchisors, meanwhile, affirmed that they were equipped with time-tested business plans and marketing strategies, and that they would provide guidance at every step. McDonald's minority recruitment executive Robert M. Beavers underscored the centrality of his company's assistance to franchisees in a 1984 *Ebony* article: "A guy doesn't have to have a tremendous amount of management success to be a success with us, but it would be rough without our support."[30] As long as McDonald's franchisees possessed "good people skills, the ability to manage money and a good practical sense about the world," they would be set on the path toward success.[31] Everything else, Beavers promised, "we will teach them."[32]

Other fast food chains also reached out to potential franchisees in *Black Enterprise*. In the June 1996 issue, both Wendy's and Popeyes emphasized their commitment to the 1990s buzzword, "diversity." Wendy's ad announced that "we believe that future growth will depend on an increasingly diverse marketplace."[33] On the same page of the magazine, Popeyes echoed, "We Made Minority Business Development Our Business" (in large font). The burger chain Hardee's similarly showcased a photograph of two African-American franchisees in St. Louis, replete with contact information for the company's Director of Minority Affairs.[34] And perhaps in reference to Burger King's $1.5 million net worth requirement for franchisees, the Hardee's ad included a quote by the two featured franchisees: "They [Hardee's] require a lesser financial net worth for minority candidates."

But while the fast food industry wooed prospective African-American franchisees—one survey by the International Franchise Association in 1992 found that 74 out of 180 franchise companies (not just fast food) claimed to have minority recruitment programs—they seldom reached into their own pockets to assist minority entrepreneurs.[35] The financial assistance they provided was generally limited to modifying asset and down payment requirements for minorities. When Burger King signed a covenant with the civil rights organization Operation PUSH (People United to Save Humanity) in 1984, for example, it agreed to raise the number of African-American franchises from less than 100 (out of 3,800) to 540 by 1987. To achieve this goal, the company pledged that it would reduce the down payment for African-American franchisees from $125,000 to $25,000. But that was where the burger chain's "assistance" ended. As the company's spokesperson John Weir told *Black Enterprise*, "The rest of the financing is arranged by the owner himself."[36] The same had been true of many other restaurant franchisors in earlier years. In 1971, the Senate's Select Committee on Small Business found that only 38 of 180 franchisors surveyed made financing help available.[37] This assistance, moreover, frequently meant that the franchisor participated in minority recruitment programs sponsored by the SBA or the Commerce Department. So when franchisors vaguely touted "minority financing program available," as the Subway chain did in an ad appearing in *Black Enterprise* in 1996, they meant that they could refer prospective franchisees to sources of government funding like the SBA.[38]

◆◆◆

African-American franchisees came on the radar of fast food companies when the industry looked to expand to predominantly minority inner-city locations starting in the late 1960s and early 1970s. By the 1980s, black franchise owners were sought after to draw and retain the African-American consumers who were becoming indispensable to the fast food industry's bottom line. In 1985, African-American customers accounted for 15 percent of all fast food sales, despite registering 11.7 percent and 12.1 percent of the total U.S. population in the 1980 and 1990 Censuses, respectively.[39] Black franchisees seemed like an obvious way to reach African-American restaurant-goers in urban communities.

Once in those urban communities, fast food companies saw African-American franchise owners as a way to manage some of the difficulties of opening outlets in what were deemed "risky" inner-city locations. While they could be enormously profitable, inner-city franchises could also pose particular challenges. This was especially true after the 1960s riots, when white-owned businesses were not always welcome in black neighborhoods.[40] Recruiting African-American franchisees was seen as a way to mitigate potential conflicts, as well as a means of outsourcing the everyday difficulties and dangers of operating restaurants in inner-city locations. As Brady Keys bluntly explained in a 1974 interview with *Black Enterprise* magazine:

> They [fast food corporations] know that doing business in my area is hell. There's cutting, shooting, killing. So they say, we really don't want to do this ourselves, so why don't we get this black cat over here and franchise him?[41]

Roland L. Jones offered a similar account of the practical hazards of doing business at a McDonald's franchise in the Northeast quadrant of Washington in the late 1960s. As Jones explained:

> The lack of consistent police presence contributed in a major way to the high rate of armed robberies at inner-city stores. Night shifts were especially dangerous, and managers and assistant managers who closed their stores in the wee hours of the morning were always at risk. In the past, whoever cashed out had taken that day's receipts directly to the bank for night deposit, but that practice was scrapped when the rate of physical attacks soared. Every store had a safe, so managers started locking up the daily receipts overnight and then

taking their deposits to the bank in broad daylight. That helped, but it didn't stop the muggers and thieves, and eventually the company [McDonald's] turned to armored car services. In the tense weeks and months after the riots, some restaurant managers began carrying guns, although this was against company policy.[42]

Jones, who cofounded the National Black McDonald's Operator Association (NBMOA), recalled how the organization's members shared tips on dealing with potentially dicey situations at their inner-city franchises. During one meeting in the early 1970s, Lee Dunham, a New York City franchise owner as well as a former member of the New York Police Department, put on an "eye-opening video presentation" for his fast food colleagues that included a tutorial titled, "How Do You Recognize a Drug Addict, and Why Is It Important?"[43]

Franchisees also took dramatic measures to ensure the security of their restaurants. In their 1976 book on the history of McDonald's, Max Boas and Steve Chain reported that on Chicago's West Side, some McDonald's franchise owners maintained a cache of firearms "near the grill," while franchisees in New York City and San Francisco employed security guards "dressed as managers and muscular 'customers' with handcuffs tied to their belts."[44] Such measures continued into the 1980s, as one New York City McDonald's franchisee told the *New York Times* in 1984.[45] Echoing Brady Keys's remark that operating outlets in high-crime areas was "hell," McDonald's franchisee Charles Griffis related:

> My stores are in hellholes . . . They get robbed once or twice a month, and I pay $20,000 a month in security services they don't pay in good neighborhoods. We had a murder in one and we still get the windows smashed and the bathrooms vandalized.[46]

In the 1990s and 2000s, neighborhoods in cities like New York and Washington were gentrifying, but some inner-city fast food outlets that remained relatively untouched by the onslaught of white professionals, luxury condo developments, yoga studios, and upscale coffee shops were still fortified as if in a war zone. La-Van Hawkins, who owned over two dozen Burger Kings in Atlanta, Baltimore, Chicago, Detroit, and Washington, employed Nation of Islam security guards at his restaurants.[47] But unlike the guards at McDonald's franchises in Chicago in the 1970s, Hawkins's security men were not dressed to blend in; consistent with Nation of Islam sartorial predilections, they wore bow ties and suits.[48] (Ironically, Nation of Islam leader Elijah Muhammad would not have approved of fast food. Muhammad authored a two-volume series in the 1960s titled *How to Eat to Live,* in which he advocated an abstemious, primarily vegetarian, one-meal-a-day diet.)[49]

◆◆◆

Civil rights and community activists have justifiably demanded that businesses in their communities be black-owned and hire African-American employees. (Placing African-American franchise owners in the literal line of fire in high-crime areas without provision of sufficient financial support for added security was most likely not what they had in mind, however.) To compel stores to employ African Americans, community activists have staged protests and called for boycotts. Some two decades before the more familiar civil rights activism in the southern states in the 1950s and 1960s, Harlem residents organized "Don't Buy Where You Can't Work" campaigns in New York City in the 1930s.[50] In the world of fast food, civil rights groups began pressuring McDonald's and other chains to place more African-American entrepreneurs at the helm of inner-city franchises in the late 1960s. Community activists of that period also did not appreciate that while McDonald's extracted profits from inner-city customers, the company appeared to show little interest in contributing to the well-being of the communities of which they were a part.[51]

Such grievances informed a boycott of Cleveland-area McDonald's restaurants in 1969. In the spring of that year, a Cleveland minister and rabbi teamed up to lobby the burger chain for a black-owned franchise;

at the time, there were only four black-owned McDonald's outlets nationwide.[52] McDonald's demurred, maintaining that it could not force existing franchisees to sell their outlets. At this time when the black power movement was fomenting, a newly established black nationalist group called Operation Black Unity (OBU) joined the two clergymen's campaign. The OBU wrote to Edward A. Bood, a McDonald's corporate vice president in charge of franchising. Bood did not respond favorably. According to historian Nishani Frazier, Bood rationalized McDonald's lack of confidence in black entrepreneurs by claiming that African Americans "lacked business expertise and resources." Bood also refused to meet with OBU on the matter, noting that he would not "capitulate to threats, harassment, coercion, intimidation, and violence."[53]

Bood's response to OBU prompted the organization, along with a coalition including the Cleveland chapters of the National Association for the Advancement of Colored People (NAACP) and the National Urban League, to begin boycotting four McDonald's outlets on the east side of Cleveland in July 1969. The boycotts quickly led to the closing of the affected McDonald's franchises. After two months, the office of Cleveland mayor Carl Stokes stepped in and facilitated negotiations between OBU and McDonald's. McDonald's eventually agreed to sell its four east side Cleveland franchises to African Americans or organizations representing African Americans; the company also promised that a future Cleveland franchise would be black-owned.[54]

The new African-American owners of McDonald's franchises on Cleveland's east side included the Hough Area Development Corporation (HADC). Community leaders formed the HADC in 1967, after devastating riots in the Hough section of Cleveland. Like many other riot-stricken neighborhoods, jobs and economic development had been scarce in Hough. The HADC was established to revitalize the neighborhood by launching small businesses and offering banking services and job training programs. Federal officials at the Office of Economic Opportunity learned of the HADC through the organization's applications for financial support from foundations and corporations. Nishani Fra-

zier points out that the Johnson administration was particularly keen
to support economic development in Cleveland, as it deemed the city's
African-American voters (and more broadly, Ohio's electoral votes) to
be crucial to Vice President Hubert Humphrey's prospects in the 1968
presidential election. With the encouragement of the Office of Economic
Opportunity, the HADC applied for, and received, a grant of $1.5 million
from the federal government. The HADC was the first community development organization to receive a grant of this size. According to Frazier,
this made the organization "the most well funded [organization of its
kind] in the nation."

With its grant, the HADC invested in small businesses on Cleveland's east side, including two McDonald's outlets. The restaurants were
largely staffed by Hough residents, and the profits were divided between
the organization and the Hough community.[55] The HADC would later sell
its east Cleveland McDonald's outlets, however, because the restaurants
proved unprofitable.[56] Even so, the HADC's onetime ownership of the
two Cleveland McDonald's restaurants—however ephemeral—was significant. It represented another instance of the U.S. federal government underwriting the fast food industry. The government, after all,
had provided the $1.5 million grant enabling the HADC to purchase its
McDonald's franchises. The Cleveland community organization's purchase of McDonald's also signaled a shift from white-owned fast food
restaurants in African-American neighborhoods to increasing numbers
of black-owned franchises, and even a handful of outlets owned by community groups such as the HADC. In Chicago, for instance, two urban
nonprofit organizations called the Better Boys Foundation and the West
Side Organization for Better Boys, pooled their resources and purchased
a local McDonald's outlet in 1970.[57]

Meanwhile, the Cleveland boycotts that preceded the HADC's ownership of McDonald's had pushed McDonald's to diversify its franchise
ownership more swiftly. Robert M. Beavers, the former McDonald's
senior vice president and the company's officer in charge of minority

franchise recruitment in the late 1960s and 1970s, recalled that the Cleveland boycotts made corporate headquarters aware of "the need to move a lot faster on minority licensing."[58] Roland L. Jones similarly noted that Cleveland "accelerated the sense of urgency at corporate headquarters in Chicago," as it made apparent that "the company *had* to pursue a more aggressive minority franchising program."[59] To this end, the McDonald's Corporation delivered a "directive requesting that white owners in inner-city areas sell to interested Black owners," according to Frazier. As a result of this directive, African-American franchisees acquired twenty-one McDonald's outlets in Detroit, Oakland, Kansas City, St. Louis, Los Angeles, Chicago, Denver, and Dayton, Ohio—a development that Burger King sought to replicate in its own inner-city franchises.[60]

McDonald's broader response to the Cleveland boycotts included a modification of its asset requirements for prospective minority franchisees; the company also pursued federally sponsored programs intended to promote minority entrepreneurship. These approaches yielded some results, however modest. As one celebratory history of the company proudly noted, McDonald's counted "nearly fifty" African-American-owned franchises by 1972—almost 10 percent of all of its franchisees.[61] And by 1980, the city of Cleveland counted 16 black-owned McDonald's restaurants.[62] Nationwide, African Americans owned some 300 McDonald's outlets by the mid-1980s; the company liked to boast that this accounted for half of all black-owned restaurant franchises (representing all chains) in the country at the time.[63]

Nevertheless, the relationship between African-American franchisees and the fast food industry would continue to be marked by episodic tension. In 1972, McDonald's held its first international convention attended by company executives and franchisees. The convention featured a speech by Paul Harvey, a conservative radio talk show host and personal friend of McDonald's chairman Ray Kroc.[64] Harvey's speech, according to one account, faulted America's poor for their condition and castigated them for being "too lazy to work." To African-American franchisees in the audience, Harvey's speech smacked of racism.[65] As Roland L. Jones recalled:

> [Harvey] didn't specifically single out black people, but he con-demned welfare recipients and condoned the recent police brutality during the Attica prison uprising in upstate New York. The whole speech seemed to be about race. When he equated laziness and fail-ure with rioting, you had to be really dense not to know to whom he was referring.[66]

In response to Harvey's speech, a contingent of African-American franchisees from Chicago and Cleveland fired off a letter to Kroc and McDonald's executives conveying their disappointment and anger over the speech. The letter also included an inventory of other grievances with the McDonald's Corporation, including the company's exclusion of African Americans from its decision-making and its inattention to the unique difficulties African-American franchisees faced in operat-ing inner-city outlets.[67] It is unclear how McDonald's Corporation re-sponded to this letter. African Americans had only been McDonald's franchisees for a few years, but their relationship with the company was already strained. A decade later, another issue—redlining—would come to the fore.

African-American franchisees and civil rights groups charged chains like McDonald's and Burger King with redlining, or confining African-American franchise owners to restaurants in black neighborhoods. (The term is most commonly associated with racial discrimination in real estate practices.)[68] Although African Americans had initially fought for the opportunity to operate fast food franchises in their own communi-ties in the late 1960s, by the early 1980s some African-American franchi-sees also sought ownership of fast food outlets outside of majority-black neighborhoods. A number of franchisees were stymied, however, by what they suspected was redlining. In 1984, Charles Griffis, an African-

American McDonald's franchisee in southern California, was embroiled in one such dispute with the burger company. McDonald's sued Griffis, claiming he owned two Popeyes restaurants—a violation of McDonald's policy barring franchisees from maintaining financial interests in other fast food chains. Griffis countersued, charging McDonald's with racial discrimination. He alleged that the company relegated him to a Los Angeles restaurant that was "an old store in real bad shape," located "on Santa Barbara Street, right in the middle of the ghetto."[69] (Griffis would eventually accumulate three more McDonald's franchises, all located in what he referred to as "the ghetto.") The case settled with McDonald's paying Griffis $4.7 million, a sum the burger chain characterized as merely a buyout of Griffis's four franchises rather than a capitulation to his "bogus racial discrimination claims."[70]

The Griffis case was not an isolated one. The New York chapter of the National Black McDonald's Operators Association lodged a formal complaint with a McDonald's regional vice president in 1982, accusing the company of redlining African-American franchisees in the New York area.[71] While members of the NBMOA wanted the freedom to purchase franchises where they pleased rather than be restricted to inner-city sites, they also felt cheated by redlining for the practical consequences and challenges it posed in the everyday operation of their restaurants. As noted earlier in this chapter, urban franchise owners bore the additional security costs associated with running inner-city outlets. These security concerns also affected the service and attention inner-city franchise owners received from the front office of fast food chains and the various contractors working with those fast food companies. As Roland L. Jones recalled of his experience as a McDonald's franchisee in 1970s Chicago:

> Normally, when an operator reported that his cash register was acting up, a representative of the equipment company went immediately to the store to make the repair on site. But white repair reps were refusing to go into black neighborhoods in Chicago, and black operators

had no option but to take their equipment to the supplier and leave it until the repair was made. This caused delays and serious inconvenience until the register could be retrieved and re-installed.[72]

Jones, who also became a McDonald's executive, subsequently reassured readers that the burger chain rectified this by training and hiring African-American tradespersons who, presumably, *were* willing to go to black neighborhood restaurants to repair equipment.[73] (It would seem that McDonald's might also have done more to compel white tradespeople to venture to inner-city franchises, but Jones's narrative makes no mention of this.) Jones's praise of McDonald's responsiveness notwithstanding, the notion that even the relatively mundane task of getting a cash register repaired could be considerably more difficult in inner-city restaurants than elsewhere points to one of the various ways redlining disadvantaged African-American fast food entrepreneurs.

Civil rights organizations such as Operation PUSH and the NAACP also took on the fast food industry for redlining. In 1982, the high-profile Operation PUSH leader (and presidential candidate in 1984 and 1988) Jesse Jackson, protested that African-American McDonald's franchisees were assigned the least desirable, "recycled" outlets that came with steep security and maintenance expenses.[74] Similarly, Los Angeles NAACP director John T. McDonald III (no relation to the burger chain's eponymous founders, Richard and Maurice McDonald) noted that in 1984 only one out of 137 African-American McDonald's franchisees owned a restaurant in a white neighborhood. The NAACP leader relayed to the *New York Times* that his organization was "very concerned about what seems to be McDonald's redlining in the Los Angeles area."[75] Los Angeles NAACP chapters subsequently waged a partial boycott, or "selective buy" campaign, against McDonald's; Los Angeles mayor Tom Bradley eventually intervened and brokered a negotiation between the civil rights organization and the burger chain.[76] In Chicago that same year, local NAACP chapters also organized a boycott of McDonald's over what they regarded as redlining, as well as to protest that the company did not employ enough African Americans as company executives and consultants.⁷⁷

Burger King was also accused of redlining. In 1988, twelve African-American franchisees from across the country brought a class-action lawsuit against the number-two burger chain (a subsidiary of the Pillsbury Company at the time) for restricting African-American, Hispanic, and Asian franchisees to blighted inner-city locations.⁷⁸ The suit sought compensatory and punitive damages totaling $500 million, and alleged that the chain discriminated against minority and women franchisees by taking longer to approve their applications for new franchises. Plaintiffs also charged that Burger King prevented them from opening multiple franchises simultaneously—a privilege the company granted its white franchisees.⁷⁹ The case, which later expanded to include twenty-four franchisees, was eventually dismissed after the plaintiffs rejected Burger King's settlement offer of $40 million. Operation PUSH's campaigns fared better, with the organization eventually signing covenants with Burger King, Kentucky Fried Chicken, Hardee's, Wendy's, and McDonald's. In the covenant with Operation PUSH, fast food companies promised to allocate more black-owned franchises, recruit more African Americans for their boards of directors, and contract with more African-American restaurant supply vendors.⁸⁰

◆◆◆

The process of diversifying fast food franchise ownership was prompted by both pulls and pushes. In the wake of the civil rights movement, fast food companies were drawn to diversify because it offered possibilities for reaching the urban market with "home-grown" personnel. When new franchisees were recruited, fast food corporations and the franchise fees they could collect also grew. And in the aftermath of the urban riots of the mid to late 1960s, the fast food industry could also expand in the name of diversity with financial support from the U.S. federal government. But as charges of redlining against particular fast food companies illustrated, the diversity they implemented was incomplete at best and exploitatively opportunist at worst. It took civil rights organizations and African-American franchisees themselves to force the fast food industry toward a more just diversity that is arguably still a work-in-progress.

The responsiveness of fast food corporations to concerns about franchisee redlining and equity, moreover, was in their own financial interest, just as initial efforts toward franchisee diversity in the late 1960s and early 1970s had been. The major fast food chains' participation in covenants with civil rights organizations, Burger King's attempt to settle the class-action suit brought against it, and even McDonald's hiring of African-American repairpersons to fix equipment in its inner-city franchises all signaled that the fast food industry could not afford to alienate African-American franchise owners. Black franchise owners were, after all, conduits to urban African-American consumers. And as the next chapter explains, fast food companies vigorously cultivated black consumers as they became increasingly vital to fast food's bottom line.

FIVE

Shoring Up the Urban Market

An image of everyday life in the Jim Crow South has remained with Roland L. Jones for over half a century. It is the scene of African-American customers placing their orders from a side window at a McDonald's outlet in Birmingham, Alabama.[1] Jones, who would one day become a McDonald's franchisee and executive, first noticed that window when he was a child visiting the southern city with his parents. Just as the South had separate "colored" and "white" water fountains before the Civil Rights Act of 1964 outlawed them, this McDonald's also drew a color line. Whites entered the restaurant through its main entrance. African Americans had to queue up outside a side window.[2]

That Birmingham McDonald's was not the only place that discriminated against its African-American customers. Black diners often also received second-class service in northern cities throughout the 1950s and 1960s. Even in places like New York City, they had difficulty obtaining reservations at restaurants where whites faced no such problem. When African Americans asked to be seated in majority-white restaurants, they were sometimes met with awkward responses or hesitations from restaurant staff. And once seated—possibly near swinging doors, bathrooms, or out of sight from white diners—it was not unusual for African Americans to be served substandard food while being neglected by waitstaff.[3]

Today, McDonald's no longer accords its African-American patrons

second-class status, in Birmingham or anywhere else (at least not systematically or by decree). And for the most part, African Americans
do not confront the same degree of routine restaurant discrimination
that they encountered in all areas of the country before the federal civil
rights legislation of the 1960s. The reality, however, is that some restaurants still make particular customers feel more welcome than others
based on race, socioeconomic status, sexual orientation, and myriad
other considerations. Herein lies part of the appeal of dining at fast food
restaurants from major national or regional chains.[4] They are relatively
democratic.[5] They aim for standardization and consistency not just in
their menu items (though there may be regional variations), but also in
customer service. One can enter a McDonald's or a Burger King looking like a pauper and still be served. As legal scholar Andrea Freeman
observes:

> Many of the defining elements of fast food restaurants help to reduce
> or eliminate potentially discriminatory behavior. Employees wait on
> customers according to their place in line, which avoids demonstra-
> tions of preference for a more desirable clientele. Posted signs clearly
> announce food prices, ensuring that employees will not charge some
> customers more than others. Food quality and appearance are also
> consistent across fast food chains and within individual restaurants,
> providing no opportunity to discriminate by adjusting portion size
> or taste. The practice of paying for food before receiving it reduces
> employees' anxiety about their customers' inability to pay and makes
> tipping a non-issue.[6]

This egalitarian character of fast food restaurants and their relative affordability, speed, convenience, ubiquity, and safety all contribute to
the draw of fast food among inner-city minority customers who may
feel unwelcome at more exclusive eating establishments.[7]

As this chapter shows, however, these considerations do not entirely
explain the appeal of major fast food chains like McDonald's and Ken-

tucky Fried Chicken to inner-city minorities. Since fast food companies began investing in inner-city locations starting in the late 1960s, they have, for the most part, aggressively cultivated African-American consumers. But while racial equality in customer service and the end of racially segregated McDonald's were unequivocally positive developments, it is less certain that the fast food industry's targeting of African Americans has been anything to commend.

◆◆◆

According to one report in 2011, black customers accounted for about 18 percent of McDonald's total receipts—6 percentage points more than the total population classified as "Black or African American" in the 2010 U.S. Census.[8] This did not happen by chance. For more than forty years, McDonald's and other fast food chains have been devising strategies to get African-American patrons in the door and keep them coming back. As discussed earlier in this book, the fast food industry seized upon the relatively untapped urban market as their suburban and highway locations became increasingly saturated. African Americans were a crucial part of this urban market, particularly as they made economic gains and because, as one U.S. Commerce Department official put it, "the Black consumer market [was] a big market."[9] That black population growth from 1960 to 1970 outpaced that of whites (20 percent to 12 percent) only made it more likely that African Americans would become the targets of sales pitches for everything from houses to hamburgers—especially hamburgers.[10] By 1971, a marketing guide to "the black consumer" would proclaim that "black ghettos in this country, if they were evaluated as a nation, would rank tenth in annual income among the nations of the world."[11]

Seventies popular culture and media also seemed to pick up on the upswing in African Americans' economic circumstances; that decade witnessed a number of depictions of the affluence of fictional and real African Americans. In the now-classic sitcom *The Jeffersons*, which debuted on the CBS network in January 1975, patriarch George Jefferson was a prosperous Harlem entrepreneur who had accumulated a chain of dry cleaners in New York City. (Notably, the theme song accompanying the show's opening credits was called "We're Movin' On Up.")[12] Some six months earlier, the June 17, 1974, issue of *Time* magazine had featured a middle-class African-American family (a mother, father, daughter, son, and their German shepherd) on its cover. The headline read: "Middle-Class Blacks: Making It in America."[13]

The Jeffersons and the *Time* magazine cover were not necessarily fantasies. African Americans did make notable gains in income between the 1960s and 1970s. As *Time* itself reported, only 13 percent of African Americans took home an annual income of $10,000 in 1961, but that percentage rose to 30 percent a decade later. White incomes also climbed during this period, but there were signs that gains in income, higher education, and white-collar jobs among African Americans outpaced those of whites. In 1964, the median black family income was 54 percent of median white family income, but by 1972, that number had risen slightly, to 59 percent. A greater share of African Americans were also attending college and obtaining professional employment. Roughly 727,000 African Americans were attending college in 1972, double the number of black college students in 1967. (College enrollment was 18 percent among blacks between the ages of eighteen and twenty-four, and 26 percent among whites in the same age cohort).[14]

African Americans had also made comparable gains in white collar employment between the 1950s and 1960s. In 1956, they made up 3.7 percent of the professional and technical workforce; that number rose to 5.9 percent a decade later.[15] Similarly, in 1971, some 756,000 African Americans were employed as doctors, lawyers, teachers, engineers, and in other professional capacities; this represented a 128 percent increase from 1960.[16] To put this into perspective, these types of jobs grew by only 49 percent in the overall U.S. economy. Such numbers led Herman P. Miller, a U.S. Census Bureau official charged with analyzing historical Census data, to remark in 1968 that "most Negro men and women are succeeding against overwhelming odds."[17]

But Miller's perspective was perhaps too sanguine. While note-worthy, progress in income, education, and jobs among African Americans should have been qualified. Due to severely limited opportunities before the federal civil rights legislation of the mid-1960s, African-American income, rates of college attendance, and representation in the professions were low enough that subsequent gains appeared especially striking. Media reports that African American gains outpaced those of whites also obscured the reality of continued economic disparities between blacks and whites. And even though *Time* trumpeted increasing white collar employment among African Americans in its 1974 cover story on "America's Rising Black Middle Class," it acknowledged that African-American business professionals were often "isolated from real decision making," and that "almost all top corporate officers are white." More than half of all working African Americans were not employed in professional capacities, but in semiskilled or unskilled labor—precisely the types of work that had been contracting as America's factories continued to mechanize.[18]

Given these considerations, Elsworthy Taylor, an African-American hospital administrator from Chicago, offered what was perhaps the most apt characterization of African-American economic mobility in the 1970s. "There are many middle-class blacks," Taylor observed in *Time*, "but there is no black middle class."[19] That about one-third of African Americans were middle-class by the 1970s gave credence to Taylor's observation. That figure was most certainly an improvement from the 13 percent of middle-class African Americans in 1960, but it was still considerably below the overall percentage of Americans—50 percent—in the middle class in 1970s.[20]

The existence of increasing numbers of middle-class African Americans in the 1970s should also be considered alongside the reality of a persistent black "underclass"—the racially tinged, culturally laden term used to describe the chronically unemployed and impoverished. Although the percentage of African Americans living below the poverty line declined from about one-half to one-third in 1969, that percentage plateaued in the 1970s. (The poverty line in 1972 meant an income below $4,500 for a nonfarm family of four.)[21] Poor African-American families were also especially hard hit by 1970s inflation, as a substantial share of their limited income was being spent on more costly essential goods and services. And in cities like Detroit and Cleveland, the deindustrialization that had already been under way was especially devastating to African Americans who had relied on manufacturing jobs.[22] These jobs gradually disappeared. The former African-American factory workers who remained unemployed lived in neighborhoods increasingly in decline, as black families with the wherewithal to move out of these communities did so.[23] As sociologist William Julius Wilson has pointed out, such developments contributed to the transformation of relatively heterogeneous African-American communities with both middle-class and working-class inhabitants, to neighborhoods with greater concentrations of poverty and attendant problems like joblessness, crime, and out-of-wedlock births.[24]

In spite of these caveats to the notion of a "growing black middle class," the fast food industry and other purveyors of goods and services sought to capture a share of the African-American consumer market in the 1970s. Trans World Airlines, for instance, began special vacation tour packages aimed at African-American travelers. They developed Afrocentric tours to Europe, which included excursions to African museums, black neighborhoods, and meet-and-greets with African-American servicemen stationed on the continent.[25] The 1970s was also the decade when companies like McDonald's and Coca-Cola began making an effort to feature African Americans in their advertising campaigns.[26] The now-disgraced comedian and actor Bill Cosby became one of the most high-profile African-American pitchmen when Jell-O hired him to promote its brand of gelatin desserts in 1974.[27]

Marketers were buoyed by the discovery that African-American households consumed a number of everyday consumer goods at a rate that exceeded their proportion of the U.S. population. While African Americans made up less than 12 percent of the population in the mid-

1970s, their shoe and music cassette purchases, for example, accounted for nearly a quarter of the total sales for those items.[28] Similarly, a team of researchers led by Harvard Business School professor Raymond A. Bauer found that African Americans purchased one-quarter of all the Scotch whisky sold in the United States in the late 1960s; among African Americans with discretionary income, Scotch was the preferred "status drink."[29] By 1969, three-quarters of all African-American residences also reported owning at least one television set—a household centerpiece that would, incidentally, become a key conduit by which fast food chains would reach out to African-American consumers in subsequent decades.[30] These examples of African Americans' acquisition of retail goods illustrated what a black college administrator succinctly shared with *Time* magazine: "Blacks want[ed] the same things as whites."[31] For some African Americans—including those in low-income inner-city communities—this meant the burgers, fries, and milkshakes that were becoming more prevalent in their neighborhoods and that were being increasingly marketed to them.

◆◆◆

Fast food companies' aggressive pursuit of African Americans since the early 1970s has been reflected by the inordinate share of their promotional budgets dedicated to reeling in minority consumers. One report in 1990 found that the three major fast food chains—McDonald's, Burger King, and Wendy's—earmarked up to one-fifth of their advertising budgets on African-American consumers even though African Americans made up only about 12 percent of the total U.S. population at the time.[32] And this just referred to television and radio advertising. Fast food companies have also promoted images of their burgers, fried chicken, pizza, and tacos on billboards, and this billboard advertising is more likely to appear in low-income African-American areas than in low-income white neighborhoods.[33] More recently, a 2014 study in the *American Journal of Preventive Medicine* revealed the extent to which fast food chains have targeted African-American children in particular. The study, which included a survey of 6,716 fast food outlets, found that restaurants in African-American neighborhoods had a more than 60 percent greater chance of featuring advertisements directed toward children than fast food restaurants in white areas.[34]

All this suggests, of course, that the fast food industry has made especially concerted efforts to market to African Americans. That African Americans are, as researchers Sonya A. Grier and Shiriki K. Kumanyika have observed, "more likely than are any other U.S. ethnic group to live in racially segregated neighborhoods, even when suburban neighborhoods are included"—only reinforces the likelihood that they will be subject to more directed marketing.[35] (The concentration of African Americans in segregated neighborhoods is partly a consequence of historical developments, including: violence and intimidation meant to drive African Americans out of white neighborhoods, racial discrimination in the form of restrictive covenants and reluctance to sell to black homebuyers, and white flight.)[36]

In conjunction with their concentration in segregated neighborhoods, for much of the twentieth century African Americans have also been more likely to be urban and to reside in the nation's major cities. (This is starting to change, as greater numbers of African Americans have been moving to suburban neighborhoods and to more rural areas in the southern states in response to the increasing unaffordability of formerly black neighborhoods in cities like Washington and New York.)[37] In the late 1960s, just as the major fast food chains were setting their sights on the urban market, one-third of African Americans were residing in America's twenty-five largest cities. By comparison, the white population was much more dispersed, with only one-seventh of whites living in the same twenty-five cities.[38] Accordingly, African Americans were considerably more represented in urban areas than in the nation as a whole. At the dawn of the urban fast food offensive in 1969, African Americans made up 11 percent of the total U.S. population. But in seventy-eight U.S. cities, they were 25 percent or more of the population.[39]

The concentration of African Americans in segregated neighborhoods within the major cities was a boon to national companies hoping
to reach African-American consumers. African Americans were, according to the jargon of marketers, "compact sales target[s]," and ripe for
"geographic targeting."⁴⁰ But while the residential segregation and concentration of African Americans in particular cities have accounted for
a degree of the disproportionate fast food marketing to which they have
been exposed, fast food companies have still gone to exceptional lengths
to attract African-American (and increasingly, Latino) consumers.

National fast food chains, especially McDonald's, have been so in-
dustrious in their attempts to appeal to minority consumers that they
have even been recognized by trade associations for "minority outreach." In 1993, McDonald's won an award from the International Franchise Association for "outstanding achievement in initiating minority
programs." Noting that McDonald's was the "largest single-brand advertiser on Hispanic television and the largest advertiser in black and
Hispanic media in the quick-service industry," the franchise advocacy
group representing some 10,000 franchisees in myriad industries presented the burger chain with its Free Enterprise Award for "devot[ing]
enormous resources to marketing programs specifically designed to
reach minorities."⁴¹ For McDonald's, the investment had been paying
off since the mid-1970s. In a 1974 survey by the minority marketing research firm D. Parke Gibson International, McDonald's ranked as the
number-one preferred fast food chain of African-American consumers,
followed by Burger King, Chicken Unlimited, Kentucky Fried Chicken,
and Burger Chef.⁴²

The major chains realized that enlisting the help of minority marketing firms would help them reach, and connect with, African-American
and Latino consumers. McDonald's was first out of the gate, signing on
the African-American advertising agency Burrell McCain (now called
Burrell Communications), in 1971. Burger King and Wendy's eventually
followed McDonald's by teaming up with African-American agencies in
1983 and 1984, respectively.⁴³ The chains also sought help from minority

agencies for help with particular product launches. When Wendy's introduced its "crispy chicken nuggets" in 1986, it hired the black-owned ad agency Lockhart & Pettus; the agency, which had established relationships with African-American television and radio stations, bought enough airtime on those stations so that commercials for Wendy's chicken nuggets blitzed viewers of black television and radio programming for six weeks.[44] And as the country's Latino population grew in the 1990s, the chains also began partnering with advertising agencies specializing in the Spanish-language consumer market. In the mid-1990s, McDonald's hired the Denver-based Solis Group to facilitate its purchase of airtime on Spanish-language television and radio programs.[45]

In conjunction with booking airtime on African-American networks like Black Entertainment Television (BET), national fast food chains also aired commercials on major network programs starring African-American cast members. McDonald's, for instance, was a major sponsor of popular NBC sitcoms like *The Cosby Show* and *A Different World* in the 1980s and early 1990s.[46] Some of these fast food commercials would be identical to those that aired on majority-white programming, while others targeted minority television viewers by prominently featuring African Americans as smiling, satisfied customers.

One such McDonald's ad, which aired in 1988, was called "Really Cookin.'" Meant to promote McDonald's breakfast menu, the commercial featured African Americans from all walks of life—two construction workers in yellow hard hats, a white-collar worker in a suit and tie, a postal service employee in uniform, and two teenage girls clutching book binders—all jauntily dropping by McDonald's for breakfast sandwiches on their way to work or school.[47] Incidentally, the "Really Cookin'" commercial, like numerous other McDonald's print and television ads targeting African Americans, incorporated what linguists refer to as g-dropping. This conflation of African Americans with "g-dropping" has a fraught history in marketing. In the mid-twentieth century, for instance, print ads for the Aunt Jemima brand pancake mix featured a smiling plantation mammy character proclaiming, "Mm-m-m! Every bite is happyfyin' light."[48] Even Barack Obama has associated African Americans with g-dropping. In a 2011 speech to the Congressional Black Caucus, the forty-fourth president g-dropped numerous words in his address. "Stop complainin'. Stop grumblin'. Stop cryin'," Obama told his audience.[49]

"Really Cookin'" also sought to appeal to African-American consumers by featuring black actors. Though African Americans have been perennially underrepresented on prime-time television programming and in Hollywood films—even in a "postracial" America—they have actually been overrepresented in commercials pitching fast food, convenience foods, candy, and soft drinks since at least the 1990s. In a survey of 825 commercials that aired during thirty-one prime-time television programs in the spring of 1999, communications scholars Jennifer Jacobs Henderson and Gerald J. Baldasty found that a remarkable 64.2 percent of fast food television advertisements included people of color. And in a reversal of the racial makeup of the country, 55 percent of fast food commercials included people of color in speaking roles, compared with 45 percent of such commercials with whites in speaking roles.[50] Fast food companies' readiness to cast African Americans in their television spots has continued into the 2000s. Data from the media research company Nielsen IAG, Inc. revealed that five of the ten most frequently aired McDonald's commercials in 2009 and 2010 featured casts made up entirely of African Americans.[51]

But racial minorities were not equally represented in all commercials. They made up 37.5 percent of total ads on prime-time television, and were significantly less likely than whites to appear in commercials for luxury cars, home goods, cosmetics, and relatively nutritious food.[52] Henderson and Baldasty also found that commercials frequently showed whites cooking at home, and African Americans opting for convenience and fast foods. A typical commercial might have depicted a white family "preparing foods such as eggs or pancakes with syrup, and using products such as 'PAM' cooking spray to complete a homemade dinner." In contrast, African Americans and other minorities were less likely to be represented in cooking or other domestic scenes. They were seen in ads for Ball Park hot dogs or Quaker granola bars—items which, Henderson and Baldasty point out, "required no skill to prepare."[53]

In conjunction with the fast food industry and processed food manufacturers' readiness to represent African Americans in their commercials, a number of studies published in public health and nutrition journals have found that black television programs aired more food advertisements overall than programming for general audiences.[54] According to one study that analyzed 553 food commercials during 101.5 hours of prime-time television programming in the fall 2003 season, there were almost 4 food commercials for every thirty minutes of African-American television programing. This compared to 2.4 commercials for every half hour of "general market" programming.[55] For the most part, these commercials were not selling carrots (even though such commercials do actually exist). They were pitching processed foods low in nutrition and high in calories.

As a 2003 study by Manasi A. Tirodkar and Anjali Jain found, prime-time television commercials accompanying African-American television shows were more likely to promote candy and sodas, and feature overweight and young actors (the latter suggesting a targeting of young viewers, of course), than those commercials airing during television programming for general audiences.[56] Similarly, a 2005 study by Vani R. Henderson and Bridget Kelly found that television commercials airing during prime-time African-American programming were more likely to be promoting fast food, candy, soda, and processed meat products than general programming. These ads appeared instead of commercials for cereals, grains, pasta, fruits, vegetables, 100 percent juices, desserts, and alcoholic beverages, which were more likely to appear during general programming. The food companies whose commercials aired the most during African-American programming in this analysis of 553 commercials were all national fast food chains, with McDonald's leading the way, followed by Kentucky Fried Chicken, Wendy's, Pizza Hut, and Burger King.[57]

◆◆◆

While the fast food chains' appeals to minority consumers have been driven by profit motives, African-American franchisees and customers have also nudged, and at times demanded, that the chains accord more attention and respect to African-American patrons. At McDonald's, a handful of African-American franchise owners representing Midwestern cities such as Chicago, Milwaukee, St. Louis, and Kansas City began to convene as a group starting in the late 1960s; by 1972, they had formally established the National Black McDonald's Operators Association.[58] The group advocated on behalf of its members in its dealings with McDonald's corporate headquarters in Oak Brook, Illinois, and it also offered support to one another on the everyday practicalities of operating franchises.

From its start, the NBMOA called on the McDonald's Corporation to launch minority marketing campaigns.[59] Given that most of the NBMOA's members at the time owned franchises in inner-city black neighborhoods, having McDonald's direct more advertising dollars toward prospective African-American consumers could translate into more business for NBMOA members. For McDonald's, expanding its customer base to include more urban African Americans was also a no-brainer. It meant more lucre from the royalties and rent on building leases that franchisees would owe Oak Brook as a result of being part of the Golden Arches empire. (Around the time that the NBMOA formed, McDonald's franchisees were required to pay royalties of 2.8 percent of gross sales, in addition to 8 percent of gross volume to cover rent on twenty-year leases.)[60] So starting in the early 1970s, McDonald's hired African-American advertising and public relations consultants, and began serving up print ads and commercials featuring African Americans in black and "mainstream" media alike.

Around the same time the NBMOA urged the McDonald's Corporation to market to African Americans, some black consumers also spurned McDonald's as a symbol of the white power structure. In an incident that reportedly occurred during the height of black power in the late 1960s and early 1970s, African-American youth in Chicago ran the chalky-faced, flame-haired McDonald's mascot Ronald McDonald out of their neighborhood. "Don't come back till you're black!" the Chicago youth were said to have barked. The iconic clown sprinted away, ironically with his "red afro flying," according to one account.[61] In a less dramatic instance of African-American Chicagoans' challenge to McDonald's, rumors swirled in the city's predominantly black South Side and West Side in 1973 that the chain had been selling burgers prepared with rotting meat in outlets serving African Americans.[62] Although the rumor was unsubstantiated, it sent a message to McDonald's and company: black consumers demanded respect.

◆◆◆

By the early 1990s, some two decades after Chicago youth reportedly chased away Ronald McDonald, the hamburger clown did come back as black. Either in response to African-American customers' assertions of black pride or as a marketing gimmick (or both), individual outlets of the major fast food chains became more "ethnic," adopting elements of Afrocentric or Latino culture. These franchises, which tended to be located in minority communities, celebrated their neighborhood's culture by refashioning their décor, menus, music, and even employee uniforms.

Kentucky Fried Chicken led the way. In the early 1990s, the chain founded by the folksy Colonel Harland Sanders (1890–1980) revamped 300 of its outlets serving predominantly African-American customers in cities such as Washington, Baltimore, and Chicago.[63] Calling this project Neighborhood KFC, the poultry chain added and changed the music, uniforms, and menu items at selected franchises.[64] Rap, rhythm and blues, and soul music replaced the bland "elevator music" common in public spaces. Employees were given new Afrocentric uniforms consisting of kente cloth dashikis.

To reinforce Kentucky Fried Chicken's reputation as a purveyor of "soul food," menus were also expanded to include special items such as red beans and rice, macaroni and cheese, slow-cooked greens, peach cobbler, and sweet potato pie.[65] (The addition of these items also suggested Kentucky Fried Chicken's attempts to compete with rival Popeyes' selection of zesty "Cajun" sides.) Kentucky Fried Chicken also hosted special events in some of its urban restaurants to promote new menu items. When the chain introduced its "popcorn chicken" in 1993, it sponsored parties with free samples, prizes, and even dance contests at twenty-nine of its predominantly African-American outlets in Chicago.[66]

Kentucky Fried Chicken also established a prominent presence on the campuses of the country's 106 historically black colleges and universities (HBCUs). This presence extended beyond opening franchises on HBCU campuses. In 2009, the chain launched KFC Pride 360°, an initiative that a press release from one participating HBCU, Norfolk State University, described as "a community program focusing on inspiring African Americans to acknowledge and uphold the four pillars of family, community, individuality and heritage." As part of its efforts to support these "four pillars," Kentucky Fried Chicken sponsored Black History Month commemorations, awards shows on Black Entertainment Television, and African-American essay and songwriting contests. The fast food chain also sponsored football games at HBCUs, including a homecoming tailgate reception at Norfolk. The event featured a professional deejay, and most likely, plenty of the Colonel's fried chicken.[67]

McDonald's has similarly banked on Afrocentric, community-based marketing. In 1994, McDonald's outlets serving urban African-American neighborhoods in places like Philadelphia and New York also began celebrating black life (and not just during Black History Month in February). One West Philadelphia franchise located near 52nd and Chestnut Streets was transformed into a veritable museum of black culture and history. At this outlet, which was black-owned and where 95 percent of patrons were African American, walls were lined with kente cloth and artwork depicting African Americans, by African-American artists.[68] A representative piece was visual artist Cal Massey's *Patriots of African Descent*, which showed three black Revolutionary War soldiers armed and in full uniform—a particularly validating image in this city known for its role in the American Revolution.

While the artwork in Afrocentric fast food restaurants might have varied depending on the city—franchises liked to display paintings from local artists—one could find similar black-themed McDonald's restaurants in other urban centers, such as at one franchise located near the Apollo Theater in Harlem. Like some of Kentucky Fried Chicken's urban restaurants, kente cloth was also incorporated into employee uniforms at McDonald's Afrocentric outlets. Employees wore aprons emblazoned with a colorful design motif symbolizing African culture, and female employees also put on kente-inspired visors while their male counterparts donned baseball caps with the design.[69] Franchises serving Latino customers have made similar attempts to celebrate Hispanic culture. In the mid-1990s, for example, McDonald's took note of increasing numbers of Latinos settling in Colorado. In response, the company made sure that its franchises registered for booths at Mexican Independence Day celebrations in the state.[70]

At McDonald's, such strategies for drawing minority consumers represented a departure from the regime of franchise uniformity under the burger chain's influential late chairman Ray Kroc. While Kroc was at the helm of McDonald's (he died in 1984), he touted the consistency of each outlet bearing the Golden Arches sign. A hamburger would taste the same in Springfield, Illinois, as it did in Springfield, Massachusetts. And a McDonald's restaurant would have the same look, feel, and scrupulously clean bathrooms (by the standards of public accommodations, anyway) everywhere.[71] But as food studies scholars have shown, by the 1990s even the Golden Arches had adapted to the palates of its customers abroad by modifying menu items and ingredients to appeal to local tastes.[72] (This cultural adaptation has gone both ways, as McDonald's and other U.S.-based fast food chains have likewise exposed overseas consumers to American fast food culture.)[73]

McDonald's has also adapted its menus domestically. The burger chain has sold taro pies in Hawaii (a cousin of apple pie, but with a filling of chunks of the tropical tuber in a purple sauce) and lobster rolls (the seasonal "McLobster") in Maine. The special "soul food" menus and Afrocentric restaurants in urban Kentucky Fried Chicken and McDonald's outlets, then, can perhaps be seen as another instance of niche marketing by fast food companies. The fast food chains' adaptations to regional and ethnic palates and its minority marketing programs are not entirely analogous, however. While McDonald's may offer taro pies to Hawaiians, it has not spent inordinate advertising dollars cultivating the Aloha State's residents as it has with African-American consumers, and increasingly, with Latinos.

That Latinos are McDonald's next target is evident in its media marketing expenditures. In 2006, the chain spent $57.4 million on television advertising for Hispanic viewers, which was 60 percent more than what the fast food giant had devoted to Spanish-language television just four years earlier. In their appeals to Latino consumers, fast food companies have focused on representing their restaurants as family gathering places, even more so than ads for blacks and whites. As McDonald's director of Hispanic consumer marketing Rick Mariquen told the *New York Times*, this was because Latinos "come to the [McDonald's] stores in large groups, often families, and see the experience as a social one."[74] Accordingly, the chain has rolled out the welcome mat to Latinos by installing extended tables to accommodate larger parties and families.[75] McDonald's has also introduced spicier "fiesta" versions of its menu items (e.g., salads and wraps), as well as burritos and tortas, to appeal to what it interprets as the Latino palate.[76] As with African Americans in previous decades, Latino consumers are becoming indispensable to the success of McDonald's and other fast food companies, particularly as their share of the total population continues to grow. A 2005 study published in the *Journal of the American Dietetic Association* surveyed 357 Latina women in southern California and found that fast food was their preferred choice for dining out, and that McDonald's was their favorite restaurant.[77]

◆◆◆

Perhaps the only other demographic that the fast food industry has targeted to the same degree as racial minorities is children. One could make the case that fast food companies' attempts to attract minority customers have been similar to the cartoon characters, storefront playgrounds, toys, games, and even cardboard crowns that the major chains have used to entice children. And indeed, at least one McDonald's franchisee has explicitly equated marketing to children with marketing to racial and ethnic groups. Frank Sandoval, McDonald's first Hispanic franchisee in Denver, was candid in an interview with the now-defunct Denver newspaper *Rocky Mountain News* in 1997. "Targeting black and Hispanic customers is no different than going after the children's market," Sandoval said.[78]

Today, Sandoval might not be so quick to go on the record with such an admission. And if he did, McDonald's headquarters in suburban Chicago would likely have to perform damage control. That is because in more recent years the fast food industry (and the food industry more broadly) has been disinclined to acknowledge that it targets children in its marketing. To do so would imply some culpability in the tripling of childhood obesity rates from roughly 1980 to the mid-2000s, especially in a post-"McLawsuit" era in which two New York teenagers sued the McDonald's Corporation for making them obese in 2002 (*Pelman v. McDonald's*).[79] In the years since the McLawsuit, public health advocates, including Duke University's Kelly D. Brownell and municipal governments like the San Francisco Board of Supervisors, have pointed to fast food children's meals as culprits in childhood obesity and type 2 diabetes.[80] (In 2010, San Francisco tried to ban the toy giveaways in fast food children's meals.)

Public policy and public health researchers have also drawn inevitable comparisons between Big Tobacco and fast food companies (as well as manufacturers of junk foods), observing that Joe Camel was to cigarettes what the Happy Meal is to fast food—insidious bait intended to lure children into ingesting harmful substances that would addict them for life.[81] The fast food industry, in turn, has highlighted changes to its children's meals, such as smaller portions of french fries, the addition of fruits and vegetables, and low-fat milk and fruit juices as alternatives to soda. The industry has also promised to "self-regulate" its marketing to children. Such responses by the fast food industry suggest that it is no longer kosher to openly push fast food to America's children.

Why, then, have fast food companies been free to continue aggressive marketing to African-American consumers, especially when African-American women in particular are disproportionately affected by the obesity epidemic?[82] There is, of course, the notion that children are especially vulnerable to industry messaging, and that they are categorically distinct from adults, who are putatively imbued with powers of volition. But even if one accepts this rationale—a rationale that was ultimately insufficient to shield the tobacco industry from legal culpability for the harm done to adult smokers—is it permissible for the fast food industry to continue targeting African-American *children*?

Recent analyses of media data have shown that, as with adults, black youth have been exposed to considerably more fast food advertising than their white counterparts. According to a 2012 report by the Rudd Center for Food Policy and Obesity at Yale University, African-American children (ages two through eleven) and teenagers viewed nearly 60 percent more television advertisements for fast food than white children and teens.[83] In some of these commercials, youth viewers were encouraged to visit fast food chains' websites. As might be expected, this greater exposure to television ads seemed to have resulted in African-American youth visiting fast food websites (where they are exposed to even more advertising) more frequently than their white counterparts. Black children and teenagers were 44 percent more likely to check out the cartoon-styled McDonald's website, "HappyMeal.com," than white youth.[84]

As of 2012, young African Americans saw approximately 75 percent more television commercials for fast food chains such as Papa John's, Domino's, Wendy's, and Burger King than white children and teens; this disparity exceeded the difference in television viewing habits between black and white youth.[85] This finding, according to Yale researchers, suggested that these restaurants "appeared to target TV advertising for some or all of their products to black youth."[86]

As a 2015 study by researchers at the Geisel School of Medicine at Dartmouth College found, greater exposure to commercials for fast food kids' meals can result in significantly more family visits to fast food restaurants. As one might imagine, this is likely a consequence of children begging their parents to buy them the kids' meals and accompanying toys they see advertised.[87] Although the Dartmouth study only included 100 children between the ages of three and seven, these children resided in rural areas where the nearest fast food restaurant could be miles away.[88] That these rural children's parents would succumb to their kids' entreaties for fast food meals and toys suggests that inner-city children who are surrounded by fast food might have an even easier time convincing *their* parents to purchase fast food kids' meals.

◆◆◆

The idea of targeting specific consumers—a strategy sometimes referred to as "market segmentation"—has been around for a long time, long before McDonald's, Wendy's, and other fast food companies began hiring black ad agencies in the 1970s. According to the cultural historian Kathy L. Peiss, as early as the 1910s advertisers marketed women's products by appealing to female consumers' "supposedly universal desire for beauty, their inherent taste, and their natural sense of duty to the family's well-being."[89] A decade later, advertisers routinely marketed the same products to women that were also sold to men, but in different ways. An enterprising adman of the 1920s noticed that women and men gravitated toward different sections of the newspaper, and parlayed this otherwise banal observation into one of the key strategies on which modern marketing came to be based.[90] A consequence of this observation was that, by the end of the 1920s, automakers advertised their vehicles to American women by suggesting that they select cars based on the exterior paint color that would best complement their wardrobes.[91]

At the same time, Madison Avenue and the companies it represented also developed ways to slice and cultivate consumer groups by race. Buoyed by low sugar prices in the 1920s, local confectioners and national candy companies ("big retail candy") proliferated.[92] But the candy market was stratified, both by class as well as race and ethnicity. In San Francisco, for example, candy makers targeted middle-class white children for pricier treats such as hand-dipped chocolate bonbons; they marketed cheaper stick candy to children of African-American, Irish immigrant, and Chinese backgrounds.[93]

By the mid to late twentieth century, race-based marketing also became a strategy to draw new consumers to offset declining or plateauing sales in the white, or "general," market. Fast food companies were not alone in taking this approach. Another industry at odds with public health advocates, Big Tobacco, made appeals to African Americans when U.S. smoking rates started to decline in the 1970s and 1980s. In some ways, the tobacco industry's comprehensive marketing playbook mirrored that of fast food. As historian of medicine Allan M. Brandt points out, cigarette manufacturers sought a foothold in black America by making contributions to civil rights organizations and educational institutions.[94] Leading tobacco company Philip Morris, for example, gave money to the NAACP, the National Urban League, and the United Negro College Fund; Philip Morris and tobacco giant R. J. Reynolds were also major sponsors of the 1988 annual meeting of the Congressional Black Caucus, along with beer companies Anheuser-Busch, Miller Brewing Company, and Coors.[95] (McDonald's has also been deeply involved with the Congressional Black Caucus, so much so that in 2010, the group of legislators officially honored the fast food company for having "brought the past to light with its Black History 365 Days a Year Campaign.")[96]

Big Tobacco marketed directly to African Americans in magazine advertisements and billboards in the 1970s and 1980s. A 1987 survey found that billboards for cigarettes were much more prevalent in African-American communities than in white neighborhoods.[97] In 1989, R. J. Reynolds even developed a brand of high-nicotine menthol cigarettes called Uptown that it intended for African-American smokers (although the company only conceded that African-American smokers *might* be attracted to the brand).[98] R. J. Reynolds withdrew Uptown after the NAACP and other civil rights organizations, the American Cancer Society, and U.S. Health and Human Services Secretary Louis Sullivan objected to the brand's potential to harm the health of African Americans—a group already more likely than whites to be diagnosed with lung cancer and to die from the disease.[99]

More recently, the soft drink industry has also marketed aggressively to African Americans and Hispanics, using philanthropy to secure goodwill and brand loyalty. As the New York University nutrition and food studies scholar Marion Nestle has shown, soda companies like PepsiCo and Coca-Cola have targeted African-American and Hispanic children in their advertising. To influence adult minority consumers, the soda industry supplements traditional print and television advertising with "sponsored events featuring athletes and celebrities, and through music concerts, cultural festivals, dance competitions and business and professional conferences." And like the major fast food chains and tobacco companies, Big Soda has treated philanthropy as another way to reach potential consumers. Nestle notes, for example, that Coca-Cola has donated to the United Negro College Fund, while PepsiCo has supported the National Association of Hispanic Journalists.[100] Such philanthropic gestures, of course, pose a conundrum. On one hand, contributions to scholarships and other charitable causes for historically marginalized groups are commendable. But when benefactors manufacture products that have the potential to adversely affect the health of those same communities, corporate philanthropy can seem somewhat unsettling.

The coming years will likely continue to see fast food engaged in targeted marking. The future portends greater marketing resources directed to other growing racial and ethnic groups in the United States. McDonald's for example, has already rolled out custom websites for Hispanics (MeEncanta.com) and Asians (MyInspirAsian.com).[101] The burger chain is banking on some of the same market segmentation strategies that were so effective in its pursuit of African Americans to attract these groups. In pursuing this strategy, McDonald's and company are likely well aware of market research indicating that historically marginalized groups may be more susceptible to the messages they receive from targeted advertising, and more loyal to the brands and products that are marketed specifically to them.[102] As the cultural historian Lizabeth Cohen notes, from the 1930s to the 1950s, publishers of African-American magazines like *Ebony* and *Jet* prevailed upon predominantly white national brands and companies to advertise in their publications. Johnson Publishing Company, the publisher of these two popular magazines, obviously profited from additional advertising. But there was more to it. When a leading national brand such as Lucky Strikes advertised its cigarettes in *Ebony*, that conferred a measure of what Cohen calls "symbolic recognition" from mainstream America.[103] On the consumer end, after years of discrimination and relative neglect by the dominant culture, it was no wonder that African Americans may have been receptive to targeted marketing. Someone was finally catering to *them*.

The fast food industry has counted on such a response for the past four decades. Its marketing to African Americans, therefore, has been especially high-volume and insidious. It was not inevitable that African Americans would be counted among fast food's most reliable consumers, or that a quarter of all burgers sold would be sold in America's inner cities. A confluence of the historical developments described in this book—including the fast food industry's targeted marketing—helped make it all happen.

SIX

Making Sense of Recent Fast Food Policies

The federal government has had a relationship with the fast food industry lasting over forty years. That relationship has been complicated in recent years. The public has increasingly regarded fast food as unhealthy, and lawmakers, federal agencies, and First Lady Michelle Obama have correspondingly sought to present themselves as health promoters. For the most part, however, federal lawmakers and regulatory agencies have not posed a real threat to fast food, even in the era of public health campaigns against obesity and other diet-related chronic conditions. And in the few instances in which the federal government has been a nuisance to the fast food industry, it has been a relatively minor, quick-to-retreat nuisance, and one that lags behind progressive municipal and state governments. Cities like New York and San Francisco, for example, have been swifter and more forceful in regulating the types of products fast food restaurants can sell, and even how much they must pay their employees.

It is impossible to determine precisely how many inner-city fast food franchises resulted from federal support. Government Accountability Office figures nevertheless suggest that in the 1960s and 1970s the Small Business Administration, at least, was a deep-pocketed accomplice in making what Eric Schlosser disapprovingly calls our "fast food nation." The GAO's 1980 review of the SBA revealed that the agency's eighty-one district field offices were most generous to three types of businesses: fast food franchises, automobile dealerships, and gas stations.[1] Another

GAO finding was that, between 1959 and 1979, the SBA disbursed about $1 billion in loans to 16,379 fast food and other franchised businesses.[2] By the spring of 1979, the agency had approved 225 individual loans and $29.6 million worth of loan transactions to McDonald's alone; similarly, Burger King had received $24 million in SBA loan guarantees and loans by 1981.[3] A smaller chain, the ice cream and fast food company Dairy Queen, received less SBA loan assistance overall, but a greater number of individual loan guarantees. (This outcome is likely due to the lower start-up costs of Dairy Queen franchises.) As of April 1979, the agency had approved 256 Dairy Queen loans totaling $13.5 million.[4] All of these transactions contributed to the explosion of fast food franchising in the 1970s, which grew by 82 percent from 1970 to 1976, and by 11.2 percent (from 46,898 to 52,163) from 1976 to 1977 alone.[5]

In 1996, the SBA guaranteed $410 million in 1,500 individual loans representing 150 corporate franchisors. Of these, $106 million went to 600 outlets of fifty-two chains. Subway received the most SBA-backed loans that year, with $11.2 million guaranteed to 109 of its outlets. One out of every 7 of the 755 new Subways built in 1996 was SBA-guaranteed.[6] In the 2000s, the SBA continued to finance Subway's ascent to the top spot among the country's fast food chains. Between October 2000 and October 2009, the sandwich franchise received 2,292 SBA-backed loans worth $392 million, with individual outlets averaging loans totaling $170,928.[7]

That fast food companies and other franchised businesses received the lion's share of loan guarantees in the 1960s and 1970s even though the SBA was supposed to help jumpstart *small* businesses is also note-worthy. The government's audit of SBA loan guarantees and loans through the spring of 1979 found that of the 16,379 franchise loan trans-actions the agency approved, $449.8 million of the roughly $1 billion went to the country's 25 largest franchise corporations. From 1969 to 1979, just 110 of 1,975 franchise companies received three-quarters ($674 million of $901 million) of SBA loan assistance. As the 1980 GAO review pointed out, "Many of these franchisors were very large corporations, such as automobile companies, oil companies, and fast food chains, that might have been able to finance all or a major part of the franchisees' costs connected with purchasing a franchise." According to the GAO, the SBA should have at the very least split loan guarantees with corporate franchisors, especially those companies that had their own subsidiary loan corporations (which most often applied to franchisors representing automobile dealerships).[8] But rather than foot the bill themselves, corporate franchisors' franchisee recruitment ads steered prospective franchise owners toward government financing programs.

The SBA not only helped underwrite the expansion of the major fast food chains; it also assumed vast financial risks for the industry and absorbed franchisors' losses. Individual recipients of SBA loan assistance were, at times, considered too high-risk (typically due to lack of liquid assets or insufficient collateral) to qualify for conventional commercial loans, but the fast food industry nonetheless encouraged prospective franchisees—however financially insecure or inexperienced—to go into business.[9] The SBA's alacrity in helping large franchisors was also reflected in its willingness to guarantee 90 percent (the maximum permitted) of franchisees' loans. As the GAO noted, however, the SBA "should [have been] in a good position to negotiate with banks to reduce SBA's share of loan guarantees."[10] That the SBA showed scant interest in doing so was of great benefit to franchisors. Since franchisors did not invest in loan transactions involving the SBA, they had little to lose and plenty to gain. Even when individual franchises ultimately failed, corporate franchisors profited from licensing and leasing fees, royalties, equipment and supply sales, and an opportunity to extend their brand's reach. As one SBA critic has pointed out, the agency's willingness to lend to fast food franchisees enables the multi-billion dollar international conglomerates that oversee the franchises to "tap into a lending program for the small guy," and shift the burden of risk onto the federal government.[11]

Franchises of large corporations have been eligible for SBA assistance since 1966, when the agency amended its Small Business Size

Standards Regulation. Unsurprisingly, this occurred after aggressive lobbying, or what two business administration scholars have called "extensive consultations," by corporate franchisors.[12] The SBA's recognition of franchises as small businesses was significant because it meant that a sizeable portion of SBA resources would be given to franchises tied to some of the world's largest corporations, rather than to fully independent small businesses. (SBA loan guarantees to franchisees accounted for 8 to 10 percent of the total.)[13] After the Small Business Size Standards Regulation was amended to include franchises, size still mattered, but varied according to numerous considerations.[14] Since 1966, the primary criterion for SBA eligibility for franchisees was whether they bore the "right" to profit and loss. That franchisees often had to abide by franchisors' strict rules regarding the management of outlets, in addition to paying start-up fees and royalties to corporate headquarters, did not matter; they were still considered bona fide small businesses.[15] And while "almost all" SBA officials working in the agency's regional and district offices in 1980 acknowledged to GAO auditors that franchisees enjoyed certain competitive advantages such as name recognition, national advertising campaigns, and management training over unaffiliated business owners, those SBA officials saw no need to revisit SBA guidelines regarding franchise eligibility.[16]

◆◆◆

Almost two decades after the GAO audit, and some thirty years after the urban riots of the mid to late 1960s, Washington policymakers still saw fast food restaurants as an antidote to the economic woes in America's inner cities. In 1996, the U.S. Department of Health and Human Services partnered with Burger King to bring 125 franchises to inner-city neighborhoods within five years; cities for the proposed new outlets included Washington, Chicago, Detroit, Camden (New Jersey), Philadelphia, New York City, Baltimore, Los Angeles, and Oakland.[17] The Clinton administration had created the Empowerment Zones/Enterprise Communities (EZ/EC) program under the aegis of the Department of Health and Human Services, to promote what it called "comprehensive urban renewal—particularly economic growth and social development—in distressed urban neighborhoods and rural areas across the country."[18]

Officials at the EZ/EC program teamed up with Burger King under the assumption that helping to finance businesses like fast food restaurants in economically depressed areas would contribute to these communities' revitalization. The idea was that by providing tax breaks to new Burger King franchises and other participating businesses that hired local residents, the federal government would generate scores of new jobs in communities where jobs were wanting.[19] Burger King seemed like a promising beneficiary of this latest government largesse; company spokespersons stated that the burger chain's partnership with Health and Human Services was expected to yield 20,000 new jobs in predominantly minority communities. Burger King chairman Robert Lowes also candidly revealed that his company participated in the EZ/EC initiative in hopes of commanding a larger share of the crowded inner-city fast food market.[20]

Although Burger King was not the only company involved with the EZ/EC initiative, it was the public face of business for the program. At the public launch of EZ/EC on February 22, 1996, then-president Bill Clinton posed for photo ops with Robert Lowes and La-Van Hawkins.[21] Hawkins, then thirty-six, was a prolific African-American franchisee who had already amassed over one hundred fast food franchises under the banners of Pizza Hut and the hamburger and hot dog chain Checkers Drive-In.[22] Through his participation in the EZ/EC program, Hawkins expected to open dozens of new Burger King franchises in less than two years. All of the burger outlets would be located in urban areas nominated as Empowerment Zones or Enterprise Communities; Hawkins's first EZ/EC-supported Burger King franchise was slated to open right across from Washington's historically black Howard University.[23] At the time, Hawkins and Burger King were enjoying a symbiotic relationship. Hawkins had benefited from the fast food chain's $100 million investment in minority outreach, and Burger King could showcase

Hawkins as the embodiment of its efforts to diversify its franchisee and supplier networks. This was a public relations boon for Burger King, which had received complaints by African-American franchise owners that the company had engaged in redlining and doled out substandard restaurant equipment to its black franchisees.[24]

Four years after their 1996 photo op with Clinton, Hawkins and Burger King would be embroiled in a legal dispute that saw Hawkins filing a $1.9 billion lawsuit against the fast food chain for only allowing him to open 25 franchises; according to Hawkins, the two parties had agreed to up to 225 restaurants.[25] Hawkins alleged that Burger King "used me as a pawn to make them look good to black people and black leaders."[26] Civil rights activist Al Sharpton also intervened, supporting Hawkins's claim that Burger King broke its promise to open more inner city outlets. Sharpton threatened a boycott of the nation's number-two burger chain, urging Burger King to enlist a black-owned investment firm to help roll out the company's proposed equity offering; he also said the company should hire a black-owned advertising agency. The eminently quotable Sharpton charged that "Burger King is pulling a whopper over the black community."[27]

For its part, Burger King defended its commitment to diversity. Company spokespersons maintained that the chain had recently doubled the number of African-American suppliers it used, and that it had boosted the proportion of Burger King minority franchisees from 11 percent in 1994 to 15 percent in 2000.[28] The company also countersued, claiming that it had only guaranteed Hawkins twenty-five restaurants, and that Hawkins still owed the company millions in loan repayments and franchise fees.[29] Unfortunately for Hawkins, in 2005 he would be sentenced to thirty-three months in federal prison for perjury in an unrelated corruption case. (Hawkins eventually served an eighteen-month prison term, and upon his release, pledged to rebuild his fast food empire.)[30]

Empowerment Zones/Enterprise Communities was, as previous chapters of this book would suggest, a recycled initiative under a new name. And like its predecessors, EZ/EC was a well-meaning attempt to promote economic development in urban (and rural) communities in urgent need of resuscitation. The establishment of federal programs intended to boost minority enterprise was also much-needed, considering the history of considerable racial disparities in business ownership. But given that government health agencies currently identify obesity as a leading public health crisis, should the federal government continue to look to fast food for answers?

◆◆◆

In the years since the EZ/EC initiative, the federal government and the fast food industry have intersected in ways beyond loan guarantees for fast food franchisees and tax breaks to fast food companies signing on to urban revitalization initiatives. Historian Susan Levine has chronicled how, in the mid-1990s, federal rules changed to allow nine major fast food chains—Subway, McDonald's, Domino's, Chick-fil-A, Pizza Hut, Taco Bell, Little Caesar's, Arby's, and Blimpie—the privilege of doing business in public school cafeterias nationwide. PepsiCo (part of Yum! Brands, Inc., which owns Taco Bell, Pizza Hut, and a handful of other fast food companies) also debuted its sodas, processed snacks, and other vending machine drinks and nibbles in 5,000 public schools.[31] The Centers for Disease Control and Prevention found that, by 2006, 23.5 percent of public schools in the federally funded National School Lunch Program (NSLP) were selling chain restaurants' fast food fare.[32] As Levine argues, the NSLP did not provide sufficient funding for schools to prepare nutritious meals, and Reagan-era budget cuts only exacerbated schools' budget shortfalls.[33] This left public school systems seeking ways to supplement their budgets, including granting fast food companies access to American children during school hours. Fast food sales were more lucrative than sales of regular school lunches, and schools used their cut of fast food and vending machine profits to finance physical education and other programs that would otherwise have been eliminated due to lack of funding.[34]

As some nutrition advocates have noted, however, funding from schools' fast food sales came at a cost—the nutrition of America's school-children, as excess sodium, saturated fat grams, and calories were added to their diets.[35] Some agency officials and lawmakers had anticipated this outcome when federal rules were modified to permit fast food chains into schools. Ellen Haas, the inaugural Undersecretary for Food, Nutrition, and Consumer Services at the USDA from 1993 to 1997, warned that this policy change would result in "short-term malnutrition and a lifetime of serious and costly health problems."[36] Missouri Democratic Congressman Dick Gephardt went further, charging that the move constituted "a dagger pointed at the hearts of our children."[37]

In the roughly two decades since brand-name fast food first appeared in America's schools, some fast food companies have publicized their efforts to adapt menu standbys to nutrition standards in accordance with the Healthy, Hunger-Free Kids Act.[38] In 2010—the year the Healthy, Hunger-Free Kids became law—Domino's unveiled its "Smart Slice" pepperoni pizza featuring a crust made of white whole wheat flour (as opposed to white flour in conventional pizzas), reduced-sodium tomato sauce, and less fat in its cheese and pepperoni. As of 2014, Domino's reported that the Smart Slice was available in thirty-eight states and 3,000 school cafeterias.[39]

The U.S. government has supported fast food in other ways, perhaps most conspicuously in the case of elected federal officials who have become legal advocates for the industry. In 2002, two obese New York teenagers filed suit against McDonald's, claiming that the Illinois-based company (as well as two Bronx McDonald's franchises they patronized) were negligent in providing nutrition and health information on menu items; the plaintiffs maintained that McDonald's should therefore be held responsible for their obesity and other diet-related conditions. The case was dismissed by a federal judge in 2003 and failed in subsequent appeals. But perhaps sensing a possibility that successful lawsuits against tobacco companies might be replicated in fast food, the fast food industry lobbied members of Congress to shield them from future litigation. A result of that lobbying was Florida Republican congressman

Ric Keller's Personal Responsibility in Food Consumption Act (H.R. 544), known colloquially as the "Cheeseburger Bill" of 2004.

The Personal Responsibility in Food Consumption Act would have barred consumers from suing food manufacturers, distributors, retailers, restaurants, and marketers for causing weight gain and obesity. According to Keller—a beneficiary of campaign contributions from McDonald's, Burger King, Pizza Hut, Wendy's, Domino's, and White Castle, as well as food manufacturers and grocery retailers—his bill aimed to restore "common sense and personal responsibility" to consumers' dealings with food purveyors.[40] James Sensenbrenner (R-WI), then Chair of the House Judiciary Committee and a supporter of Keller's bill, added that "if a person knows or should know that eating copious orders of super-sized McDonald's products is unhealthy and could result in weight gain, it is not the place of the law to protect them from their own excesses."[41] Although the bill failed to pass in the Senate, it was backed by the George W. Bush White House, and received considerable bipartisan support. It sailed through the House by a vote of 276–139 in 2004, and 307–119 when it was reintroduced in 2005. The National Restaurant Association, which represented numerous fast food chains and also lobbied for similar legislation, was more successful at the state level. By 2011, two dozen "pro-business" states had passed their own versions of the Cheeseburger Act.[42]

◆◆◆

In recent years, food industry watchdogs have applauded the federal government for taking measures to regulate how fast food companies and the restaurant sector more broadly do business. The FDA's proposed ban on artificial trans fats (vegetable oils that are hydrogenated to become more solid), and its directive that some restaurants post calorie counts, have been cited as examples.[43] Both the federal government's artificial trans fat ban and the calorie-posting mandate are expected to be relatively undisruptive to the fast food industry, however.

Many of the major fast food chains have already phased out artificial trans fats, which they previously favored because it was cheaper than butter and gave foods a longer shelf life than those made from liquid vegetable oils. Citing concerns that artificial trans fats contributed to heart disease by elevating low-density lipoprotein ("bad" LDL cholesterol), New York City's Board of Health voted to ban the item in restaurant cooking in late 2006. A number of progressive city and county governments nationwide followed New York City's example, as did the state of California in 2008. Meanwhile, federal action has lagged. Although the FDA has required that foods containing artificial trans fats be listed as such on ingredient labels since 2003, it was only at the end of 2013 that the agency proposed that artificial trans fats be stripped of their "generally recognized as safe" designation. In June 2015, the FDA announced that the food industry would have until 2018 to phase out the product. When a federal ban does take effect, it is likely to be met with a yawn by the likes of McDonald's and Burger King, where artificial trans fats are already no longer in use (though natural trans fats may still be found in meats and cheeses).

In 2015, the FDA also announced that proprietors of fast food and sit-down restaurants with twenty or more locations, along with movie theaters, vending machine operators, amusement park food vendors, and some supermarket retailers selling prepared foods, had to comply with new rules requiring them to post calorie counts on food items. Affected eating establishments had five years to prepare; the 2010 healthcare overhaul (the Patient Protection and Affordable Care Act) had already included this mandate.[44] And as with the FDA response to artificial trans fats, the federal government has been behind municipal and state governments on calorie labeling. New York City began requiring calorie labeling at chain restaurants in 2008, and as of late 2014, some eighteen city, county, and state governments had enacted similar laws.[45]

Fast food companies and other affected businesses, then, were already acclimated to posting calories in swaths of the country. And some chains, including McDonald's and Panera Bread, had already provided calorie information nationwide. When the FDA announced its new rules, the National Restaurant Association was already behind a national, standard calorie-labeling law; it wanted to spare its members from having to adhere to an array of city, county, and state regulations.[46] The federal government's "new" calorie posting law, then, is hardly radical, rushed, or onerous to the major fast food chains. The law's efficacy may also be dubious when one considers compelling evidence suggesting that the mandate may have negligible effects—if any—on the overweight Americans it is intended to help.[47] Those most deterred from ordering high-calorie menu items when apprised of calorie counts tend to be educated and high income—a demographic *least* likely to be obese in the contemporary United States.[48]

◆◆◆

After First Lady Michelle Obama announced her antiobesity "Let's Move" initiative in 2010, there were signs that the Obama White House might finally take the fast food industry to task for obesity and diet-related conditions. In 2011, while urging American schoolchildren to toss their burgers and fries in favor of whole grains and fresh fruits and vegetables, Mrs. Obama lamented that, "fast food has become the everyday meal."[49] And when sixteen-year-old American gymnast Gabby Douglas revealed on a late-night talk show that one of her postcompetition meals at the 2012 London Olympics was a McDonald's Egg McMuffin, Mrs. Obama, who was appearing on the same talk show as the newly minted gold medalist, good-naturedly ribbed, "You're setting me back, Gabby."[50] (Predictably, McDonald's subsequently hired Douglas as a celebrity spokesperson for its egg-white breakfast sandwich.)

These two instances of Mrs. Obama's very mild verbal disapprovals of fast food—and in Douglas's case, the disapproval was meant to be feigned—were hardly damaging attacks on the $191 billion fast food industry.[51] The fast food industry was safe, even with a First Lady championing antiobesity as her signature cause. If anything, one could make the case that Mrs. Obama has actually burnished the reputations of fast food companies like McDonald's and Subway.[52] When McDonald's announced in 2011 that it would add apple slices and reduce the portion of french fries in Happy Meals, the First Lady publicly praised the burger chain:

> McDonald's is making continued progress today by providing more fruit and reducing the calories in its Happy Meals . . . I've always said that everyone has a role to play in making America healthier, and these are positive steps toward the goal of solving the problem of childhood obesity.[53]

Given that McDonald's was (and still is) attempting to shake off its reputation as one of the world's largest purveyor of fattening foods, the company could not have paid for a better endorsement. The First Lady's remarks could help the company recast itself as a combatant in the fight against the obesity epidemic rather than a culprit in the making of it.

Mrs. Obama offered even more effusive praise for the Subway sandwich chain in 2014. In response to the company's announcement that it would undertake a three-year campaign to market healthy eating to children and offer healthier kid's menu options, the Office of the First Lady issued a press release rhapsodizing that, "in addition to strengthening its already nutritious menu offerings to kids, SUBWAY® will launch a new series of campaigns for kids aimed at increasing fruit and vegetable consumption and will set new standards for marketing products to families." Mrs. Obama even appeared at a Subway outlet in Washington, D.C., to celebrate the fast food chain, where she raved:

> I'm excited about these initiatives not just as a First Lady, but also as a mom . . . Subway's kids' menu makes life easier for parents, because they know that no matter what their kids order, it's going to be a healthy choice.[54]

The First Lady's earnest plaudit for Subway was a public relations gift to the company, which had long been cultivating a public image as the "healthy" fast food alternative. In 2000, Subway had launched a successful advertising campaign showcasing loyal customer Jared Fogel. (Subway would end its ties with Fogel in 2015 when it emerged that the sandwich pitchman had sex with minors and distributed child pornography—crimes that would eventually land him a fifteen-year prison sentence.)[55] Fogel, who once weighed over 400 pounds, shed 245 of those pounds by eating six-inch turkey and foot-long vegetarian Subway sandwiches (without mayonnaise, cheese, or oil dressing) every day for a year.[56] Noting that Subway's menu was "already nutritious" even before the proposed changes to its kids menu in 2014, the press release from Mrs. Obama's office seemed to affirm the pitch from the company's famous "Jared" marketing campaign. Far from stigmatizing fast food and damaging the industry, the First Lady's antiobesity initiative, then, has actually provided fast food companies like McDonald's and Subway with a golden opportunity to reinvent themselves as healthy places where, rather than gobbling down calorically dense, high-sodium foods, kids can munch on nourishing apples slices and sip nonfat milk.

◆◆◆

One of the most contentious issues related to the fast food industry, and one on which the Obama administration and fast food companies are currently at odds, is not related to dietary health, but to labor. In the past few years, labor groups, often led by fast food employees, have demanded that the $7.25 per hour U.S. minimum wage (as of 2016) be raised. On August 29, 2013, fast food workers in eight cities across the country participated in a "national day of strikes," calling for a living wage of $15 per hour. The fast food industry, as well as other sectors dependent on low-wage labor, has vigorously opposed minimum wage hikes. Fast food industry spokespersons and franchise owners have insisted that a $15 per hour minimum wage would result in considerably higher prices for consumers, as well as major job cuts, since workers would be replaced by more economical automated service mechanisms.[57] The validity of such claims, however, is contested. A 2015 study by labor economists at the University of Massachusetts at Amherst found that the fast food industry could "fully absorb" a minimum-wage increase to $15 within four years, due to: (1) projected growth in fast food sales revenues; (2) reductions in employee turnover, which would result in greater labor productivity (lower turnover and higher productivity would be expected outcomes of higher wages); and (3) the implementation of modest price increases that would not be expected to diminish consumer demand.[58]

The current White House has supported minimum wage increases, but only up to a point. In 2014, Obama signed an executive order raising the minimum wage to $10.10 an hour for workers on federal contracts; the previous year, he had also backed a bill sponsored by two congressional Democrats—Senator Tom Harkin of Iowa and Representative George Miller of California—that would have mandated a $10.10 minimum wage for all workers. (The bill, called the Minimum Wage Fairness Act, has so far been unsuccessful.) The president has also peppered his speeches on income inequality with calls for wage increases, but to the disappointment of labor activists, he has only endorsed a $12 per hour minimum.[59] With a Republican-controlled House and Senate in 2016, it is unlikely that federal legislation raising the minimum wage to $10.10 per hour, much less $15 per hour, will be passed in the 114th Congress.

Numerous cities and states, however, are ahead of the curve (as they were with artificial trans fats and calorie labeling). Major U.S. cities, including Los Angeles, Seattle, and San Francisco, have approved measures to phase into a $15 per hour minimum wage, and twenty-nine states (as of June 2015) require employers to pay hourly wages above the federal minimum. In July 2015, a New York State government panel officially advised that the state phase into a $15 minimum wage for employees working at fast food chains with at least thirty restaurants; fast food employees in pricey New York City would receive expedited wage hikes relative to the rest of the state. The New York State panel's recommendations are expected to be implemented by the state's acting labor commissioner. This means that hourly fast food wages in New York City would reach $15 by the end of calendar year 2018, and fast food workers in the rest of the state would earn the same wage by 2021.[60] Whether fast food will become more costly (a development some nutrition advocates would actually welcome), and whether fast food orders will soon be processed by robots, remains to be seen.

◆◆◆

It is a safe bet that local and state governments will continue to pass laws affecting the fast food industry in some form or another, and the federal government will trail behind by a few years. But it is unlikely that any of those future laws will be truly damaging, as the major fast food chains have shown themselves to be wizards of adaptation and circumvention. In 2011, San Francisco banned free toys from fast food kids' meals unless those meals adhered to the city's nutrition standards. The San Francisco ordinance was, of course, meant to extinguish the allure of children's fast food options like the iconic Happy Meal. But McDonald's cleverly responded by charging a meager ten cents for toys accompanying Happy Meals. The burger chain even added an incentive for purchasing the toys—proceeds from toy sales would go toward its Ronald McDonald House charity. If this example is any indication, the coming years will likely see the fast food industry continue to be one step ahead of government attempts to police its practices.

SEVEN

Unpacking Links Between Fast Food and Obesity

That we are a "fast food nation" has become self-evident, especially after the publication of Eric Schlosser's book by the same name. In many ways, the "fast food nation" moniker is a fitting descriptor of contemporary American food culture. Consider that potatoes are currently America's best-selling vegetable—a phenomenon owing to the popularity of the french fry.[1] Eighty percent of all potatoes produced in the United States become french fries; twenty-nine of the thirty-six pounds of potatoes the average American consumes every year are in the form of french fries.[2] Many of these french fries are, of course, from fast food outlets. In 1960, when the major fast food chains were just getting established, Americans took in an average of only 6.6 pounds of frozen spuds.[3]

In this french fry–loving fast food nation, 96 percent of American children can correctly identify Ronald McDonald; Santa Claus is the only figure kids recognize more than the McDonald's mascot.[4] And in this fast food nation, the Golden Arches and its ilk are ubiquitous—found along interstates and on Main Street, as well as in strip malls, food courts, airports, office buildings, stadiums, military bases, college campuses, museums, zoos, Walmarts, and countless other spaces.[5] Even hospitals make room for fast food chains. Surrounded by scrub-wearing patrons, I have ordered french fries and soft serve at McDonald's franchises tucked inside the Vanderbilt University Medical Center and the Cleveland Clinic.[6] (The Vanderbilt McDonald's has since been replaced by an Au Bon Pain, and the Cleveland Clinic franchise shuttered in September 2015.)[7] And as of 2012, there were 24,722 Subways, 14,098 McDonald's, 7,600 Pizza Huts, 7,231 Burger Kings, 7,015 Dunkin' Donuts, 6,594 Wendy's, 6,187 Dairy Queens, 5,670 Taco Bells, 4,907 Domino's Pizzas, and 4,780 KFCs (as Kentucky Fried Chicken is now known) in this fast food nation.[8] It is estimated that over 200 million Americans—nearly two-thirds of the total U.S. population—consume fast food at least once in any given month; McDonald's alone welcomes 26 million customers in its U.S. restaurants every day.[9]

This "fast food nation" moniker should also be qualified, however.

Generic pronouncements of the abundance and ubiquity of fast food do not consider that a growing segment of Americans do not eat fast food (or profess that they do not). Nutrition-conscious consumers avoid fast food because they regard it as unhealthy (although that may not prevent them from patronizing more upscale boutique fast food chains or independent restaurants serving more homespun versions of fast food standbys). "Foodies" may snub fast food because of their discriminating palates. Still others spurn fast food for political reasons—they object to the low wages chains pay their employees, they are concerned about food sourcing, or they are inherently suspicious of behemoth chains like McDonald's for homogenizing and degrading American culture, and squeezing out smaller independent businesses in the process.[10] In 2015, McDonald's closed more of its U.S. restaurants than it opened; this had not happened since 1970.[11] One 2013 survey of consumers found that McDonald's was especially unpopular among Americans in the eighteen-to-thirty-four age cohort, ranking seventeenth among the major fast food chains; Subway, Burger King, and Pizza Hut claimed the top three spots in the survey.[12]

Meanwhile, Subway has ceded its reputation as America's favorite "healthy" fast food chain to Chipotle Mexican Grill (before the spate of foodborne illnesses in late 2015, anyway).[13] The very definition of "fast food" may be changing. The *New Yorker*'s Michael Specter recently made this observation about the increasingly popular Sweetgreen salad chain: "Sweetgreen serves meals you can purchase in three minutes and eat in five; that's fast food. But it consists of salads and fresh soups, not processed meat, fattening sodas, or fries." Sweetgreen, Chipotle, Lyfe Kitchen, Shake Shack, Panera, and a handful of other "fast casual dining" chains that lie somewhere between full-service restaurants and the traditional fast food restaurants are now the fastest growing type of quick-service restaurants.[14]

But despite the rise of fast casual dining and some consumer demand for healthier quick-service meals, in most parts of the United States the fast food nation Schlosser described is in no danger of extinction. Expenditures at traditional fast food restaurants like McDonald's still surpass what Americans spend on movies, books, magazines, newspapers, and music, put together.[15] Staple menu items at fast casual restaurants are still slightly—and sometimes more than slightly—pricier than those found at traditional fast food restaurants.[16] Hungry Americans with only change and maybe a dollar bill or two in their pockets have more options at Taco Bell, Burger King, and McDonald's than fast casual spots. Brian Wansink, an expert on eating behavior and the director of Cornell University's Food and Brand Lab, has been quoted as saying that he and his wife "take our three girls to Taco Bell and buy five tacos for the price that one of us could eat at Chipotle."[17] As Wansink's example illustrates, traditional fast food restaurants still generally offer the best bang for one's buck (if one's object is to fill one's stomach or feed as many mouths as possible, that is).

Traditional fast food restaurants also continue to be part of the food landscape in just about every type of community—in suburbs, exurbs, and rural areas all across America. In inner cities, they often predominate. According to a widely cited statistic of the 1990s and 2000s, inner-city fast food outlets accounted for a quarter of all burgers sold in the United States.[18] What this means is that these burgers have been sold disproportionately to African Americans. In part this is because, for much of the twentieth century, "urban" has been a proxy for "black"—a consequence of the Great Migration of some six million African Americans from the rural South to cities across the country from the 1910s to 1970s. So far in this century, however, there has been a Great Migration reversal of sorts. African Americans are leaving northern cities and relocating to the South, and to suburbs and exurbs, seeking economic opportunities and lower costs of living. Demographics of inner cities are also in flux, as increasing numbers of white professionals in places like New York, Washington, Boston, and Philadelphia move to formerly blighted center-city neighborhoods.[19]

In spite of these recent shifting demographics in some of America's cities, the decades-old indispensability of African-American consumers to fast food's bottom line has not been lost on the industry. In a memoir chronicling his experiences climbing the ladder at McDonald's Corporation as an African American, Roland L. Jones, who was the owner of three urban franchises as well as the company's director of urban operations from 1974 to 1976, recounted: "From the company's own research, we knew that the number of heavy users of McDonald's was higher among blacks than whites and that per person, blacks spent more than whites."[20]

Some two decades later, Frank Sandoval, McDonald's first Hispanic franchisee in Denver, told the Rocky Mountain News that "the ethnic consumer frequents us more often, and their visits translate into higher check averages."[21] What Jones and Sandoval described continued into the 2000s. In 2006, African Americans and Hispanics accounted for 18 percent and 17 percent of McDonald's sales respectively, even though they comprised 12 percent and 14 percent of the U.S. population.[22]

SO WHO EATS FAST FOOD?

During the heyday of fast food in the United States—roughly the 1970s to 1990s—Americans' appetite for Big Macs and Whoppers seemed to cut across socioeconomic divides more than they do now. According to an advertising industry survey in the mid-1980s, 93 percent of Americans had patronized a fast food restaurant within a six-month period. (Sixty percent had eaten at Kentucky Fried Chicken alone.) Most were repeat customers, frequenting fast food establishments an average of nine times per month.[23]

Today's typical fast food habitué is more likely to be relatively young, low-income, and African American. A Centers for Disease Control and Prevention survey of 11,000 respondents from 2007 to 2010 found that overall, fast food makes up about 11 percent of all the calories consumed by the average U.S. adult. Among those ages twenty to thirty-nine, fast food accounts for 15 percent of total calories. Consumers who are twenty to thirty-nine years old with annual incomes of less than $30,000 obtain 17 percent of their calories from fast food, compared to 13 percent for those earning $50,000 or more. African Americans also took in higher-than-average fast food calories—15 percent in contrast to 11 percent for Hispanics and whites.[24] (But as Marion Nestle cautions, perhaps all of these figures underreport actual fast food consumption—survey respondents may be embarrassed to disclose the true extent of their fast food habits given the stigma of fast food among the health- and status-conscious.)[25]

Not long before the CDC released its findings on the demographics of fast food consumption, a 2011 study by DaeHwan Kim and J. Paul Leigh published in the journal *Population Health Management* suggested a more complex understanding of the relationship between fast food and socioeconomic status. Examining survey data from 4,972 adults, the study found that fast food consumption actually increased as people's incomes rose, but only up to $60,000; fast food consumption beyond that income threshold declined. (The survey also reported that those who were either obese or African American were more likely than others to consume fast food, regardless of income.)[26]

Although its conclusions about the demographics of fast food consumption may complicate conventional wisdom, the Kim and Leigh study does not mean that well-to-do Americans are first in line at the

McDonald's drive-thru. The study's finding that fast food consumption actually *dropped* in groups earning more than $60,000 is notable. (This detail tended to be obscured or buried in media reports underscoring fast food's putative popularity among the middle class.) And in contrast to the study, numerous other investigations of socioeconomic status and fast food consumption show that the poor and working class are indeed the most frequent consumers of fast food—a consequence of the relative affordability, palatability, and convenience of quick-service meals.[27] In recent years, the introduction of "value menus" at McDonald's, Burger King, Wendy's, Taco Bell, Arby's, and a handful of other chains has made fast food even more appealing to low-income customers. As Steve Levigne, a McDonald's vice president for United States business research, told the *New York Times* in 2006: "The Dollar Menu appeals to lower-income, ethnic consumers . . . It's people who don't always have $6 in their pocket."[28]

The geographic characteristics of consumers of the dollar menu and other fast food items may not be so clear-cut, however. While this book focuses on the expansion of fast food in inner-city minority communities since the late 1960s, McDonald's and its peer chains dot every state in the Union. Vermont, the District of Columbia, Maine, Montana, and Rhode Island are the states (and district) with the most fast food restaurants per capita.[29] And as one might expect, the states that are among the most populated—California, New York, Texas, Florida, and Pennsylvania—also have the greatest number of fast food restaurants overall.[30] Regionally, Americans residing in the South and Midwest lead the nation in fast food consumption.[31]

FAST FOOD: ONE OF MANY POSSIBLE PIECES IN THE OBESITY PUZZLE . . .

The question of the degree to which fast food is responsible for obesity among low-income inner-city Americans has been taken up by many researchers. Most studies have ascertained that the more people eat fast food, the higher their BMIs; residing or attending schools near fast food restaurants has also been correlated with more frequent fast food consumption and higher BMIs.[32]

There have been a few studies, however, that challenge the assumption that fast food and obesity go hand-in-hand. A 2015 study by Cornell University researchers David Just and Brian Wansink used CDC data of 5,000 adults from 2007 to 2008; the most underweight and the most obese were excluded from analysis.[33] Just and Wansink found that when the diet patterns of Americans belonging to these two weight categories were not considered, there did not appear to be a relationship between BMI and frequency of soda, candy, and fast food consumption. While this study received considerable media attention for its conventional wisdom–defying findings, critics of the study pointed out that the Cornell researchers did not consider how much junk food people consumed, only how often they consumed it. As science journalist Faye Flam pointed out, the question of "who ordered a large and who ordered a small" was left unexamined.[34]

In another study questioning links between fast food and obesity, researchers at the think tank RAND Corporation discovered that not all low-income inner-city communities with high rates of obesity are cornucopias of fast food. South Los Angeles was a case in point. The 2009 study found that, despite having fewer fast food chains per capita than the more affluent West Los Angeles, rates of obesity in South Los Angeles eclipsed those in West Los Angeles. But why were South Angelenos more overweight? According to the study, those in South LA may have loaded up on calories by consuming calorie-laden processed foods and soft drinks purchased from numerous neighborhood convenience and small food stores.[35]

Another RAND study—this one published in 2015—concluded that a 2008 Los Angeles city ordinance barring new fast food restaurants from opening in South Los Angeles did not result in reduced rates of obesity among area residents.[36] The study's lead author, economist Roland Sturm (who was also the lead author of the 2009 RAND paper), noted that the Los Angeles ordinance was too limited to effect meaningful change, as it applied only to "stand-alone" fast food restaurants, leaving numerous fast food outlets located in strip malls, as well as convenience stores, free to do business as usual.[37] That full-service restaurants were allowed to carry on business as usual likely did not assist in Los Angeles's antiobesity efforts, either. In a 2015 analysis of National Health and Nutrition Examination Survey (NHANES) data of 18,098 adults, University of Illinois researcher Ruopeng An found that full-service restaurants could be just as unhealthy as fast food outlets in terms of the calories, dietary fat, cholesterol, and sodium that diners consumed in both types of eating establishments.[38]

Other studies have discounted the influence of the food environment in body weight altogether.[39] Using data from 13,465 children in California (ages five through seventeen), a 2012 study concluded that there is "no evidence to support the hypothesis that improved access to supermarkets, or less exposure to fast-food restaurants or convenience stores within walking distance, improves diet quality or reduces BMI among Californian youth."[40] Perhaps because many Los Angelenos (and Californians more broadly) drive, their diet and BMI may be less affected by food options available in their local neighborhoods than those who walk to food stores and restaurants for their daily sustenance.[41]

These studies encourage a more complex understanding of obesity as the function of a multitude of environmental factors that influence exercise and diet, as well as the possible interaction of environmental conditions with biological mechanisms that affect appetite and weight.[42] Fast food is just one component of the obesity-promoting environment in low-income communities lacking access to healthy foods. The presence of exercise-friendly sidewalks, parks, and recreational facilities, for example, also matters. While studies pinpointing a single explanation for obesity may elicit considerable media attention—high fructose corn syrup was a favorite culprit in the mid-2000s—most obesity researchers would agree that obesity's causes are multifaceted. And because there is no magic bullet, significant population-wide reductions in obesity will not be achieved easily or swiftly.

. . . FAST FOOD: BUT A PIECE IN THE OBESITY PUZZLE NONETHELESS

But while the causes of obesity are multifarious, it is undeniable that burgers, fries, milkshakes, pizza, fried chicken, tacos, and other standard fast food fare are generally unhealthy. To exceed the American Heart Association's recommended fat intake for an entire day, all one has to do is polish off a Double Whopper with cheese from Burger King; the same could be said for a host of other items from Burger King's rivals.[43] Burger chains may boast that their menus now feature salads, skinless grilled chicken, apple wedges, parfaits, and other healthier items, but burgers and fries remain their bread and butter. In 2006, Richard Adams, a former McDonald's franchisee as well as McDonald's Corporation's director of franchising for the western United States, reported that the typical McDonald's franchise received about 50 orders for salads, and 50 to 60 orders of Premium Chicken Sandwiches per day. This may seem impressive. But Adams also revealed that every day the same franchise would sell 300 to 400 Dollar Menu double cheeseburgers.[44]

The hit 2004 documentary *Super Size Me* may have been the first time many ordinary Americans gave serious thought to fast food in relation to obesity, but public health researchers and advocates have been publicly critical of fast food for almost as long as McDonald's and its peers have pervaded the urban food landscape—more than four decades. In 1974, Jean Mayer, a nutrition professor at the Harvard School of Public Health (and later the president of Tufts University), gave the *New York Times Magazine* his assessment of fast food:

> The typical McDonald's meal—hamburgers, french fries, and a malted
> [milkshake]—doesn't give you much nutrition . . . It's very low in
> Vitamins B and C, but very high in saturated fats. It's typical of the
> diet that raises the cholesterol count and leads to heart disease.[45]

Around the same time, Mayer's colleague George Christakis, the head
of the nutrition program at New York's Mount Sinai School of Medicine,
also cautioned against fast food consumption in an address at an American Public Health Association convention. Christakis warned that regular meals of McDonald's could raise cholesterol levels, "set[ting] the
stage for chronic disease later in life." "We must change our hamburger-
malted way of life or change the content," he declared.[46]

Beyond the public health community, other voices had been articu-
lating concerns about industrial agriculture and food processing more
broadly. The counterculture had critiqued industrially processed food
(and industrial capitalism itself) in the 1960s and 1970s, and a growing
number of authors and activists like Wendell Berry and Frances Moore
Lappé had been advocating sustainable agriculture.[47] Fewer authors
singled out fast food and its nutritional profile in particular, but the
popular assault on the healthfulness of fast food was already germinat-
ing. In a 1974 New York magazine article opposing the opening of a Mc-
Donald's franchise on the Upper East Side of Manhattan, the food critic
Mimi Sheraton cited nutrition experts and lectured readers that Mc-
Donald's meals were packed with "large amounts of fat, carbohydrates,
calories, and sodium."[48] (It should be noted that dietary fat is, in some
ways, less maligned today than it has been in previous decades, as researchers find that consumption of fats—even saturated fats—may not
be as detrimental to heart health as once thought.)[49]

Not all 1970s health and nutrition advocates explicitly denounced
fast food, of course. But the public health consensus was that the American diet contained too many calories and too much saturated fat, sugar,
and salt—all of which fast food contained in spades. That decade, even

the federal government began to relay this message. In a 1977 press conference introducing the first publication of *Dietary Goals of the United States*, George McGovern (the head of the Senate Select Committee on Nutrition and Human Needs who later became a casualty of cattle industry lobbying) stood before an eye-catching display of 125 pounds of sugar, 100 pounds of lard, and 300 cans of soda.[50] All this, McGovern announced, was what had been consumed by "every man, woman, and child in the United States" in the previous year.[51]

Dietary Goals of the United States would also inform Americans that they were averaging about 3,300 calories per day (500 in excess of the recommended caloric allowance for adult men), and choosing too many "empty calorie" and "junk" foods at the expense of fruits and vegetables.[52] McGovern's committee emphasized that such dietary trends were reaching crisis level because diet contributed to escalating health care costs and played a key role in the leading causes of death, including heart disease, stroke, hypertension, cancer, diabetes, arteriosclerosis, and cirrhosis of the liver.[53] To reverse this scourge of diet-related morbidity, McGovern urged Americans to:

> eat less food in general and specifically eat less meat, fat, especially saturated fat, cholesterol, and sugar; and eat more unsaturated fat, fruits, vegetables, and cereals, especially whole grain cereals.[54]

Given that standard fast food fare tended to be meat-heavy, as well as laden with saturated fat, cholesterol, and sugar, McGovern's dietary recommendations implied the prudence of fewer visits to McDonald's, Kentucky Fried Chicken, and other fast food chains. (This was before McGovern's about-face on meat consumption.)

Since the publication of *Dietary Goals of the United States* four decades ago, there has been heightened scrutiny of the health effects of a fast food diet. Nowadays, some obesity researchers implicate the growth of fast food for the rise in obesity rates.[55] Obesity rates soared from roughly 1980 to the mid-2000s, doubling in adults and tripling in children. (While the CDC revised the BMI criterion for obesity downward in 1998, this alone cannot account for the rise in obesity.) National Health and Nutrition Examination Survey data from 2009 to 2010 found that 36 percent of American adults and 17 percent of children and adolescents (ages two to nineteen) were obese.[56]

The years that saw obesity rates climb coincided with increasing fast food consumption, as evidenced by the mounting share of fast food calories in Americans' overall diet. One 2004 study noted that between the mid-1970s and mid-1990s, fast food calories rose from 3 percent to 12 percent of Americans' total calorie intake.[57] Similarly, another study reported that fast food made up just 14.3 percent of all spending on foods eaten outside the home in 1967, but 35.5 percent in 1999.[58] It is no wonder that from 1970 to 2000, the amount Americans spent on fast food rocketed from $6 billion to $110 billion.[59] The fast food industry both created and fueled this demand; between 1972 and 1997, the number of per capita fast food restaurants in the United States doubled.[60]

According to some obesity researchers, this stupendous growth in fast food translated directly into expanding waistlines. A 2004 statistical analysis concluded that from 1984 to 1999, "the increase in the per capita number of restaurants makes the largest contribution to trends in weight outcomes, accounting for 61% of the actual growth in BMI and 65% of the rise in the percentage of obese."[61] Not all of these restaurants were fast food outlets, of course. But fast food did make up 35.5 percent of all spending on food consumed outside the home in 1999.[62]

Perhaps because of such links between fast food and obesity, some epidemiologists have even begun referring to fast food as a health metric. In 2012, for example, researchers at the University of Wisconsin Population Health Institute developed health rankings for the nation's roughly 3,000 counties. In determining the health of each county, the Wisconsin researchers considered the fast food density of each county as part of the overall healthfulness of its "physical environment." (Scores for "daily fine particulate matter," "drinking water safety," "access to recreational facilities," and "limited access to healthy foods" rounded out researchers' assessments of each county's physical environment.)[63]

SURROUNDED BY FAST FOOD, EATING MORE FAST FOOD, AND CONSUMING MORE CALORIES

Living near fast food restaurants may indeed constitute a "risky" physical environment, at least if one is low-income and male. A 2011 analysis of a longitudinal nationwide survey of 5,155 U.S. adults between the ages eighteen and thirty found that low-income men who lived within 3 kilometers (1.9 miles) of fast food chain restaurants consumed fast food more frequently than those who did not. These low-income men, researchers reasoned, were less likely to own cars, which made them more dependent on their immediate environs for meals and other services.[64] This geographic constraint, coupled with limited cash for food, made it more likely that these low-income men would be ordering double cheeseburgers (subsequently marketed as "McDoubles") off McDonald's Dollar Menu.

As might be expected, regular consumers of McDoubles and other fast food fare generally take in more calories than those who skip such items. A 2004 study found that men who reported eating fast food on a given day consumed 500 more calories than those who did not.[65] With 3,500 calories amounting to roughly one pound, it would not take long to gain weight on a fast food diet, as filmmaker Morgan Spurlock famously dramatized in *Super Size Me*.

A 2009 study showed that children who attended schools located near fast food restaurants were more likely to be overweight than those residing in communities without nearby fast food outlets. The study analyzed data representing 500,000 California schoolchildren between 2002 and 2005, and found that students whose schools were within half a mile of fast food outlets ate fewer fruits and vegetables, drank more soda, and had higher rates of obesity than students attending schools without fast food restaurants nearby. This relationship between body

mass index and proximity to fast food outlets was particularly pronounced among African-American schoolchildren and children attending schools in urban areas.[66]

Researchers outside the United States have also observed associations between fast food exposure, fast food consumption, and body
weight, although these links have not been discerned in all countries.[67]
In a 2014 study in Britain, researchers at the University of Cambridge
found, in a survey of over 5,000 adults, that an abundance of take-out
fast food restaurants (including both the major chains and mom-and-
pop establishments) near people's homes, workplaces, and commuting
routes "was associated with marginally higher consumption of takeaway food, greater body mass index, and greater odds of obesity." The
researchers reported that the group with the greatest exposure to take-
out establishments consumed a larger volume of take-out food, and
weighed 21 percent more than those who were least likely to encounter
such food vendors in their daily routines.[68]

Those surrounded by a greater concentration of fast food outlets may
also be predisposed to higher body weights because fast food takes the
place of alternative foods that may be lower in fat and calories. In 2014,
University of Michigan researchers found that areas of Genesee County,
Michigan with a higher concentration of fast food restaurants were also
home to heavier residents who consumed fewer fruits and vegetables.
Notably, this relationship between fast food surroundings and fruit and
vegetable consumption was observed independent of socioeconomic
factors; the Michigan researchers pointed out that this "suggest[ed] that
the presence of fast food is a risk factor for the advantaged as well as the
disadvantaged."[69] It should be noted, however, that while people may be
tempted to consume fast food if they are surrounded by it regardless of
their economic circumstances, a study published in 2011 discovered that
lower-income groups were most influenced by the geographic availability of fast food from the major chains (in this case, McDonald's, Burger
King, Wendy's, Arby's, Pizza Hut, and Kentucky Fried Chicken).[70]

Finally, among the numerous studies exploring relationships between fast food and weight, some suggest that obese Americans obtain a higher-than-average proportion of their total calories from fast food. According to the CDC's survey of 11,000 adults from 2007 to 2010, "the percentage of total daily calories from fast food increased as weight status increased," with obese adults deriving the largest share of their total calories from fast food.[71] This particular nexus between fast food and obesity appears to apply regardless of socioeconomic status. As a 2011 study found, "people who were obese and had high incomes visited fast food restaurants more frequently than their high-income, nonobese counterparts."[72]

FAST FOOD AND OBESITY IN INNER-CITY MINORITY COMMUNITIES

McDonald's and other fast food chains are the default dining options in many inner-city minority neighborhoods. Studies investigating the geographic distribution of fast food restaurants have found that in many of America's cities, minority communities are home to more fast food restaurants than majority-white areas. In one 2004 study, researchers mapped fast food restaurants in New Orleans and discovered that shopping districts in communities that were 80 percent African American averaged six more fast food outlets than predominantly white areas of the same size.[73]

With a population that was roughly 52 percent Hispanic and 31 percent African American in 2008, Bronx County, New York was similarly deluged with fast food.[74] Sixty-two percent of all restaurants in the county were fast food outlets, compared to an average of 45 percent in New York State.[75] Along with poverty and lack of quality health care, fast food has helped make more disadvantaged parts of Bronx County unhealthy places to live.[76] University of Wisconsin population health researchers determined that Bronx County had the highest premature death rates of any county in New York State.[77] Findings such as this, as well as the statistic that nationwide, African Americans' life expectancy is four years shorter than that of whites, scream for more attention.[78] While there are multiple contributing factors, this gap in life expectancy will not close completely without addressing the socioeconomic and racial dimensions of the obesity epidemic.

CONCLUSION: *Proposing Solutions*

Fast food is not the sole culprit in obesity, and eradicating fast food restaurants in inner-city minority communities will not stamp out health inequalities. Zoning laws intended to prevent new fast food restaurants from opening may also be ineffective in some cities, as the last chapter noted.[1] And if such restrictions are proposed on a larger scale, the fast food industry is likely to wage a well-financed campaign against them. Big Soda's response to New York mayor Michael Bloomberg's attempt to ban the sale of oversized sugary beverages from restaurants and other venues showed us that.[2]

The federal government could certainly reconsider whether franchises of large corporations (be they fast food or other sectors) should to be eligible for SBA 7(a) loans. But this would not halt the expansion of all the major fast food chains. McDonald's, for example, has hardly relied on this loan program in recent years (see appendix, table 2). Meanwhile, those fast food chains that *do* continue to benefit from the SBA 7(a) loan program—Subway chief among them—would likely lobby against any measure to restrict their eligibility. In short, ending fast food chains' participation in the 7(a) loan program would not be easy or wholly effective in curbing fast food expansion. It is clear, however, that fast food companies should no longer be privileged in urban revitalization and jobs programs, as Burger King had been when the Clinton administration launched the EZ/EC initiative. More fast food restaurants in low-income minority communities already acutely affected by obesity, type 2 diabetes, and other diet-related diseases are not the answer.

Given the difficulties of banishing fast food outlets, how can residents in places like the South Bronx maintain healthy diets when the only food options for blocks around may be fast food outlets and bodegas supplying soda and processed foods? Answers to this question have come from a range of sources, even from fast food companies. Major chains like McDonald's point to their healthier options, such as salads, grilled chicken sandwiches and wraps, yogurt parfaits, and fruit slices.[3] The problem with this advice is that most consumers don't visit the major fast food chains for these healthier items; at McDonald's, fries and burgers still rule.[4] Traditional fast food menu standbys are often cheaper than the healthier options, and they also contain liberal quantities of fat and salt (and in some cases, sugar) that render them irresistible to many palates.[5] While commendable and welcome, healthier menu items at the major fast food chains are unlikely to significantly reduce rates of obesity among America's poor.

Numerous health advocates and commentators on food and nutrition have also proposed that Americans eschew fast food in favor of home cooking. But car-less Americans living in neighborhoods where obtaining fresh, affordable groceries is a challenge need more than lectures on the virtues of cooking. They need a food environment that is conducive to cooking both healthfully and affordably. This is where federal, state, and municipal governments can intervene.

One of the ways policymakers can help bring about healthy food environments is by inducing supermarket operators to open in underserved communities. This is already being done in places like New York, where the city launched the Food Retail Expansion to Support Health (FRESH) program in 2009. This program offers "zoning and financial incentives" for supermarket operators and real estate developers to open or build stores in areas the city has identified as lacking in grocery stores.[6] Other U.S. cities, such as New Orleans, Newark, Cleveland, and Louisville, and states such as Pennsylvania, have experimented with similar initiatives in which tax credits, loans, or grants have been used as carrots to bring supermarkets to urban food deserts. With such financial incentives to assist grocers with the start-up costs of opening stores in urban areas, their grocery stores can be economically viable. Fourth-generation grocer Jeffrey Brown attests to this. Brown operates eleven supermarkets (as of 2015) with the ShopRite chain in the Philadelphia area; six of his stores are located in previously underserved inner-city locations. These six supermarkets have been profitable for Brown, who informed the *New York Times* that "the profit margins on my urban stores are comparable to those in my suburban stores."[7]

Simply building supermarkets is not enough, however. As anyone who has visited supermarkets of the same chain in different neighborhoods knows, these supermarkets can vary widely in the quality of food for sale, as well as in selection and price. Even though journalist James F. Ridgeway made this observation about Washington, D.C., supermarkets over fifty years ago, this inequality between urban supermarkets in poorer communities and those in more affluent locations persists. For inner-city supermarkets serving low-income customers to have the best chance of success, they should be just as clean and inviting as those in more privileged neighborhoods. And perhaps most importantly, those supermarkets need to be stocked with high-quality, attractive, and fresh foods. They should not serve as dumping grounds for expired castoffs from supermarket chains' more valued stores.[8]

Policymakers can also improve food environments in underserved areas by more widely instituting food access programs currently funded by private foundations or municipal governments. These programs, which have been implemented in a number of U.S. cities, including New York and Philadelphia, make it easier for convenience stores to carry fresh fruits and vegetables by linking produce distributors with store owners; in some cases, the programs even provide shopkeepers with refrigerators to store healthy items that are perishable. When the fruits and vegetables in convenience stores that participate in such programs are of relatively high quality, they actually get purchased.[9] Similar initiatives include supporting traveling produce vendors such as those with vans, trucks, or mobile carts to park in communities with shortages of fresh, healthy foods. New York, for instance, has issued over 200 "green carts" to vendors selling "local and ethnically relevant" fruits and vegetables.[10] Other programs that could be expanded to more cities include those that link farmers directly with customers in underserved communities. This could be in the form of neighborhood farmers' markets or community-supported agriculture (CSA), in which urban customers buy farm shares and pick up the fruits and vegetables yielded from those shares at appointed locations near their homes. As one 2016 study of a farmers' market in Flint, Michigan, has shown, the location of farmers' markets matters.[11] When residents of low-income, "distressed neighborhoods" are able to get to farmers' markets by walking or public transport, they are considerably more likely to patronize those markets than when those markets are located in more difficult-to-reach neighborhoods.[12]

New supermarkets, bodegas with healthy items, mobile produce vendors, fresh farm deliveries to underserved communities, and farmers' markets still may not be enough to lure people away from fast food, however. It is essential that the food sold at these venues be affordable to Americans on tight budgets. While geographic accessibility is important, studies also indicate that cost is a primary consideration in determining where consumers shop. Consumers may skip the closest grocery store in favor of those farther away with lower prices.[13] There may be a number of ways to help make produce cheaper for American consumers—not just in low-income inner-city communities, but everywhere. As author Michael Pollan and others have proposed, U.S. agricultural policy can subsidize fresh fruits and vegetables so that these items can better compete for the wallets of shoppers who might otherwise be drawn to inexpensive soft drinks and junk food made from government-subsidized corn and soy.[14] To be sure, grain subsidies alone have not been responsible for the low costs of processed foods relative to fruits and vegetables. In complicating the notion that subsidies determine the cost of particular food items, food studies scholar Julie Guthman notes that grains and potatoes can be grown and harvested with highly efficient machines, while the cultivation of fruits and vegetables still requires considerable manual labor.[15] This is certainly a logical point, but government subsidies to offset the costs farmers incur in the production of fruits and vegetables could also result in lower produce prices for consumers, and those lower prices for fruits and vegetables might make junk food seem less appealing by comparison (at least in terms of cost).

To help address obesity among low-income Americans eligible for the Supplemental Nutrition Assistance Program (SNAP, as the Food Stamp Program has been officially called since 2008), the USDA could also implement changes to encourage participants to purchase more fruits, vegetables, and other healthy items such as whole grains and nuts. In March 2015, the USDA announced $31.5 million in pilot grants toward such an effort. The grants, which were awarded to private foundations as well as city and state governments, included programs raising SNAP participants' purchasing power at grocery stores, farmers' markets, and farm share arrangements; some of these programs enable SNAP recipients to double their benefits if they apply them toward fruits and vegetables from participating food purveyors.[16] Such programs have shown promise in cities like Boston, Philadelphia, and New York; they should be much more widely implemented so that SNAP participants everywhere have an economic incentive to maintain healthy diets.[17] This wish list of greater agricultural subsidies for fruits and vegetables, and increasing the value of SNAP benefits for healthy items is, however, in large part contingent on whether Congress has the will to make healthy diets—especially among America's poor and working classes—a priority.

But even if Congress did grant this wish list, and healthy foods were suddenly made accessible—both geographically and economically—obesity might still disproportionately affect America's poor. The linguist and cultural commentator John McWhorter has argued that more supermarkets in inner-city minority neighborhoods is not a panacea for obesity, as African Americans are culturally predisposed to consuming unhealthy foods because "slavery and sharecropping didn't make healthy eating easy for black people back in the day."[18] I would argue that McWhorter underestimates the healthfulness of earlier African-American diets, even during the days of sharecropping. As noted earlier in this book, dietary surveys of African Americans in the South found that staple foods included highly nutritious foods such as fresh sweet potatoes, turnips, and greens, in addition to unhealthier items such as lard, salt pork, and flour. But while McWhorter may ascribe undue influence to African Americans' putative "cultural preferences" for unhealthy foods in accounting for the popularity of fast food and junk food in black neighborhoods today, he is right to point out that "parents are often unaware of how unhealthy it [fast food and junk food] is." It is this unawareness that needs to be rectified.

Solutions must target children. They represent the future of the American diet, and more immediately, they can influence the foods their parents purchase and prepare. To this end, the curricula in America's public schools should include at least a modicum of education on nutrition and healthy food preparation starting at the elementary school level. While some children may come from "foodie" or food-literate families, other children's lack of familiarity with nonprocessed foods cannot be underestimated. In 2010, ABC aired a six-episode series called *Jamie Oliver's Food Revolution*, in which celebrity chef Jamie Oliver visited Huntington, West Virginia, to campaign for healthier school lunches and bring attention to the obesity epidemic. One episode from the series featured Oliver visiting a classroom of first-graders and asking them to identify sundry vegetables and fruits. Students were unable to correctly identify the tomatoes Oliver presented them; one student guessed that the tomatoes were potatoes, and when an actual potato was shown, none of the students could identify it, either. When Oliver held up an eggplant, the students guessed "pear" and "turnip." After the celebrity chef gave them a hint and said that the name of the item started with "egg," one student confidently blurted, "egg salad!" Perhaps *Jamie Oliver's Food Revolution* was edited for shock value, and students who could correctly identify the selected fruits and vegetables were cut from the scene. But even if the program had been edited, it is nevertheless concerning that more than a few six-year-olds are mystified by the sight of raw tomatoes, yet quick to recognize ketchup as a condiment for their fast food fries and burgers.

Children nationwide, but particularly those in underserved communities, should be exposed to a rudimentary nutrition education that would equip them with knowledge about what constitutes a healthy diet. And given that the Federal Trade Commission has yet to effectively regulate fast food marketing to children, nutrition education that provides American schoolchildren with information that could help them make informed choices—in the face of the fast food advertising they encounter on television, billboards, and the internet—is especially needed. Of course, the most financially strapped school districts may balk at proposals to hire new staff or train existing teachers in nutrition. For such school districts, it may be worth considering dispatching nutrition educators such as those working on behalf of the FoodCorps initiative.

Established in 2009 when the Edward M. Kennedy Serve America Act was signed into law, FoodCorps is part of the extensive network of service programs, AmeriCorps. Describing itself as "a nationwide team of AmeriCorps leaders who connect kids to real food and help them grow up healthy," FoodCorps service members have been sent to school districts all over the country to provide nutrition education, teach students gardening and cooking skills, and connect school cafeterias with local farmers. But the program is relatively small, with fewer than 250 service members for the entire United States. Its service members currently serve 500 schools in seventeen states and the District of Columbia—a drop in the bucket considering that there are over 14,000 public school districts in the country.[19] Federal policymakers should consider earmarking additional funding for FoodCorps or similar initiatives in order to reach more school districts. (The federal government provides about one-third of FoodCorps' funding, with private foundations underwriting the remainder.) FoodCorps staff cost money, but not as much as one might think—each service member receives a modest living allowance of $17,500 per year.[20] And despite this fairly low compensation, entrance to the FoodCorps service program is highly competitive.

In lieu of initiatives like FoodCorps, school districts could also consider reinstating home economics, an idea a number of food commentators have proposed in the last few years.[21] This updated home econom-ics curriculum, however, should be shorn of its traditional association with female homemaking and target all students regardless of gender. It should include nutrition education and a "laboratory" component in which students learn to prepare foods that are both nutritious and palatable; if schools have working gardens or access to locally sourced foods, all the better. Ideally, students would apply the nutrition edu-cation and practical cooking instruction they learn at school to their own households, thereby influencing their families' everyday diets in positive ways.

To reinforce healthy habits among schoolchildren, and cultivate their taste for nutritious foods, schools must also serve meals that are both healthy and palatable. This doesn't just mean reducing fat, sodium, and calories from school lunches, as mandated by the Healthy, Hunger-Free Kids Act of 2010. In fact, students have complained that school lunches made to comply with the law have been unappetizing, too meager, or both.[22] One of the consequences of this dissatisfaction with school lunches is greater food waste, particularly of dreary-looking fruits and vegetable items. Fewer students may also opt to purchase these austere school lunches.[23]

As the School Nutrition Association (an organization representing food service staff at America's schools) has advocated, school districts should be given more flexibility on nutrition standards so that they have more options in preparing meals that are both wholesome and appealing to students. As Jean Ronnei, the chief operations officer of public schools in St. Paul, Minnesota, points out, the Healthy, Hunger-Free Kids Act's restrictions on sodium in school lunches means that her school district cafeteria would not be able to serve barbeque sauce with rotisserie chicken.[24] Considering that the barbeque sauce could mean the difference between students devouring the chicken or tossing it in the trash bin, relaxing sodium restrictions on school lunches in such cases seems sensible.

Instead of requiring school districts to conform to rigid guidelines on sodium, calories, and even fat grams, the USDA should focus its efforts on encouraging school districts to use fresh ingredients and prepare meals from scratch that students will want to eat. As Yale University discovered in 2005 when one of its residential colleges first began serving wholesome meals made from fresh ingredients, students respond rapturously to nourishing meals made from quality ingredients.[25] (Food activist/restauranteur Alice Waters, who happened to be the parent of a Yale undergraduate at the time, was largely behind the idea of this dining hall intervention.) And it's not just ultra-wealthy, elite universities that can afford to serve wholesome, well-prepared food and gain a following from student diners as a result. According to Jean Ronnei, before the sodium requirements of the Healthy, Hunger-Free Kids Act went into effect, public school students in St. Paul got "excited" over school lunches like "fresh roasted chicken [with barbeque sauce], cornbread that's homemade, apple kohlrabi slaw and strawberries."[26]

Empirical evidence suggests that when students are fed well-prepared and nutritious school lunches and exposed to nutrition education, basic food preparation training, and even gardening, they adopt healthier diets. In a 2010 study commissioned by Alice Waters's Chez Panisse Foundation, researchers at the University of California at Berkeley tracked 238 fourth- and fifth-graders in Berkeley's public schools from 2006 to 2009. They compared students whose schools had "hands-on cooking and gardening classes, system-wide changes in food and dining services, and the integration of school lunch and hands-on learning with regular classroom lessons," to students in schools without such a comprehensive nutrition intervention.[27] Students in schools with the integrated nutrition programs consumed more fruits and vegetables, and these healthy habits continued long after students had graduated from the schools with these programs in place.[28] There is also anecdotal evidence suggesting that students armed with nutrition education will make healthier choices themselves, and even become missionaries for healthy eating within their peer groups and their families.[29] Instead of children begging their parents for Happy Meals at the sight of a McDonald's commercial, perhaps students who have been schooled in nutrition might even ask their parents for kale.

All of what's been proposed here—nutrition education, cooking instruction, improved school lunches, SNAP rewards for healthy purchases, agricultural subsidies for fruits and vegetables, and tax credits for new supermarkets and related interventions to facilitate underserved communities' access to healthy foods—will, of course, cost money. But reducing rates of obesity, type 2 diabetes, and other diet-related diseases would, it has been shown, result in billions saved in the form of fewer health care outlays and greater workplace productivity.[30] Perhaps even more important than potential savings, such nutrition interventions also have the potential to reduce health inequalities and improve quality of life for millions of Americans by promoting healthfulness and people's everyday enjoyment of wholesome food.

Critics of the types of proposals I have outlined may object to them on the grounds that they "laud the lifestyles of those with class and race privilege."[31] This is a valuable and thoughtful critique, but what I have proposed in these pages is foremost about facilitating equitable access to nutritious food, not about making low-income and minority Americans adopt the specific diets of the privileged. It is crucial that food and nutrition interventions take the existing food culture of the communities they serve into account, and provide what has been called "culturally appropriate" and "ethnically relevant," healthy foods and nutrition education. Similarly, these proposals are not meant as prescriptions for making low-income and minority Americans conform to white, middle-class aesthetic ideals of thinness. These proposals are about finding ways to help close the gap in life expectancy between America's haves and have-nots.

It is also important to recognize that these proposals are not a cure-all for obesity. This is in part because some people may be genetically predisposed to obesity.[32] Unfortunately, there are currently few effective and widely available therapies targeting genetic predispositions to weight gain. (Bariatric surgery is one of the few effective interventions against obesity, but it is not targeted gene therapy.) In the absence of such therapies, democratizing access to healthy foods and nutrition education could help countervail Americans' urge to consume those foods that most promote obesity. There are, however, still other limitations to these policy proposals. As Julie Guthman points out, we need to acknowledge that "our food system is part of a political economy that systematically produces inequality."[33] Low wages for workers at every point in the industrial food chain are perhaps the most obvious manifestation of this inequality, and those low wages affect the type of diets households can afford.[34] Our policymakers need to address this systemic inequality, and as I have argued elsewhere, a comprehensive plan to eliminate obesity also requires an all-out assault on poverty.[35] But in the meantime, equipping all Americans with the resources to make healthy choices may be the most feasible and promising way forward.

ACKNOWLEDGMENTS

The support of people who believed in this book from its earliest stages helped motivate me to continue working on it even though there always seemed to be other obligations and distractions. Karen Merikangas Darling at the University of Chicago Press was foremost in this camp; I could not be more thankful for her stewardship of this project. This book also benefited from Michael Koplow's meticulous and deft manuscript editing (although I am responsible for any remaining mistakes). I am also grateful to Evan White and Kristen Raddatz, as well as to the referees the Press commissioned for their constructive comments on the proposal and manuscript that developed into this book.

A number of other scholars read portions, or all, of what became this book. Rachel Bernard edited a rough draft of the first chapter I ever wrote. Jonathan Bean imparted his encyclopedic expertise on the Small Business Administration when I first started researching the government agency in 2010; his comments on the manuscript five years later were similarly invaluable. Dov Weinryb Grohsgal read the lengthiest chapter of the manuscript, and gave exceedingly thorough feedback on everything having to do with Richard Nixon. Leah Wright-Rigueur also helped me get a better sense of Nixon, and could always be counted on for encouragement. In the home stretch, Alice Fabbri passed on a number of references to relevant sources in science journals. Daniel Bowman Simon's close reading of the entire manuscript, informed comments, and trove of additional references and digitized sources were an unexpected boon in the last few months of writing and revising. And finally, Marion Nestle's unparalleled expertise, encouraging feedback, and generous support at the very beginning and end of the writing process, were vital.

Others helped with locating sources, their willingness to be interviewed, or providing lodging during research trips. This includes the staff at the National Archives in College Park, Maryland; librarians at the National Institutes of Health (NIH), Princeton University, Harvard University, and the University of Sydney; Shawn McKeehan, Sloan Coleman, and Karen Gordon Mills at the SBA; and Brady Keys, Sarah Milov, and Henry and Melissa Chou.

The American Academy of Arts and Sciences and the National Institute of Diabetes and Digestive and Kidney Diseases at the NIH, offered funding and resources to launch and develop this book. I am especially indebted to the late Robert Martensen, David Cantor, Anne Sumner, and all the Stetten Fellows from 2009 to 2011, as well as to Mary Maples Dunn and my cohort of Visiting Scholars at the American Academy.

Former advisors and professors at Princeton also helped make this book possible in varying ways. Liz Lunbeck has promoted my work and facilitated numerous academic and professional opportunities, including linking me with the University of Chicago Press. Liz's cheerleading, mentorship, and friendship over the years have meant the world. Years after I graduated, Dan Rodgers still reads drafts (including the entire manuscript that became this book) with great care and expeditiousness. He is the teacher and scholar his graduate students have wanted to emulate, and for good reason. Christine Stansell taught me so much about writing and urban history. Carolyn Rouse's "Race and Medicine" seminar sparked my interest in the medical humanities. Nell Painter was generous and encouraging, and Dirk Hartog was always benevolent and ready to help.

In the two years I spent teaching in the Harvard history of science department, Janet Browne and Anne Harrington were extraordinarily kind and supportive. Lindy Baldwin, Allie Belser, Cara Kiernan Fallon, Jeanne Haffner, Emily Harrison, Lisa Haushofer, David Jones, and Sean O'Donnell, as well as my teaching fellows, students, and advisees, were also terrific.

From the University of Sydney, I'd like to thank Thomas Adams, Robert Aldrich, Warwick Anderson, Pru Black, Barbara Caine, Huw Calford, Frances Clarke, Marco Duranti, Nick Eckstein, Jenny Ferng, Andrew Fitzmaurice, John Gagné, Sebastian Gil-Riaño (and Adriann Moss), Conor Hannan, Ari Heinrich, Chris Hilliard, Peter Hobbins, Miranda Johnson, Judith Keene, Sophie Loy-Wilson, Pam Maddock, Iain Mc-Calman, Cindy McCreery, Mike McDonnell, Kirsten McKenzie, Richard Miles, Jane Park, Hans Pols, Penny Russell, Hélène Sirantoine, Sarah Walsh, Shane White, and my students and tutors over the past two years.

Friends during the five years I spent researching and writing this book were indispensable. They include Catherine Abou-Nemeh, Mark Broomfield, Shereene Brown, Annina Burns, Liz Cresswell, Melissa D'Anello, Pete Daniel, Gil Davis, Debbie Doroshow, Carrie Eisert, Tara Failey, Yang Hu, Mina Kim, Zoe Kwok, Jenny Martin, Todd Olszewski, Monika Serrano-Riedlinger, Yael Sternhell, Jill Wertheim, former graduate school and postdoctoral comrades, and the former Chevy Chase and Davis Square running buddies who offered buoyant encouragement when the proverbial finish line for this book seemed so distant.

These acknowledgments would be incomplete without a heartfelt thanks to my parents, and Henry, Melissa, Zoe, and Rory; I appreciate them more than I let on. My mother Chian-Hua has always been my cardinal supporter. This book is dedicated to her.

APPENDIX

Table 1. Small Business Administration (SBA) 7(a) Loan Program to Fast Food Franchises in 2009*

Fast food franchisor (includes burger, sandwich, poultry, pizza, taco, hot dog, pretzel, and dessert establishments)	Number of 7(a) SBA loan guarantees	Dollar amount of SBA loan guarantees (all figures over a million rounded to the nearest hundred thousand)
Arby's	5	$3.9 million
Auntie Ann's	9	$2.5 million
A&W Restaurant	2	$462,000
Baja Fresh Mexican Grill	10	$2.0 million
Baskin-Robbins	16	$1.8 million
Bellacino's Pizza	1	$187,500
Belleria Pizzaria	1	$67,230
Ben & Jerry's Ice Cream	2	$164,750
Big Boy	1	$585,000
Blimpie	2	$85,500
Bojangles	2	$1.3 million
Buffalo Wild Wings Grill and Bar	5	$4.8 million
Buffalo Wings & Rings	1	$971,010
Burger King	5	$1.8 million
Carvel	1	$128,720
Charlie's Chicken	1	$161,250
Checkers Drive-In	3	$1.4 million
Cheeburger-Cheeburger	1	$375,000
The Cheese Steak Shop	1	$168,750
Chester Fried Chicken	1	$5,000
Church's Fried Chicken	1	$300,000
CiCi's Pizza	12	$3.8 million
Cindy's Cinnamon Rolls	1	$108,000
Cinnabon	3	$435,045
Cold Stone Creamery	7	$1.1 million
Cookie Company	1	$168,480
Creno's Pizza	1	$107,100
Culver's Frozen Custard	4	$2.3 million
Dairy Queen	35	$11.2 million
Del Taco	5	$3.1 million

Fast food franchisor (includes burger, sandwich, poultry, pizza, taco, hot dog, pretzel, and dessert establishments)	Number of 7(a) SBA loan guarantees	Dollar amount of SBA loan guarantees (all figures over a million rounded to the nearest hundred thousand)
Domino's Pizza	14	$3.0 million
Donut Connection	1	$138,750
D.P. Dough	3	$319,125
Dunkin' Donuts	36	$18.3 million
East of Chicago Pizza	1	$62,500
Figaro's Italian Pizza	5	$428,260
Firehouse Subs	7	$2.3 million
Five Guys Famous Burgers and Fries	8	$2.3 million
Fox's Pizza Den	7	$709,960
Friendly's	1	$12,500
Fudrucker's	2	$1.1 million
Gambino's Pizza	3	$124,500
Garlic Jim's Famous Gourmet Pizza	1	$153,000
Global Donuts and Deli	1	$99,000
Godfather's Pizza	6	$714,045
Golden Chick	1	$187,500
Great American Cookie Company	1	$170,100
Gumby's Pizza International	1	$148,500
Hogi Yogi	1	$10,000
Honey Dew Donuts	2	$307,500
Hungry Howe's Pizza	1	$217,500
Idaho Pizza Company	1	$27,050
IMO's Pizza	1	$33,000
Jerry's Sub Shop	3	$614,250
Jets Pizza	3	$239,500
Jimmy John's	29	$7.7 million
Jimmy's Pizza	3	$607,350
Johnny Rockets	5	$2.0 million
Johnny's New York Style Pizza	2	$238,550
Kentucky Fried Chicken	9	$3.2 million
Kolache Factory	1	$129, 600
La Salsa	2	$549,000
Ledo Pizza	1	$161,250
Lee's Famous Recipe Chicken	1	$409,500
Lenny's Sub Shop	3	$357,300
Little Caesar's Pizza	25	$5.3 million
Little Scoops	1	$59,130
MaggieMoo's	2	$145,000

Fast food franchisor (includes burger, sandwich, poultry, pizza, taco, hot dog, pretzel, and dessert establishments)	Number of 7(a) SBA loan guarantees	Dollar amount of SBA loan guarantees (all figures over a million rounded to the nearest hundred thousand)
Maid-Rite Sandwich Shoppe	2	$207,525
Marble Slab Creamery	3	$547,350
Marco's Pizza	1	$80,750
McDonald's**	1	$25,000
Me-N-Ed's Pizzeria	1	$319,650
Mellow Mushroom	2	$634,500
Milio's Sandwiches	1	$110,500
Moe's Southwestern Grill	3	$868,350
Mr. Gatti's	1	$283,500
Mrs. Field's Cookies	1	$12,500
Nancy's Pizza	2	$164,540
Nathan's Famous	1	$25,000
Nestlé Toll House Café	2	$190,000
Noble Roman Pizza	1	$225,000
Paciugo Italian Gelato Rennaissance	1	$178,500
Panchero's Mexican Grill	4	$1.1 million
Papa John's Pizza	11	$4.4 million
Papa Murphy's Take 'N' Bake Pizza	15	$2.3 million
Papa's Pizza To Go	1	$76,500
Philly's Soft Pretzel Factory	2	$130,375
Pizza Inn	1	$933,750
Pizza Patron	1	$162,000
Pizza Ranch	5	$815,026
Pizza Schmizza	1	$5,000
Pizza Street	2	$545,400
Port of Subs	2	$72,250
Pretzel Time	2	$193,750
Qdoba Mexican Grill	5	$6.3 million
Quiznos	33	$3.3 million
Red Brick Pizza	1	$75,000
Red Robin Burger and Spirits	1	$348,570
Rocky Rococo Pan Style Pizza	3	$821,250
Roly Poly Rolled Sandwiches	2	$27,510
Rosati's Pizza	3	$510,330
Salsarita's	3	$598,000
Schlotzsky's Sandwich Shop	4	$1.4 million
Shake's Frozen Custard	1	$20,700
Simple Simon's Pizza	1	$110,500

Fast food franchisor (includes burger, sandwich, poultry, pizza, taco, hot dog, pretzel, and dessert establishments)	Number of 7(a) SBA loan guarantees	Dollar amount of SBA loan guarantees (all figures over a million rounded to the nearest hundred thousand)
Sir Pizza and Subs	1	$356,250
Snappy Tomato Pizza Company	2	$361,500
Sonic	6	$2.8 million
Spicy Pickle	2	$12,500
Stevi B's Pizza	5	$633,500
Straw Hat Pizza	1	$127,500
Submarina Sandwiches	2	$379,500
Subway	152	$27.7 million
Taco Bell	1	$1.5 million
Taco Del Mar	1	$143,820
TCBY	3	$432,750
Tim Horton Donuts	1	$25,000
Togo's Eateries	1	$120,000
Topper's Pizza	1	$511,500
Wendy's	2	$1.1 million
Wetzel's Pretzel	6	$1.0 million
Which Wich Superior Sandwiches	5	$953,100
Wing Zone	1	$180,000
Wings Etc.	4	$792,750
Williams Fried Chicken	1	$622,500
Wingstop	12	$2.7 million
Wow Cafe and Wingery	2	$420,000
Z Pizza	2	$586,350
Zack's Famous Frozen Yogurt	1	$101,950
Zaxby's	2	$295,200

Total number of franchisors: 131.
Total number of loans: 679.
Total amount of SBA loan guarantees to identifiable fast food franchises: over $170 million.
Data from Small Business Administration, email attachment to author, November 24, 2010 (Excel file, SBA 7(a) and 504 Gross Loan Approval Volume to Franchise Businesses, 1970–part of 2010; originally titled "2011028"). For more on SBA loan eligibility, see Small Business Administration, "7(a) Loan Program Eligibility," accessed 1 May 2014, http://www.sba.gov/content/7a-loan-program-eligibility.
*2009 is the last year for which the author possesses complete data.
**Despite McDonald's very modest SBA 7(a) loan total in 2009, franchises representing the company received many millions worth of loan guarantees from 1970 to 1986. See table 2 for precise figures on McDonald's SBA 7(a) loan history from 1970 to 2008.

Table 2. Loan Guarantees to McDonald's Franchises, 1970–2009

Year	Number of 7(a) SBA loan guarantees	Dollar amount of SBA loan guarantees (all figures over a million rounded to the nearest hundred thousand)
1970	5	$461,250
1971	22	$2.5 million
1972	13	$1.3 million
1973	21	$2.5 million
1974	16	$1.7 million
1975	35	$4.6 million
1976	25	$4.0 million
1977	22	$4.6 million
1978	32	$6.0 million
1979	24	$4.6 million
1980	20	$4.7 million
1981	20	$4.3 million
1982	13	$3.2 million
1983	15	$3.8 million
1984	11	$2.7 million
1985	15	$4.7 million
1986	9	$2.3 million
1987	2	$331,270
1988	no entries listed	
1989	2	$514,000
1990	1	$490,074
1991	1	$412,973
1992	1	$1.4 million
1993	2	$994,700
1994	3	$943,625
1995	1	$43,650
1996	3	$421,700
1997	2	$107,800
1998	1	$28,000
1999	no entries listed	
2000	no entries listed	
2001	no entries listed	
2002	3	$3.2 million
2003	1	$240,000
2004	no entries listed	
2005	4	$262,500

Year	Number of 7(a) SBA loan guarantees	Dollar amount of SBA loan guarantees (all figures over a million rounded to the nearest hundred thousand)
2006	2	$614, 000
2007	2	$137,500
2008	no entries listed	
2009	1	$25,000

Total number of loans: 350*

Total amount of SBA loan guarantees: over $68 million.

Data from Small Business Administration, email attachment to author, November 24, 2010 (Excel file, SBA 7(a) and 504 Gross Loan Approval Volume to Franchise Businesses, 1970–part of 2010; originally titled "2011028").

* This assumes that no franchises were double-counted.

NOTES

INTRODUCTION

1. Eric Schlosser, *Fast Food Nation: The Dark Side of the All-American Meal* (New York: Perennial, 2002), 102. Note that on July 7, 2004, the General Accounting Office was renamed the Government Accountability Office.

2. Greg Critser also mentions this in *Fat Land: How Americans Became the Fattest People in the World* (New York: Mariner Books, 2004), 112.

3. Scott A. Hodge, "For Big Franchisers, Money to Go; Is the SBA Dispensing Corporate Welfare?" *Washington Post*, November 30, 1997, C1. See also "S.B.A. Aid to Major Corporations Cited," *New York Times*, October 27, 1980, D4.

4. J. Eric Oliver, *Fat Politics: The Real Story Behind America's Obesity Epidemic* (New York: Oxford University Press, 2006), 37–43.

5. Ibid.

6. Dave Carpenter, "McDonald's to Dump Supersize Portions," Associated Press, March 3, 2004, accessed December 5, 2015, http://www.washingtonpost .com/wp-dyn/articles/A26082-2004Mar3.html.

7. The idea of performing a Google Image search derives from Karen Hitchcock, "Fat City: What Can Stop Obesity"? *The Monthly*, March 2013, accessed February 19, 2015, http://www.themonthly.com.au/issue/2013/march/1361848247 /karen-hitchcock/fat-city. Hitchcock writes:

> Very few people get obese and none get morbidly obese through the consumption of home-cooked whole foods. To get that fat, for most people, takes piles of highly refined, ready-to-chow junk food and drink. Try googling "what I ate when I was fat."

8. Zachary Fowle, "Heart Attack Grill's Quadruple Heart Bypass Challenge," *Phoenix New Times*, August 31, 2010, accessed July 5, 2013, http://blogs .phoenixnewtimes.com/bella/2010/08/heart_attack_grills_quadruple.php.

9. Charlotte Martin, "World's Worst Jumbo Junk Food," *The Sun*, July 24, 2012, accessed July 5, 2013, http://www.thesun.co.uk/sol/homepage/features/2988347 /Worlds-worst-jumbo-junk-food.html?offset=1.

10. Katie Little, "Posts on McDonald's Employee Site Bash Fast Food," *CNBC*, December 23, 2013, accessed February 18, 2015, http://www.cnbc.com/id /101293024.

11. Ibid.

12. This was a second embarrassment for the McResources Line; the first

occurred in July 2013 when the website featured a sample budget for McDonald's employees on how to survive on fast food wages. The sample budget was criticized and lampooned for being unrealistic, and presuming that McDonald employees held second jobs—a presumption essentially conceding that a McDonald's wage alone was not a living wage. See Jordan Weissman, "McDonald's Can't Figure Out How Its Workers Survive on Minimum Wage," *The Atlantic*, July 16, 2013, accessed February 18, 2015, http://www.theatlantic.com/business /archive/2013/07/mcdonalds-cant-figure-out-how-its-workers-survive-on -minimum-wage/277845/.

13. Douglas Kellner, "Theorizing/Resisting McDonaldization: A Multiperspectivist Approach," in *Resisting McDonaldization*, ed. Barry Smart (London: Sage, 1999), 197. Regarding the internal memo, Kellner cites Joel Kovel, "Bad News for Fast Food: What's Wrong with McDonald's?" *Z Magazine*, September 1997, 28.

14. Some scholars have questioned whether obesity deserves its status as a public health crisis, and others have emphasized the making of the obesity epidemic. Some representative works on these topics include: Oliver, *Fat Politics: The Real Story Behind America's Obesity Epidemic*; Paul Campos, *The Obesity Myth: Why America's Obsession with Weight Is Hazardous to Your Health* (New York: Gotham, 2004); Charles E. Rosenberg, "Disease in History: Frames and Framers," *Milbank Quarterly* 67, Supplement 1 (1989): 1–15; Ian Hacking, "Making Up People," *London Review of Books*, August 17, 2006, 23–26; Abigail C. Saguy and Rene Almeling, "Fat in the Fire? Science, the News Media, and the 'Obesity Epidemic,'" *Sociological Forum* (March 2008): 53–83; Amy Erdman Farrell, *Fat Shame: Stigma and the Fat Body in American Culture* (New York: New York University Press, 2011).

15. "The Obesity Crisis in America," statement of Richard H. Carmona, testimony before the Subcommittee on Education Reform, Committee on Education and the Workforce, United States House of Representatives, July 16, 2003, accessed July 5, 2013, http://www.surgeongeneral.gov/news/testimony /obesity07162003.html.

16. "Obesity Bigger Threat than Terrorism?" *CBS News*, March 1, 2005, accessed July 5, 2013, http://www.cbsnews.com/news/obesity-bigger-threat-than -terrorism/.

17. This summary of the "Let's Move" initiative has been published online. See Chin Jou, "Fighting Obesity Requires a War on Poverty," *The Drum*, Australian Broadcasting Corporation, June 11, 2015, accessed June 15, 2015, http://www .abc.net.au/news/2015-06-11/jou-fighting-obesity-requires-a-war-on-poverty /6537888.

18. The nutrition guidelines of the Healthy, Hunger-Free Kids Act require that high school lunches contain no more than 850 calories, while middle and elementary school lunches are not to exceed 700 and 650 calories, respectively. As has been widely reported, many students have resisted the new nutrition

guidelines, claiming that school meals now leave them hungry and unsatisfied. See Vivian Yee, "No Appetite for Good-for-You School Lunches," *New York Times*, October 5, 2012, accessed July 5, 2013, https://www.nytimes.com/2012/10/06 /nyregion/healthier-school-lunches-face-student-rejection.html?pagewanted =all&_r=0.

19. The NIH budget varies from year to year. See "NIH Budget," National Institutes of Health, accessed October 10, 2015, http://www.nih.gov/about /budget.htm.

20. The phrase in quotation marks is from the NIH Obesity Research Task Force. See "About NIH Obesity Research," National Institutes of Health, accessed July 5, 2013, http://obesityresearch.nih.gov/about/.

21. There are, however, areas of research that dwarf obesity at the NIH; cancer research, for instance, was allocated $5.67 billion in 2014. See "Estimates of Funding for Various Research, Condition, and Disease Categories," National Institutes of Health, April 10, 2013, accessed July 5, 2013, http://report.nih.gov /categorical_spending.aspx.

22. Gerardo Otero, Gabriela Pechlaner, Giselle Liberman, and Efe Gürcan, "The Neoliberal Diet and Inequality in the United States," *Social Science and Medicine* 142 (2015): 47; *Accelerating Progress in Obesity Prevention: Solving the Weight of the Nation*, Report by the Institute of Medicine (Washington, DC: National Academies Press, 2012).

23. The term "toxic food environment" was coined by Kelly D. Brownell in *Food Fight: The Inside Story of the Food Industry, America's Obesity Crisis, and What We Can Do About It* (New York: McGraw-Hill, 2004).

24. For more on this, see Marion Nestle's *Food Politics: How the Food Industry Influences Nutrition and Health* (Berkeley: University of California Press, 2007).

25. Some of Michael Pollan's writings on this include *The Omnivore's Dilemma: A Natural History of Four Meals* (New York: Penguin, 2006), and "Farmer in Chief," *New York Times Magazine*, October 9, 2008, accessed July 6, 2013, https:// www.nytimes.com/2008/10/12/magazine/12policy-t.html?pagewanted=all.

26. See Nadine Lehrer, *U.S. Farm Bills and Policy Reforms: Ideological Conflicts over World Trade, Renewable Energy, and Sustainable Agriculture* (Amherst, NY: Cambria Press, 2010).

27. Michael Carlson, "Earl Butz" (obituary), *The Guardian*, February 3, 2008, accessed July 6, 2013, http://www.guardian.co.uk/world/2008/feb/04/usa .obituaries. Butz continued to serve as agriculture secretary under President Gerald Ford, but was ignominiously ousted in 1976 for making a racist joke.

28. The phrase in quotations is derived from the subtitle of the book by Greg Critser, *Fat Land: How Americans Became the Fattest People in the World*. The title of Critser's book is somewhat misleading, as South Pacific island nations like Nauru, Samoa, and Micronesia tend to have the highest rates of obesity world-

wide; the United States is currently second, behind Mexico, in the Western Hemisphere.

29. It should be noted that not all experts agree that agricultural subsidies of grains are a major culprit in rising rates of obesity in the United States. For example, the nonprofit organizations Food & Water Watch and the Public Health Institute have put forth the idea that deregulation, not agricultural subsidies, is to blame for obesity. The two organizations point out that during the 1980s and 1990s, food processors, grain traders, meat companies, and food marketers lobbied for the elimination of U.S government farm programs that limited production and stabilized commodity prices for farmers; the abolition of such programs had the potential to significantly reduce what food processors et al. paid for crops, especially grains. With the passage of the 1996 Farm Bill, Congress eliminated government programs that had limited production and the supply of commodities to the marketplace. The result was greater supply and lower prices for commodities like corn and soy, which, of course, benefited the food industry. Perversely, this led some farmers to produce even greater quantities of corn and soy to offset their declining farm income. With lower commodity prices, the food industry could charge less for processed foods, and consumers could afford to buy more calorie-dense processed foods and beverages. See Food & Water Watch and the Public Health Institute, *Do Farm Subsidies Cause Obesity?* (Washington, DC: Food & Water Watch; Oakland, CA: Public Health Institute, 2011). Food studies scholar Julie Guthman also challenges the notion that processed foods containing corn and other subsidized crops are cheaper than fruits and vegetables because of farm subsidies. She argues that fruits and vegetables are more expensive to grow and harvest than grains, which accounts for the higher costs of produce relative to many processed snack foods. See Julie Guthman, *Weighing In: Obesity, Food Justice, and the Limits of Capitalism* (Berkeley: University of California Press, 2011), 122.

30. Michael Moss, "While Warning about Fat, U.S. Pushes Cheese Sales," *New York Times*, November 6, 2010, A1. Dairy Management's attempts to cram more cheese into already fat-laden fast food products were remarkably successful. By its own estimation, the USDA's cheese promotion strategies contributed to the sale of an additional 30 million pounds of cheese in 2007.

31. See Nestle, *Food Politics*.

32. Michael Moss, *Salt Sugar Fat: How the Food Giants Hooked Us* (New York: Random House, 2013); David Kessler, *The End of Overeating: Taking Control of the Insatiable North American Appetite* (New York: Rodale, 2009).

33. For reports by Nader's group, see James S. Turner, *The Chemical Feast: Ralph Nader's Study Group Report of the Food and Drug Administration* (New York: Grossman Publishers, 1970); Harrison Wellford, *Sowing the Wind: A Report for Ralph Nader's Center for Study of Responsive Law on Food Safety and the Chemical Harvest* (New York: Grossman Publishers, 1972).

34. Michael Pollan, "Unhappy Meals," *New York Times Magazine*, January 28, 2007, accessed July 7, 2013, https://www.nytimes.com/2007/01/28/magazine /28nutritionism.t.html?pagewanted=all&_r=0; Nestle, *Food Politics*, 41–42.

35. Pollan, "Unhappy Meals"; "McGovern Releases Second Edition of Dietary Goals for the United States" (press release from Senator McGovern's Office), July 24, 1978, Box 617, George S. McGovern Papers, Mudd Manuscript Library, Princeton University, Princeton, New Jersey.

36. Reports of the precise dollar amount that the Texas cattle ranchers sought from Winfrey varied; the $12 million figure is derived from the *New York Times*. See Sam Howe Verhovek, "Talk of the Town: Burgers v. Oprah," *New York Times*, January 21, 1998, accessed November 7, 2015, http://www.nytimes.com /1998/01/21/us/talk-of-the-town-burgers-v-oprah.html.

37. Patricia Wells, "Fast Food Companies Defend Themselves; 100 Percent Domestic Beef," *New York Times*, February 10, 1979, 44.

38. "Bill Summary & Status 102nd Congress (1991–1992) H.R. 82," *Library of Congress* (THOMAS), accessed February 16, 2015, http://thomas.loc.gov/cgi-bin /bdquery/D?d102:1:./temp/~bdPCJr; National Institutes of Health Director's Files, Document + 87607, National Institutes of Health, Bethesda, Maryland.

39. Duff Wilson and Janet Roberts, "Special Report: How Washington Went Soft on Childhood Obesity," Reuters, April 27, 2012, accessed July 7, 2013, http:// www.reuters.com/article/2012/04/27/us-usa-foodlobby-idUSBRE83Q0ED 20120427.

40. For more on lobbying by the soft drink industry, see Marion Nestle, *Soda Politics: Taking On Big Soda (and Winning)* (New York: Oxford University Press, 2015).

41. To calculate BMI, divide weight in kilograms by the square of height in meters. The NIH offers a BMI calculation tool here: http://www.nhlbi.nih.gov /guidelines/obesity/BMI/bmicalc.htm (accessed December 6, 2015). For criticisms of the BMI as an indicator of health, see Oliver, *Fat Politics*.

42. "Obesity and African Americans," Office of Minority Health, U.S. Department of Health and Human Services, accessed July 25, 2013, http:// minorityhealth.hhs.gov/templates/content.aspx?ID=6456.

For more on obesity among African-American children (as well as Hispanic and white children), see Shiriki K. Kumanyika, "Environmental Influences on Childhood Obesity: Ethnic and Cultural Differences in Context," in *Physiology and Behavior* 94 (2008): 61–70.

43. R. Rogers, T. F. Eagle, A. Sheetz, A. Woodward, R. Leibowitz, M. Song, R. Sylvester, N. Corriveau, E. Kline-Rogers, Q. Jiang, E. A. Jackson, and K. A. Eagle, "The Relationship between Childhood Obesity, Low Socioeconomic Status, and Race/Ethnicity: Lessons from Massachusetts," *Childhood Obesity* 11.6 (December 2015): 691–95.

44. "Obesity and African Americans."

45. See Sara N. Bleich, Roland J. Thorpe Jr., Hamidah Sharif-Harris, Ruth Feshazion, and Thomas A. LaVeist, "Social Context Explains Race Disparities in Obesity among Women," *Journal of Epidemiology and Community Health* 24 (2010): 465–69; Kumanyika, "Environmental Influences on Childhood Obesity: Ethnic and Cultural Differences in Context." There are a host of explanations for why African-American women are particularly affected by obesity. Foremost, perhaps, is that they are more likely to be of low socioeconomic status, which is linked to constraints in access to healthy foods and physical recreation. Studies also show that African-American women tend to be less body-obsessed than middle-class and affluent white women. They are more apt to accept their own bodies and not to conflate beauty with body size. See Christine M. Lawrence and Mark H. Thelen, "Body Image, Dieting, and Self-Concept: Their Relation in African-American and Caucasian Children," *Journal of Clinical Child Psychology* 24 (1995): 41–48; Lonnae O'Neal Parker, "Black Women Heavier and Happier with Their Bodies Than White Women, Poll Finds," *Washington Post*, February 27, 2012, accessed July 29, 2013, http://www.washingtonpost.com/lifestyle/style/black -women-heavier-and-happier-with-their-bodies-than-white-women-poll -finds/2012/02/22/gIQAPmcHeR_story.html. African-American women and children who live in urban areas may not necessarily be more obese than their rural counterparts, however. A 2012 study in the *Journal of Rural Health* found that the obesity rate for rural Americans (of all races) is 39.6 percent, compared to 33.4 percent for those living in cities. Authors of the study hypothesized that this is due to rural Americans' high-fat diet and geographic isolation in a modern era in which fewer of them are likely to be engaged in physically strenuous agricultural labor given the the mechanization of farming. See C. Befort, N. Nazir, and M. G. Perri, "Prevalence of Obesity among Adults from Rural and Urban Areas of the United States: Findings from NHANES (2005–2008)," *Journal of Rural Health* 28.4 (Fall 2012): 392–97.

46. "Obesity and African Americans."

47. See Guthman, *Weighing In*; Farrell, *Fat Shame*; April Michelle Herndon, *Fat Blame: How the War on Obesity Victimizes Women and Children* (Lawrence: University Press of Kansas, 2014).

48. See Farrell, *Fat Shame*; Campos, *The Obesity Myth: Why America's Obsession with Weight is Hazardous to Your Health*; Marilyn Wann, *FAT!SO? Because You Don't Have to Apologize for Your Size* (Berkeley: Ten Speed Press, 1998); Harriet Brown, *Body of Truth: How Science, Culture, and History Drive Our Obsession with Weight— and What We Can Do About It* (Boston: Da Capo Lifelong Books, 2014); Gina Kolata, "Some Extra Heft May Be Helpful," *New York Times*, April 20, 2005, accessed December 9, 2015, http://www.nytimes.com/2005/04/20/health/some-extra-heft -may-be-helpful-new-study-says.html.

49. "Adult Obesity Causes & Consequences," Centers for Disease Control and

Prevention, updated June 15, 2015, accessed December 9, 2015, http://www.cdc.gov/obesity/adult/causes.html.

50. Legal scholar Andrea Freeman's compelling point about the "myth of personal choice" is: "Too often, advocates of 'personal choice' blame low-income people of color for their own weight issues and health crises, linking these problems to individual moral and cultural failures instead of placing the problems in the broader, historical context of long-entrenched policies and practices." See Andrea Freeman, "Fast Food: Oppression through Poor Nutrition," *California Law Review* 95.6 (December 2007): 2222.

51. Charlotte Biltekoff, *Eating Right in America: The Cultural Politics of Food and Health* (Durham, NC: Duke University Press, 2013), 104.

52. Ibid.; Barbara Kingsolver with Steven L. Hopp and Camille Kingsolver, *Animal, Vegetable, Miracle: A Year of Food Life* (New York: HarperCollins, 2007), 130.

53. Tara Weingarten, "Alice's Wonderland," *Newsweek*, August 26, 2001, accessed March 21, 2015, http://www.newsweek.com/alices-wonderland-151609.

54. Ibid; Biltekoff, *Eating Right in America*, 104; Alice Waters, "Slow Food, Slow Schools: Teaching Sustainability through the Education of the Senses," paper presented at the Program in Agrarian Studies at Yale University, New Haven, Connecticut, 2003; Alice Waters, "Fast Food Values," keynote address at REAP [Resource Efficient Agricultural Production] Conference, Madison, Wisconsin, September 2002.

55. B. R. Myers, "The Moral Crusade against Foodies," *The Atlantic*, March 2011. Myers points to what he sees as Waters's hypocrisy, that is, her championing of sustainable food while serving meat at Chez Panisse. For a book-length critique of the foodie movement's focus on local and organic foods as antidotes to the obesity epidemic, see Guthman, *Weighing In.*

56. Stan Luxenberg, *Roadside Empires: How the Chains Franchised America* (New York: Penguin, 1985), 5.

57. Jonathan J. Bean, *Big Government and Affirmative Action: The Scandalous History of the Small Business Administration* (Lexington: University Press of Kentucky, 2001), 52.

58. Christopher Shawn McKeehan, telephone interview with author, November 18, 2010. At the time of this interview, McKeehan was a program manager with the SBA.

59. McDonald's email to author, July 4, 2013.

CHAPTER 1

1. Figures based on the author's calculations of SBA data. Data from Small Business Administration, email attachment to author, November 24, 2010 (Excel file, SBA 7(a) and 504 Gross Loan Approval Volume to Franchise Businesses,

1970–part of 2010; originally titled "2011028"). See the appendix for a break-down of these data.

2. It should be noted that not all inner-city communities are deluged with fast food outlets and bereft of supermarkets or fresh produce. See John McWhorter, "The Food Desert Myth," *New York Daily News*, April 22, 2012, accessed August 10, 2013, http://www.nydailynews.com/opinion/food-desert -myth-article-1.1065165; Roland Sturm and Deborah Cohen, "Zoning for Health? The Year-Old Ban on New Fast-Food Restaurants in South LA: The Ordinance Isn't a Promising Approach to Attacking Obesity," *Health Affairs* 28.6 (2009): 1088–97. Additionally, the relationship between grocery store density and obesity is not firmly established. See Gina Kolata, "Studies Question the Pairing of Food Deserts and Obesity," *New York Times*, April 17, 2012, accessed May 4, 2014, http://www.nytimes.com/2012/04/18/health/research/pairing-of-food-deserts -and-obesity-challenged-in-studies.html?_r=1. It should also be pointed out that it is unclear how, if at all, geographic proximity to grocery stores affects people's diets. As a 2011 study using survey data from over 5,000 relatively young adults (ages 18 to 30) nationwide concluded, "Greater supermarket availability was generally unrelated to diet quality and fruit and vegetable intake, and relationships between grocery store availability and diet outcomes were mixed." See Janne Boone-Heinonen, Penny Gordon-Larsen, Catarina I. Kiefe, James M. Shikany, Cora E. Lewis, and Barry M. Popkin, "Fast Food Restaurants and Food Stores: Longitudinal Associations with Diet in Young to Middle-aged Adults: The CARDIA Study," *Archives of Internal Medicine* 171.13 (2011): 1162. Despite all of these considerations, accessible grocery stores in underserved communities can encourage healthier eating if they sell produce and other nutritious items that are both affordable and high-quality, and government policies can help make produce more affordable for low-income Americans. See the conclusion of this book for more on grocery stores and policy proposals for making fruits and vegetables more affordable.

3. Megan McArdle, "Fast Food Strike Made Minimum Sense," *Bloomberg News*, August 2, 2013, accessed May 4, 2014, http://www.bloomberg.com/news /2013-08-02/fast-food-strike-s-minimum-sense.html; Sabouri Ben-Achour, "Groceries: A Low-Margin Business, But Still Highly Desirable," *Marketplace* (American Public Media), September 12, 2013, accessed May 4, 2014, http://www .marketplace.org/topics/business/groceries-low-margin-business-still-highly -desirable; "Workers' Protest Highlight Fast-Food Economics," Associated Press, September 1, 2013, accessed May 4, 2014, http://www.cnbc.com/id/101001870; Candice Choi and Jonathan Fahey, "Fast-Food Workers Face Problem: Who'll Fund Raises?" *Boston Globe*, September 2, 2013, accessed May 4, 2014, http:// www.bostonglobe.com/business/2013/09/01/workers-protests-highlight-fast -food-economics/4nYqt8xRm9J73vASTzcSXM/story.html.

4. In spite of the extra costs associated with doing business in inner cities,

there is empirical evidence on the long-term successes of inner-city supermarkets in low-income communities in Los Angeles, New York, Philadelphia, and other cities. See Melinda Fulmer, "Some Supermarkets Thrive in Inner City," *Los Angeles Times*, May 13, 2000, accessed December 10, 2015, http://articles.latimes.com/2000/may/13/business/fi-29527; Allen R. Myerson, "Thriving Where Others Won't Go," *New York Times*, January 7, 1992, D1, D5.

5. Stipulations for SBA 7(a) loan guarantees are as follows: "[The] SBA can guarantee as much as 85 percent on loans of up to $150,000 and 75 percent on loans of more than $150,000. 7(a) loans have a maximum loan amount of $5 million. SBA's maximum exposure is $3.75 million ($4.5 million under the International Trade Loan). Thus, if a business receives an SBA-guaranteed loan for $5 million, the maximum guaranty to the lender will be $3.75 million or 75 percent." See "7(a) Terms & Conditions," Small Business Administration, accessed May 5, 2014, http://www.sba.gov/content/7a-terms-conditions.

6. "7(a) Loans," Small Business Administration, accessed May 5, 2014, http://www.sba.gov/category/lender-navigation/steps-sba-lending/7a-loans.

7. *Table of Small Business Size Standards Matched to North American Industry Classification System Codes* (effective January 22, 2014), Small Business Administration, 24, 38, accessed May 5, 2014, http://www.sba.gov/sites/default/files/files/Size_Standards_Table.pdf.

8. "About Us," Subway, accessed April 13, 2016, https://www.subway.com.au/About.

9. "Subway," *Entrepreneur*, accessed May 6, 2014, http://www.entrepreneur.com/franchises/subway/282839-0.html#; "Top 50 Sorted by Average Sales per Unit," QSR, accessed May 6, 2014, http://www.qsrmagazine.com/reports/top-50-sorted-average-sales-unit.

10. "Company Profile" and "Welcome to McFranchise," *McDonald's*, accessed May 6, 2014, http://www.aboutmcdonalds.com/mcd/investors/company_profile.html and http://www.aboutmcdonalds.com/mcd/franchising.html.

11. "Top 50 Sorted by Average Sales per Unit." It should be noted that although McDonald's franchises received considerable SBA loan guarantees throughout the 1970s and early 1980s, since that period the chain has received relatively nominal loan guarantees from the agency. The SBA has declined to speculate as to why its loan guarantees to McDonald's franchises have fallen sharply since the 1980s.

12. "KFC Corp," *Entrepreneur*, accessed May 6, 2014, http://www.entrepreneur.com/franchises/kfccorp/282495-0.html.

13. Kate Taylor, "Wendy's Sells 70 Restaurants in Dallas, Continuing Refranchising Effort," *Entrepreneur*, February 20, 2014, accessed May 6, 2014, http://www.entrepreneur.com/article/231656.

14. "Top 50 Sorted by Average Sales per Unit."

15. While corporate supermarkets grossing over $30 million may be ineli-

gible for SBA 7(a) loans, it should be noted that federal agencies, particularly the Department of Housing and Urban Development (HUD) and the Commerce Department, do have programs that can help bring grocery stores to inner cities.

16. "2011 Top 100 Retailers," National Retail Federation, accessed May 8, 2014, http://www.stores.org/2011/Top-100-Retailers.

17. Regardless, neither chain received any 7(a) franchise loans from the agency between 1970 and part of 2010, according to data of the SBA's loan guarantees.

18. "Negro Concern Sets Supermarket Chain," *New York Times*, February 8, 1967, 37; "Super Jet Opens First Market, Tuesday Nov. 14," *Baltimore Afro-American*, November 14, 1967, 2; "Jet Food Corporation Opens Largest Branch in Cleveland," *Baltimore Afro-American*, July 5, 1969, 13. According to the *Afro-American*, Jet Food also had plans to expand to Washington, DC, and Durham, North Carolina, but it is unclear whether those plans ever materialized. See "Jet Food Corporation Opens Largest Branch in Cleveland," 13.

19. Louis Haugh, "Jet Food to Open 2 Supermarkets," *Chicago Tribune*, February 23, 1967, 8. Smith had been a marketing veteran. In 1940, he became PepsiCo's first African-American salesman, charged with helping the company market its products to African Americans. See "10 Bizarre and Daring Feats of Salesmanship," *Fortune*, accessed July 27, 2015, http://archive.fortune.com/galleries/2008/fortune/0809/gallery.Legends_of_sales_Clifford.fortune/5.html.

20. "More Jobs for Negroes as Jet Food Store Opens," *Jet*, November 30, 1967, 50.

21. Robert E. Weems, Jr., with Lewis A. Randolph, *Business in Black and White: American Presidents and Black Entrepreneurs in the Twentieth Century* (New York: New York University Press, 2009), 82.

22. This conclusion is drawn from Small Business Administration, email attachment to author, November 24, 2010 (Excel file, SBA 7(a) and 504 Gross Loan Approval Volume to Franchise Businesses, 1970–part of 2010; originally titled "2011028," 533 pages).

23. The year 2009 is highlighted because that is the most recent year for which the author possesses complete data (data from 2010 are incomplete, and the author has been unable to obtain data since 2010). Big M Supermarkets were acquired by the Tops Markets chain in December 2012.

24. All figures are based on the author's calculations of SBA data: Small Business Administration, email attachment to author, November 24, 2010 (Excel file, SBA 7(a) and 504 Gross Loan Approval Volume to Franchise Businesses, 1970–part of 2010; originally titled "2011028"). The "fast food industry" is being defined as those restaurant chains specializing in hamburgers, sandwiches, poultry (usually fried chicken or chicken wings), pizza, tacos, hot dogs, pretzels, and desserts.

25. See table 2 in the appendix for a record of SBA support of McDonald's from 1970 to 2008.

26. For more on the politics of Reconstruction and the Freedmen's Bureau, see Eric Foner, *America's Unfinished Revolution, 1863–1877* (New York: Harper and Row, 1988).

27. Weems, *Business in Black and White*, 11.

28. Ibid., 31.

29. Division of Negro Affairs document, quoted in ibid., 35.

30. For more on the Division of Negro Affairs's business clinics after World War II, see ibid., 50–51.

31. Ibid., 44, 64.

32. Max Boas and Steve Chain, *Big Mac: The Unauthorized Story of McDonald's* (New York: E. P. Dutton and Co., 1976), 184.

33. For more on race and Cold War politics, see Mary L. Dudziak, *Cold War Civil Rights: Race and the Image of American Democracy* (Princeton, NJ: Princeton University Press, 2000); Thomas Borstelmann, *The Cold War and the Color Line: American Race Relations in the Global Arena* (Cambridge, MA: Harvard University Press, 2001).

34. Robert J. Yancy, *Federal Government Policy and Black Business Enterprise* (Cambridge, MA: Ballinger Publishing Company, 1974), 65. According to Yancy, there were ten loans made from the SBA's District of Columbia office and seven from its Philadelphia office.

35. Weems, *Business in Black and White*, 74, 79, 177.

36. Yancy, *Federal Government Policy and Black Business Enterprise*, 65; Weems, *Business in Black and White*, 74.

37. Weems, *Business in Black and White*, 74–75.

38. Jonathan Cottin, "Staff Problems, Mistrust, Delay Nixon Minority Enterprise Plan," *National Journal*, June 20, 1970, 1323. Roosevelt would become chair of the Equal Employment Opportunity Commission in 1965, and serve in that capacity until the following year.

39. Weems, *Business in Black and White*, 82.

40. The August 4, 1967, cover of *Time* magazine depicted a few illustrated scenes of the Detroit riots in the summer of 1967 that came to be among the iconic images of upheaval in America's urban centers in the mid to late 1960s. The *Time* cover featured a storefront building engulfed in flames and smoke, with a water hose feebly attempting to fight the blaze, and a single rioter fleeing the scene. Surrounding that image were a helmeted white policeman holding a rifle, a press conference by members of the National Advisory Commission on Civil Disorders, a man and a woman apparently carrying armfuls of presumably just-looted merchandise, and a trio of firefighters battling the blaze at the storefront.

41. *Mobilizing for Urban Action: Challenge to Business* (New York: American Management Association, 1968), 8.

42. Weems, *Business in Black and White*, 79.

43. Jonathan J. Bean, "'Burn, Baby, Burn': Small Business in the Urban Riots of the 1960s," *Independent Review* 5.2 (Fall 2000): 169.

44. Ibid., 8–9. The quote was attributed to management expert Lawrence A. Appley.

45. The sociologist William Julius Wilson's classic study, *The Truly Disadvantaged: The Inner City, the Underclass, and Public Policy*, notes how the concentration of poverty and the propagation of antisocial mores were exacerbated by an exodus of upwardly mobile African Americans from black communities that had previously consisted of residents of varying socioeconomic status. (In noting an unintended consequence of desegregation, Wilson was not, however, advocating a return to racial segregation.) See William Julius Wilson, *The Truly Disadvantaged: The Inner City, the Underclass, and Public Policy* (Chicago: University of Chicago Press, 1987).

46. For more on the devastating effects of deindustrialization in America's inner cities, see Thomas J. Sugrue, *The Origins of the Urban Crisis: Race and Inequality in Postwar Detroit* (Princeton: Princeton University Press, 1996).

47. Memo from Eugene P. Foley to Henry Wilson, "Subject: Relieving Racial Tensions in Urban Ghettos, Aug. 15, 1966," 2, Archives II (National Archives, College Park, Maryland), Records of the Economic Development Administration, Record Group 378, Box 5 ("Records of the Office of the Executive Secretariat, Office of Administration, EDA, Subject Files, 1965–69"), folder: "Ghettos."

48. In 1966, for instance, 57 percent of all nonwhite (this meant primarily "black" in 1966) households in cities with populations of 250,000 and over were living in what the U.S. Census Bureau officially designated as "poverty areas." See Edmund K. Faltermayer, "More Dollars and More Diplomas," *Fortune*, January 1968, 222.

49. Rates of joblessness would later rise with the economic challenges of the 1970s (i.e., low growth rates, stagflation, and the energy crisis). By March 1976, 14 percent of the country's 9.4 million African-American adults (ages 16 and over) were unemployed. "Negro Exodus Slows, Reports Shows," *Washington Post*, August 1, 1968, Archives II (National Archives, College Park, Maryland), Records of the Office of the Secretary of Agriculture, General Correspondence, 1906–76," Record Group 16, Box 4870; "The Gibson Report" ("Minority Marketing/Communications Publication"), published by D. Parke Gibson International, Inc., June 1977, Archives II (National Archives, College Park, Maryland), Records of the Minority Business Development Agency, Record Group 427, Box 3 of 5, Accession No. 427-82-005, Folder: "The Gibson Report" (no page number).

50. Faltermayer, "More Dollars and More Diplomas," 141.

51. Lizabeth Cohen, *A Consumer's Republic: The Politics of Mass Consumption in Postwar America* (New York: Vintage, 2003), 372–73.

52. Contemporaneous observers also commented on this. Management expert Lawrence A. Appley noted that African Americans confronted a "two-phase struggle": "The first phase was the struggle for civil rights; the second and most decisive phase was the fight for economic equality." See *Mobilizing for Urban Action*, 9.

53. Cohen, *A Consumer's Republic*, 372–73.

54. See Bean, "Burn, Baby, Burn," 166–67.

55. Ibid., 170–71. Sociologist David Caplovitz famously discovered that poor Americans did often pay more for merchandise and services than their better-off counterparts in his study, *The Poor Pay More* (New York: Free Press, 1963).

56. For more on this, see Thomas Byrne Edsall with Mary D. Edsall, *Chain Reaction: The Impact of Race, Rights, and Taxes on American Politics* (New York: W. W. Norton, 1992).

57. Bean, *Big Government and Affirmative Action*, 50.

58. Robert E. Weems, Jr., *Desegregating the Dollar: African American Consumerism in the Twentieth Century* (New York: New York University Press, 1998), 76.

59. Memo from Eugene P. Foley to Henry Wilson, "Subject: Relieving Racial Tensions in Urban Ghettos, Aug. 15, 1966," 1, Archives II (National Archives, College Park, Maryland), Records of the Economic Development Administration, Record Group 378, Box 5 ("Records of the Office of the Executive Secretariat, Office of Administration, EDA, Subject Files, 1965–69"), folder: "Ghettos."

60. Weems, *Business in Black and White*, 76.

61. See Eugene P. Foley, *The Achieving Ghetto* (Washington, DC: National Press, 1968).

62. John Flory, "Employment and Urban Areas," U.S. Department of Commerce, Economic Development Administration, Office of Program Plans and Analysis, Archives II (National Archives, College Park, Maryland), Records of the Economic Development Administration, Record Group 378, Box 1 ("Records of the Office of the Deputy Assistant Secretary for Policy Coordination, Jonathan Lindley, Economic Development Administration, General Subject Files, 1966–1968"), untitled folder.

63. Weems, *Business in Black and White*, 86.

64. *Report of the National Advisory Commission on Civil Disorders* (New York: Bantam Books, 1968); Bean, *Big Government and Affirmative Action*, 62; *Mobilizing for Urban Action*, 13.

65. Letter from Senator Edmund Muskie, Senate Committee on Government Operations, to Ross Davis, Economic Development Administration, September 28, 1968, Archives II (National Archives, College Park, Maryland), Records

of the Economic Development Administration, Record Group 378, Box 1 ("Office of the Deputy Assistant Secretary for Policy Coordination, Jonathan Lindley, EDA, General Subject Files, 1966–68"), untitled folder.

66. Bean, "Burn, Baby, Burn," 180.

67. Bean, *Big Government and Affirmative Action: The Scandalous History of the Small Business Administration*, 65. Bean writes that the SBA's lift of the ban on businesses selling alcohol also "threatened to inflame hostilities in the ghetto," as "liquor stores were the number one target of rioters."

68. Bean, "Burn, Baby, Burn," 179. Bean adds that "policymakers responded sympathetically and paternalistically to the perceived demands of the rioters."

69. *Mobilizing for Urban Action*, 10.

70. Ibid., 33–34. Moot did not specify how many people participated in this management trainee program, but noted that "nearly 100,000 small businessmen" sought counsel from the SBA management education program, which employed 150 management assistant officers located in major cities throughout the country." See ibid., 34–35.

71. For more on how the Johnson and Nixon administrations saw the promotion of minority enterprise (and African-American economic development more generally) as antidotes to further urban unrest, see John David Skrentny, *The Ironies of Affirmative Action: Politics, Culture and Justice in America* (Chicago: University of Chicago Press, 1996); Dean Kotlowski, "Black Power—Nixon Style: The Nixon Administration and Minority Business Enterprise," *Business History Review* 72.3 (1998): 409–45.

72. "Managing for a Better America: Mobilization for Urban Action Programs: An Urgent Call for the Immediate Mobilization of Management in the Attack on Urban Despair and Decay" (pamphlet), June 3–5, 1968, Americana Hotel, New York City, the American Management Association's Special Conference, Archives II (National Archives, College Park, Maryland), Records of the Economic Development Administration, Record Group 378, Box 1 ("Records of the Office of the Deputy Assistant Secretary for Policy Coordination, Jonathan Lindley, EDA, General Subject Files, 1966–1968"), untitled folder.

73. *Mobilizing for Urban Action*, 43.

74. "Managing for a Better America."

75. *Mobilizing for Urban Action*, 43.

76. Figures are based on the author's calculations of SBA data: Small Business Administration, email attachment to author, November 24, 2010 (Excel file, SBA 7(a) and 504 Gross Loan Approval Volume to Franchise Businesses, 1970–part of 2010; originally titled "2011028," 533 pages). It is possible that Dunkin' Donuts also received SBA loan guarantees in 1968 and 1969, but the SBA has not made data before 1970 available to the author.

77. *Mobilizing for Urban Action*, 43.

78. Ibid.

79. For more on striking by fast food workers nationwide and internationally, see Steven Greenhouse, "A Day's Strike Seeks to Raise Fast-Food Pay," *New York Times*, August 1, 2013, A1; Steven Greenhouse, "Fast-Food Protests Spread Overseas," *New York Times*, May 15, 2014, B1. For more on the idea of fast food employment (in this case, at Burger King) as valuable work experience in the Bedford-Stuyvesant section of Brooklyn, see Sam Roberts, "Brooklyn Group Serves Up Hope with Fast Food," *New York Times*, March 16, 1987, accessed December 10, 2015, http://www.nytimes.com/1987/03/26/nyregion/metro-matters-brooklyn-group-serves-up-hope-with-fast-food.html.

80. For the figure on the percentage of fast food workers who are primary wage earners, see Ellie Sandmeyer, "Fox Piles on Big Business' Attempts to Smear Fast Food Protestors as 'Rent-a-Mobs,'" *Media Matters* blog, December 10, 2013, accessed May 24, 2014, http://mediamatters.org/blog/2013/12/10/fox-piles-on-big-business-attempt-to-smear-fast/197222. For an example of a sanguine historical perspective on fast food, see William B. Cherkasky, "Franchises Are Good for the Neighborhood," *Washington Post*, June 30, 1985, C8.

81. Cherkasky, C8.

82. Regina Austin, "'Bad for Business': Contextual Analysis, Race Discrimination, and Fast Food," *John Marshall Law Review* 207 (1999): 215.

83. Schlosser, *Fast Food Nation*, 4; Jacqueline Botterill and Stephen Kline, "Re-branding: The McDonald's Strategy," Emerald Management First Executive Summary (June 2007): 1. For the complete article by Botterill and Kline, see Jacqueline Botterill and Stephen Kline, "From McLibel to McLettuce: Childhood, Spin and Re-branding," *Society and Business Review* 2.1 (June 2007): 74–97.

84. Gene Demby, "The Golden Arch of the Universe Is Long . . ." Code Switch, National Public Radio, April 20, 2014, accessed November 5, 2015, http://www.npr.org/sections/codeswitch/2014/04/18/304591220/the-golden-arch-of-the-universe-is-long; *Black Enterprise*, May 1984, 15.

85. Ibid; italics in original.

86. Katherine S. Newman, *No Shame in My Game: The Working Poor in the Inner City* (New York: Knopf and the Russell Sage Foundation, 1999), 94.

87. Newman, *No Shame in My Game*, 151, 98, 102; Austin, "Bad for Business," 216–17.

88. Regarding the low-status of fast food work, legal scholar Regina Austin points out that, in the popular imagination, fast food work is "at the bottom of the employment barrel," a perception "further reinforced by the low social status of the typical jobs holders—teenagers, women, minorities, immigrants, and the elderly." See Austin, "Bad for Business," 215–16.

89. Newman, *No Shame in My Game*, 119, 123, 132; Austin, "Bad for Business," 217.

90. Steven Barboza, "How Fast Food Companies 'Super Size' African Americans," *MadameNoire*, January 31, 2011, accessed December 28, 2013, http://

madamenoire.com/107406/how-fast-food-companies-%E2%80%9Csuper-size %E2%80%9D-african-americans/.

91. Ibid. For more on Jones, see his autobiography: Roland L. Jones, *Standing Up and Standing Out: How I Teamed with a Few Black Men, Changed the Face of McDonald's, and Shook Up Corporate America* (Nashville: World Solutions, Inc., 2006).

92. National Black McDonald's Operators Association, accessed May 24, 2014, http://nbmoa.org/.

93. National Black McDonald's Operators Association; "Top 50," *QSR*, accessed May 25, 2014, http://www.qsrmagazine.com/reports/top-50. The McDonald's sales figure is from 2009.

94. See Barboza, "How Fast Food Companies 'Super Size' African Americans."

95. Nathan Skid, "Serving off the Menu: Bistro Opens with La-Van Hawkins, Questions, but No Liquor License," *Crain's Detroit Business*, October 7, 2012, accessed May 25, 2014, http://www.crainsdetroit.com/article/20121007 /FREE/310079949/serving-off-the-menu-bistro-opens-with-la-van-hawkins -questions.

96. Nichole M. Christian, "Business, A Model Partnership for Inner-City Business, Derailed," *New York Times*, May 14, 2000, accessed December 10, 2015, http://www.nytimes.com/2000/05/14/business/business-a-model -partnership-for-inner-city-renewal-derailed.html?pagewanted=all.

97. For more on the details of Hawkins's convictions, prison sentence, and post-prison comeback, see Skid, "Serving off the Menu"; Kimberly Hayes Taylor, "La-Van Hawkins Returns to Detroit," *BLAC (Black Life, Arts & Culture)*, accessed May 25, 2014, http://www.blacdetroit.com/BLAC-Detroit/November -2012/La-Van-Hawkins-Returns-to-Detroit/.

98. Boas and Chain, *Big Mac*, 186. For more on Chicken Delight's growth and market strategies in the mid-1960s, see *Proposal for a Motivational Research Study on the Sales and Advertising Opportunities of Chicken Delight* (Croton-on-Hudson, NY: Institute for Motivational Research, Inc., August, 1966).

CHAPTER 2

1. Thanks to Ben Coates for suggesting the *Coming to America* reference in an American Academy of Arts and Social Sciences Visiting Scholars' workshop.

2. Patricia Sowell Harris, *None of Us Is As Good As All of Us: How McDonald's Prospers by Embracing Inclusion and Diversity* (Hoboken, NJ: John Wiley & Sons, Inc., 2009), 62. The owner of the Harlem McDonald's was R. Lee Dunham, a retired New York City police officer and African-American fast food franchising pioneer.

3. For more on fast food restaurants' customer turnover strategies, see Luxenberg, *Roadside Empires*, and George Ritzer, *The McDonaldization of Society* (Los Angeles: Sage, 2013), 110–11.

4. Martin Plimmer, "This Demi-Paradise: Martin Plimmer Finds Food in the Fast Lane Is Not to His Taste," *The Independent*, January 3, 1998, 46.

5. Joanne Finkelstein, "Rich Food: McDonald's and Modern Life," in *Resisting McDonaldization*, ed. Barry Smart (London: Sage, 1999), 76.

6. Bruce Horovitz, "McDonald's Revamps Stores to Look More Upscale," *USA Today*, May 8, 2011, accessed June 9, 2012, http://www.usatoday.com/money /industries/food/2011-05-06-mcdonalds-revamp_n.htm. For more on McDonald's legendary cleanliness, see James L. Watson, "Transnationalism, Localization, and Fast Foods in East Asia," in *Golden Arches East: McDonald's in East Asia*, ed. James L. Watson (Stanford: Stanford University Press, 1997), 33.

7. Alix M. Freedman, "Fast-Food Chains Play Central Role in Diet of the Inner-City Poor," *Wall Street Journal*, December 19, 1990, A1.

8. Jones, *Standing Up and Standing Out*, 210.

9. As early as the 1970s, Tom Burrell, the founder of Burrell Communications, the first black advertising agency McDonald's hired, had observed that many African-American McDonald's customers seemed to frequent the fast food chain in different ways than white customers (or what the fast food company perceived as the habits of white customers, anyway). Noting that commercials directed at white audiences "would show white families piling into the car," Burrell said that white customers saw McDonald's as "a treat, a destination," for the whole family. In contrast, Burrell observed that among African-American customers, "The McDonald's was used as a place where working people would go and take a break whenever they had a chance. It was a place where children would go very often by themselves." According to Burrell, African Americans patronized McDonald's more frequently, but spent less money on each visit, than whites. White customers, Burrell discerned, were more likely to spend more on each visit to the fast food chain because they tended to go with other family members on "special occasions." See "Episode 628: This Ad's for You," Planet Money, National Public Radio, accessed November 5, 2015, http://www.npr.org /sections/money/2015/05/29/410589806/episode-628-this-ads-for-you.

10. Sarah Maslin Nir, "The Food May Be Fast, but These Customers Won't Be Rushed," *New York Times*, January 28, 2014, A1.

11. Sarah Maslin Nir and Jiha Ham, "Fighting in McDonald's in Queens for the Right to Sit. And Sit. And Sit," *New York Times*, January 15, 2014, A18.

12. Ibid.

13. Nir, "The Food May Be Fast, but These Customers Won't Be Rushed," A1.

14. Emma G. Fitzsimmons and Jiha Ham, "Elderly Patrons End Dispute with a McDonald's in Queens," *New York Times*, January 21, 2014, A17.

15. Kim Barker, "A Manhattan McDonald's with Many Off-the-Menu Sales," *New York Times*, July 20, 2015, A1.

16. Freedman, "Fast-Food Chains Play Central Role in Diet of the Inner-City Poor," A1.

17. Ibid.

18. Melanie Warner, "Salads or No, Cheap Burgers Revive McDonald's," *New York Times*, April 19, 2006. For more on inner-city African-American teenagers' eating habits and food preferences, see Thomas E. McDuffie and Richard J. George, "Eating Habits of Inner-City, African American Adolescents," *Journal of Negro Education* 78.2 (Spring 2009): 114–22. (McDuffie and George's study focuses on middle and high school students in Philadelphia.)

19. Freedman, "Fast-Food Chains Play Central Role in Diet of the Inner-City Poor," A1.

20. Sari Horwitz, "The Missing Ingredient; In Washington's Mostly African American Neighborhoods, Finding a Sit-Down Restaurant Isn't Easy," *Washington Post*, August 11, 1997, B01.

21. For more on the point that not all inner-city communities are food deserts, see McWhorter, "The Food Desert Myth."

22. Tracey Deutsch, *Building a Housewife's Paradise: Gender, Politics, and American Grocery Stores in the Twentieth Century* (Chapel Hill: University of North Carolina Press, 2010), 212; James F. Ridgeway, "Segregated Food at the Supermarket," *New Republic*, December 5, 1964, 6–7.

23. Ridgeway, "Segregated Food at the Supermarket," 6; Deutsch, *Building a Housewife's Paradise*, 212.

24. Ridgeway, "Segregated Food at the Supermarket," 6, 7.

25. Deutsch, *Building a Housewife's Paradise*, 213.

26. See Michael L. Power and Jay Schulkin, *The Evolution of Obesity* (Baltimore: Johns Hopkins University Press, 2009).

27. It should be noted that evolutionary explanations for obesity still leave some questions unanswered. For one thing, we do not know with certainty that hunter-gatherers did indeed confront regular periods of dietary privation. There is fossil evidence to suggest that hunter-gatherers may have enjoyed a diet of relative abundance. They may have even had better diets than those who followed them, as some fossil evidence indicates that hunger-gatherers were actually taller than people of the first known agricultural societies some 10,000–12,000 years ago. (One explanation for this phenomenon is that once people started farming, they had to contend with periodic famines, and consumed a less varied, more grain-centered diet.) A second challenge to the notion that we are evolutionarily predisposed to easy weight gain and fattening foods is that it is unclear whether being efficient at fat storage (i.e., likely to put on weight) was actually beneficial for hunter-gatherers. After all, would it not have been more advantageous for hunter-gatherers to be lean rather than fat in their efforts to chase down prey, or run away from predators?

28. Moss, *Salt Sugar Fat*; Kessler, *The End of Overeating*.

29. Naa Oyo A. Kwate, "Fried Chicken and Fresh Apples: Racial Segregation

as a Fundamental Cause of Fast Food Density in Black Neighborhoods," *Health and Place* 14 (2008): 38.

30. Ibid.; Brady Keys, phone interview with author, September 28, 2011.

31. Robert T. Dirks and Nancy Duran, "African American Dietary Patterns at the Beginning of the 20th Century," *Journal of Nutrition* 131 (2001): 1886, 1887.

32. See Frederick Douglass Opie, *Hog and Hominy: Soul Food from Africa to America* (New York: Columbia University Press, 2008).

33. Dirks and Duran, "African American Dietary Patterns at the Beginning of the 20th Century," 1882–83.

34. For more on the diets of African-American sharecroppers, see Harvey Levenstein, *Revolution at the Table: The Transformation of the America Diet* (New York: Oxford University Press, 1988), 27–28.

35. Dirks and Duran, "African American Dietary Patterns at the Beginning of the 20th Century," 1884.

36. For more on the history, definitions, and meanings of "soul food," see Opie, *Hog and Hominy*, chapter 7. For more on the history of "soul food" in the urban North, see Tracy N. Poe, "The Origins of Soul Food in Black Urban Identity: Chicago, 1915–1947," *American Studies International* 37.1 (February 1999): 4–33. Historians trace the term "soul food" to 1963, when Malcolm X's audio recordings for the autobiography he coauthored with Alex Haley made reference to it. (Malcolm X noted that his landlady prepared "soul food.") See Poe, "The Origins of Soul Food in Black Urban Identity," 5. Nevertheless, the *Oxford English Dictionary* cites an earlier published instance, in the *Los Angeles Sentinel* of December 29, 1960.

37. Poe, "The Origins of Soul Food in Black Urban Identity," 13.

38. Opie, *Hog and Hominy*, 64.

39. Levenstein, *Revolution at the Table*, 178.

40. Opie, *Hog and Hominy*, 156. Levenstein, however, suggests that African-American migrants to the North "neglected milk, fresh vegetables, and other 'protective' foods." See Levenstein, *Revolution at the Table*, 178.

41. Brady Keys, phone interview with author, September 28, 2011.

42. Barry M. Popkin and Anna Maria Siega-Riz, "A Comparison of Dietary Trends among Racial and Socioeconomic Groups in the United States," *New England Journal of Medicine* 335.10 (September 1996): 716–20.

43. Freeman, "Fast Food," 2233.

44. Michael Specter, "Freedom from Fries," *New Yorker*, November 2, 2015, accessed November 5, 2015, http://www.newyorker.com/magazine/2015/11/02/freedom-from-fries.

45. Boas and Chain, *Big Mac*, 147.

46. Ibid; Daniel Boorstin, *The Americans: The Democratic Experience* (New York: Vintage, 1973), 429.

47. James Trutko, John Trutko, and Andrew Kostecka, "Franchising's Growing Role in the U.S. Economy, 1975–2000," Final Report, Submitted to Office of Chief Counsel for Advocacy, Small Business Administration (Contract No. SBA-6643-0A-91), March 1993, 1–3. (Even though this report was published in 1993, it included prognostications to 2000.)

48. Ibid.; Luxenberg, *Roadside Empires*, 14; Robert Mittelstaedt and Manferd O. Peterson, "Franchising and the Financing of Small Business," in *Small Business Finance: Sources of Financing for Small Business* (Greenwich, CT: JAI Press, 1984), 175.

49. Trutko et al., "Franchising's Growing Role in the U.S. Economy," 1–2; Thomas S. Dicke, *Franchising in America: The Development of a Business Method, 1840–1980* (Chapel Hill: University of North Carolina Press, 1992), 120.

50. John F. Love, *McDonald's: Behind the Arches* (New York: Bantam, 1986), 12. Dates on the very first McDonald's restaurant vary. *Behind the Arches,* the authorized history of the chain, notes that 1937 saw the arrival of the first McDonald's.

51. Ibid.; Ray Kroc (with Robert Anderson), *Grinding It Out: The Making of McDonald's* (Chicago: Henry Regnery Company, 1977).

52. Kroc, *Grinding It Out*, 166.

53. "I Recommend Blacks Go into Business via the Franchise Route" (interview with Brady Keys), *Black Enterprise*, May 1974, 30. Keys's definition of "white suburbs" was "the outer city, the mostly white area."

54. Lisa D. Chapman, "Black Franchises under the McDonald's Arches," *Black Enterprise*, May 1974, 21. Other burger chains experienced similar growing pains and were looking for ways to overcome them. See, for example, *The Challenge of the 70's: Planning the Continued Growth of Hardee's: A Proposal for a Benchmark Motivation Research Study* (Croton-on-Hudson, NY: Institute for Motivational Research, Inc., June 1972).

55. Barboza, "How Fast Food Companies 'Super Size' African Americans"; Freeman, "Fast Food," 2226; Jacob Ward, "Better Directions: Digital Maps Are Changing How We Navigate Our Lives," *Wired Magazine* (October 2005), accessed February 9, 2014, http://www.wired.com/wired/archive/13.10/start.html?pg=3?tw=wn_tophead_6.

56. Ward, "Better Directions."

57. Jones, *Standing Up and Standing Out*, 261.

58. Ibid.

59. Ibid., 262.

60. Boas and Chain, *Big Mac*, 147.

61. Kroc, *Grinding It Out*, 167.

62. Ibid.

63. Boas and Chain, *Big Mac*, 28.

64. David Isay, "Last Day at the Automat," National Public Radio Sound Portrait, accessed August 15, 2013, http://soundportraits.org/on-air/last_day_at

_the_automat/. For more on the history of automats such as Horn and Hardart, see Nicolas Bromell, "The Automat: Preparing the Way for Fast Food," *New York History* 81.3 (July 2000): 300–312.

65. "Fast-food Franchisers Invade the City," *Business Week*, April 27, 1974, 92.

66. Jones, *Standing Up and Standing Out*, 119.

67. Ibid.

68. "Fast-food Franchisers Invade the City," 93.

69. Ibid. The average sales volume of an individual McDonald's outlet in 1974 was $590,000 annually.

70. Ibid., 92. A 2015 segment on the National Public Radio program *Planet Money* likewise reported: "[I]n the 1970s, McDonald's had one goal and one goal only—grow, aggressively grow. It had already conquered the suburbs. It wanted to move big into the cities." See "Episode 628: This Ad's for You" (quote from host Robert Smith).

71. "Fast-food Franchisers Invade the City," 92.

72. Ibid., 93.

73. Shin-Yi Chou, Michael Grossman, and Henry Saffer, "An Economic Analysis of Adult Obesity: Results from the Behavioral Risk Factor Surveillance System," *Journal of Health Economics* 23.3 (May 2004): 568; Jason P. Block, Richard A. Scribner, and Karen B. DeSalvo, "Fast Food, Race/Ethnicity, and Income: A Geographic Analysis," *American Journal of Preventive Medicine* 27.3 (2004): 211. Block et al. note that in 1995, food consumed outside the home made up 34 percent of Americans' total caloric intake, and 38 percent of total fat consumed, compared to 18 percent of calorie intake and fat intake in 1977–1978 (216). The authors also point out that "in the last 20 years, the percentage of calories attributable to fast-food consumption has increased from 3% to 12% of total calories consumed in the United States" (211).

74. Mark D. Jekanowski, James K. Binkley, and James Eales, "Convenience, Accessibility, and the Demand for Fast Food," *Journal of Agricultural and Resource Economics* 26.1 (July 2001): 58.

75. Mimi Sheraton, "The Burger That's Eating New York," *New York* (magazine), August 19, 1974, 31–35.

76. Boas and Chain, *Big Mac*, 62.

77. Ibid., 61; Sheraton, "The Burger That's Eating New York," 31; Kwate, "Fried Chicken and Fresh Apples," 40.

78. Boas and Chain, *Big Mac*, 62.

79. Kwate, "Fried Chicken and Fresh Apples," 40.

80. See Abraham J. Briloff, "You Deserve a Break' . . . McDonald's Burgers Are More Palatable Than Its Accounts," *Barron's*, July 8, 1974, 3, 14–16, 25.

81. Kwate, "Fried Chicken and Fresh Apples," 40.

82. Sheraton, "The Burger That's Eating New York," 31. The Upper East Side of Manhattan is home to a number of McDonald's outlets now, however.

83. See Diane E. Lewis, "A 'Golden Arch' in Roxbury: Controversy Remains as McDonald's Opens," *Boston Globe*, September 17, 1990, 24.

84. Ibid. This activist might have also added that entry-level fast food jobs tend to have notoriously high rates of job dissatisfaction and turnover. See Ritzer, *The McDonaldization of Society*, 134. But as noted previously, the fast food industry has emphasized that fast food jobs can also be a path to upward mobility.

85. Weems, *Desegregating the Dollar*, 80; "The Gibson Report" ("Minority Marketing/Communications Publication"), published by D. Parke Gibson International, Inc., June 1977, Archives II (National Archives, College Park, Maryland), Records of the Minority Business Development Agency, Record Group 427, Box 3 of 5, Accession No. 427-82-005, Folder: "The Gibson Report" (no page number). D. Parke Gibson International was established by its namesake, D. Parke Gibson, in 1960. It advised companies such as Avon (cosmetics and personal care products), Coca Cola USA, Columbia Pictures, Greyhound (bus lines), and R. J. Reynolds (tobacco) on how to appeal to African-American consumers. See Weems, *Desegregating the Dollar*, 75.

86. Many African Americans remained in the South, of course, and some southern cities were majority-black. Atlanta, for example, was 51 percent black in 1970.

87. Carol Morello and Dan Keating, "Number of Black D.C. Residents Plummets as Majority Status Slips Away," *Washington Post*, March 24, 2011, accessed April 24, 2016, https://www.washingtonpost.com/local/black-dc-residents-plummet-barely-a-majority/2011/03/24/ABtIgJQB_story.html.

88. Faltermayer, "More Dollars and More Diplomas," 229. Faltermayer similarly notes that, as of 1968, the African-American population was "66 percent in Washington, DC, about 50 percent in Newark, 36 percent in St. Louis, and 34 percent in Detroit and Cleveland."

89. "I Recommend Blacks Go into Business via the Franchise Route," 30.

90. Jones, *Standing Up and Standing Out*, 112.

CHAPTER 3

1. Vernon C. Thompson, "The Slow Process of Starting a Fast Food Business," *Washington Post*, April 2, 1978, DC1.

2. Ibid.; Phil McCombs, "Despite Capitalization Woes, Some Black Businesses Thrive," *Washington Post*, October 30, 1977, A1.

3. Thompson, "The Slow Process of Starting a Fast Food Business."

4. Ibid.

5. McCombs, "Despite Capitalization Woes, Some Black Businesses Thrive."

6. Thompson, "The Slow Process of Starting a Fast Food Business."

7. McCombs, "Despite Capitalization Woes, Some Black Businesses Thrive." A representative for the Greater Washington Business Center told the *Washing-*

ton Post in 1977 that the advocacy group helped some 2,000 small businesses a year.

8. Bean, "Burn, Baby, Burn," 171.

9. Cottin, "Staff Problems, Mistrust, Delay Nixon Minority Enterprise Plan," 1319. Figures on minority business ownership as a whole were similarly dismal. A missive from the Nixon White House to Congress in 1972 noted that while "the Nation's Black, Spanish-speaking and Indian and other minorities constitute about one-sixth of the American population," their combined businesses made up less than 1 percent of total gross business receipts—$10.6 billion out of $1.5 trillion. The report went on to say that "in the United States today, there are only about 4 percent of these [minority-owned] businesses, despite the fact that they constitute almost 17 percent of our population." See "Fact Sheet: Minority Enterprise Message," Office of the White House Press Secretary, March 18, 1972, Archives II (National Archives, College Park, Maryland), General Records of the Department of Commerce, Record Group 40, Box 274 ("Executive Secretariat's Subject File, 1953–74"), Folder: "Minority Business Enterprise (OMBE) Mar.–Apr., Office of the White House Press Secretary, March 18, 1972, from Nixon to Congress."

10. Weems, *Desegregating the Dollar*, 90.

11. Yancy, *Federal Government Policy and Black Business Enterprise*, 17; "Black Capitalism: A Disappointing Start," *Time*, August 15, 1969, accessed November 18, 2010, http://www.time.com/time/magazine/article/0,9171,901274,00.html; Bean, *Big Government and Affirmative Action*, 65. Yancy's figures on minority businesses were derived from Commerce Department reports.

12. "Keys Group Milestones," Keys Group Company, accessed June 23, 2012, http://keysgroup.com/milestones.html.

13. Yancy, *Federal Government Policy and Black Business Enterprise*, 17.

14. Ronald Bailey, "Introduction/Black Business Enterprise: Reflections on Its History and Future Development," in *Black Business Enterprise: History and Contemporary Perspectives*, ed. Ronald W. Bailey (New York: Basic, 1971), 9.

15. Cottin, "Staff Problems, Mistrust, Delay Nixon Minority Enterprise Plan," 1319, citing Theodore L. Cross, *Black Capitalism: Strategy for Business in the Ghetto* (New York: Atheneum, 1969).

16. *Mobilizing for Urban Action*, 37.

17. Love, *McDonald's*, 371.

18. Jones, *Standing Up and Standing Out*, 54.

19. Eighty-three percent of all loan transactions involving the SBA between 1959 and 1979 were those for which the agency served as a guarantor rather than a direct lender. See "SBA Franchise Loans: Risk of Loss Can be Reduced and Program Effectiveness Improved," GAO Report, Statement of Henry Eschwege before the Subcommittee on Commerce, Consumer, and Monetary Affairs, Committee of Government Operations, House of Representatives," May 19, 1981, 2.

20. Hodge, "For Big Franchisers, Money to Go; Is the SBA Dispensing Corporate Welfare?"

21. Tony Wilkinson, "You, Your Franchisees & the SBA Loan Program," *Franchising World*, January/February 1993, 20.

22. Hodge, "For Big Franchisers, Money to Go; Is the SBA Dispensing Corporate Welfare?"

23. Arnold Schuchter, "Conjoining Black Revolution and Private Enterprise," in *Black Business Enterprise: History and Contemporary Perspectives*, ed. Ronald W. Bailey (New York: Basic, 1971), 224–25. The EOL had previously been jointly administered by the SBA and Office of Economic Opportunity. The reasons for the bureaucratic shifting had to do with inadequate loan supervision and high rates of default under the previous arrangement—problems to which the SBA was not immune either. In an attempt to reduce loan defaults, the SBA changed EOL loan processing practices somewhat, privileging borrowers with previous successful business experience, or those the agency deemed were likely candidates for loan repayment.

24. The logic of this decision was that corporate franchisors, despite charging franchise owners various participation fees, were not interfering with franchisees' "right" to earn income. This information is derived from Sloan Coleman, telephone interview with author, July 6, 2011. According to Coleman (representing the SBA's Office of Financial Assistance in Washington as of the date of the telephone interview), what constitutes a "small business" today varies. The agency considers the nature of the business (no casinos, for example), how the loan applicant plans to use the loan money, and the size of the business. How the SBA determines the size of a business depends on whether it is a retail operation or whether it is a wholesale or manufacturing firm. If the business is a retail operation, the agency looks at total receipts, which, at the time of the phone interview, could be up to $7.5 million annually. For wholesale firms, the SBA typically regards 100 employees or fewer as "small businesses." Manufacturing firms, however, can employ up to 500 people and still be defined as "small businesses." Coleman includes the caveat that all of these numbers are general guidelines; ultimately, agency loan application requirements vary by industry and are somewhat ad hoc.

25. "Small Business Administration Franchise Loans: Risk of Loss Can Be Reduced and Program Effectiveness Improved."

26. According to the *Philadelphia Tribune* in June 1979, "the 502 Program has been employed with success throughout the country." See "Local Black Business Developers Say McDonald's Is Their Kind of Place," *Philadelphia Tribune*, June 6, 1979, 6.

27. William L. Henderson and Larry C. Ledebur, "Programs for the Economic Development of the American Negro Community: The Moderate Approach," *American Journal of Economics and Sociology* 30 (Jan. 1971): 41. See Howard J. Sam-

uels, "Compensatory Capitalism," in *Black Economic Development*, eds. William F. Haddad and G. Douglas Pugh (Englewood Cliffs, NJ: Prentice Hall, 1969), 72. It is unclear whether these ambitious minority business creation goals were met. Project OWN would later be renamed Operation Business Mainstream.

28. Kotlowski, "Black Power—Nixon Style," 416.

29. Maurice Stans initially announced the MESBIC program in 1969, but it did not officially begin until 1972, along with the Small Business Investment Act Amendment. See Arthur I. Blaustein and Geoffrey Faux, *The Star-Spangled Hustle* (Garden City, NY: Doubleday, 1972); Weems, *Business in Black and White*, 179.

30. "About Office of Investment," Small Business Administration, accessed July 29, 2012, http://www.sba.gov/content/about-office-investment-0.

31. Letter from Theodore J. Lettes (assistant to the director, Capital Development Branch) to Edgar I. Castro, May 9, 1973, from Archives II (National Archives, College Park, Maryland), Records of the Minority Business Development Agency, Record Group 427, Box 1 of 3, Accession No. 427-83-009, Folder: "Request for Info—Puerto Rico."

32. Letter from Lonnie Murray (assistant to the director, Capital Development Branch) to Charles Borges, March 12, 1974, Archives II (National Archives, College Park, Maryland), Records of the Minority Business Development Agency, Record Group 427, Box 1 of 3, Accession No. 427-83-009, Folder: "Request for Info—Puerto Rico."

33. Richard S. Rosenbloom and John K. Shank, "Let's Write Off MESBICs," *Harvard Business Review* (September–October 1970), 91, from Archives II (National Archives, College Park, Maryland), Records of the Minority Business Development Agency, Record Group 427, Box 3 of 3, Accession No. 427-83-009, Folder: "Revenue Sharing Funds for MESBICs."

34. Ibid.; letter from Theodore J. Lettes (assistant to the director, Capital Development Branch) to Edgar I. Castro, May 9, 1973. Some sources note that one dollar raised could be matched to two dollars in debentures, but economist Timothy Bates writes that MESBICs provided up to three dollars for every dollar raised by corporations, and offered not just debentures, but also participating equity. See Timothy Bates, "Is the Small Business Administration a Racist Institution?" *Review of Black Political Economy* 26.1 (Summer 1998): 89–104.

35. Arthur I. Blaustein and Geoffrey Faux, for example, wrote in 1972, "In all cases, the leverage benefits of the MESBIC go not to the minority entrepreneur, but to the owners of the MESBICs, the large white-owned corporations . . . The MESBIC therefore becomes another in the long list of devices to enrich corporate America under the guise of helping the needy." See Blaustein and Faux, *The Star-Spangled Hustle*, 193, 187.

36. Letter from J. H. Marx (director, Capital Development) to Richard Finn, June 8, 1978, Archives II (National Archives, College Park, Maryland), Records of the Minority Business Development Agency, Record Group 427, Box 3 of 3, Ac-

cession No. 427-83-009, Folder: "Request for Info—Massachusetts." This letter affirmed the eligibility of fast food franchises in the MESBIC program: "MES-BICs can make equity investments and/or loans to disadvantaged persons for the purchase, organization or expansion of a franchise."

37. Udayan Gupta, "Franchising Fever," *Black Enterprise*, February 1985, 112.

38. Letter from Lonnie Murray (Capital Development) to Joseph A. DeJesus, August 29, 1980, Archives II (National Archives, College Park, Maryland), Records of the Minority Business Development Agency, Record Group 427, Box 3 of 3, Accession No. 427-83-009, Folder: "Request for Info—Connecticut."

39. Bates, "Is the Small Business Administration a Racist Institution?" 95.

40. Boas and Chain, *Big Mac*, 196.

41. Ibid., 198.

42. Media reports of the Kroc donation ranged from $200,000 to $255,000. Public election records appear to show the sum of Kroc's donations to be $208,000. See Boas and Chain, *Big Mac*, 198-99; Jones, *Standing Up and Standing Out*, 188-90; Kroc, *Grinding It Out*, 181.

43. Kroc, *Grinding It Out*, 181; Jones, *Standing Up and Standing Out*, 190.

44. Kroc, *Grinding It Out*, 181.

45. Boas and Chain, *Big Mac*, 203.

46. Ibid., 200, 201.

47. Kroc, *Grinding It Out*, 181.

48. Boas and Chain, *Big Mac*, 201.

49. Ibid., 202. For more on Nixon's wartime stint with the OPA, see Meg Jacobs, "How About Some Meat? The Office of Price Administration, Consumption Politics, and State Building from the Bottom Up, 1941-1946," *Journal of American History* 84.3 (December 1997): 910-41.

50. Boas and Chain, *Big Mac*, 202-3; Schlosser, *Fast Food Nation*, 37.

51. Boas and Chain, *Big Mac*, 36; Ralph Novak, "The McDonald's Man: What Ray Kroc Hath Wrought around the World," *People*, May 19, 1975, accessed July 4, 2011, http://www.people.com/people/archive/article/0,,20065264,00.html; "Food: The Burger That Conquered the Country," *Time*, September 17, 1973, accessed July 4, 2011, http://www.time.com/time/magazine/article/0,9171,907911,00.html; Eric Pace, "Ray A. Kroc Dies at 81; Built McDonald's Chain," *New York Times*, January 15, 1984, accessed July 4, 2011, https://www.nytimes.com/learning/general/onthisday/bday/1005.html; Schlosser, *Fast Food Nation*, 37.

52. Novak, "The McDonald's Man."

53. Yancy, *Federal Government Policy and Black Business Enterprise*, 72.

54. See Dov Weinryb Grohsgal, "Southern Strategies: The Politics of School Desegregation and the Nixon White House" (Ph.D. diss., Princeton University, 2013).

55. Novak, "The McDonald's Man."

56. Schlosser, *Fast Food Nation*, 32.

57. Kotlowski, "Black Power—Nixon Style," 423.

58. Ibid., 416; Skrentny, *The Ironies of Affirmative Action* 67–110, 192–93. Quoted phrases are from Kotlowski.

59. Weems, *Business in Black and White*, 6.

60. Ibid; Stephen E. Ambrose, *Nixon, Vol. 2: The Triumph of a Politician, 1962–1972* (New York: Simon & Schuster, 1989), 125–26.

61. "Black Capitalism: A Disappointing Start."

62. Yancy, *Federal Government Policy and Black Business Enterprise*, 66; Bean, *Big Government and Affirmative Action*, 63.

63. Bean, *Big Government and Affirmative Action*, 63.

64. Kotlowski, "Black Power—Nixon Style," 411.

65. Yancy, *Federal Government Policy and Black Business Enterprise*, 66.

66. Cottin, "Staff Problems, Mistrust, Delay Nixon Minority Enterprise Plan," 1319.

67. Maurice Stans maintains that Nixon's support for black capitalism and the creation of the Office of Minority Business Enterprise (OMBE) were motivated not by politics, but by principles of racial fairness. According to Stans, Nixon said the following about black capitalism: "I don't think there are any votes in it for us, but we'll do it [supporting minority enterprise] because it's right." See Maurice H. Stans, *One of the President's Men: Twenty Years with Eisenhower and Nixon* (Washington, DC: Brassey's Inc., 1995), 169. Dean J. Kotlowski disputes this, asserting that Nixon believed that his support for minority enterprise could translate into electoral support from middle-class African Americans. See Kotlowski, "Black Power—Nixon Style," 421. For a comprehensive account of Nixon's political calculations in relation to civil rights, see Dean J. Kotlowski, *Nixon's Civil Rights: Politics, Principle, and Policy* (Cambridge, MA: Harvard University Press, 2002).

68. Kotlowski, "Black Power—Nixon Style," 421.

69. In 2006, Jeffrey Hart, one of Nixon's speechwriters, claimed that the Nixon campaign did not devise a Southern strategy in 1968, but rather, a border state strategy." See book discussion on *The Making of the American Conservative Mind*, C-SPAN, February 9, 2006, accessed July 19, 2015, http://www.c-span.org/video/?191295-1/book-discussion-making-american-conservative-mind. Nixon ended up splitting the southern states' electoral votes with former Alabama governor and segregationist George Wallace, who ran as a third-party (American Independent Party) presidential candidate in 1968. Nixon won Kentucky, Virginia, Tennessee, North Carolina, South Carolina, and Florida, while Wallace won Arkansas, Louisiana, Georgia, Alabama, and Mississippi.

70. Nor was the Nixon campaign team's courtship of African-American voters confined to 1969. When Nixon ran for reelection in 1972, he continued to reach out to black voters despite implicitly conceding that his Democratic opponent had an edge in the black community. In an ad in a November 1972 issue

of *Ebony* magazine, for example, a Nixon campaign ad pitched: "Senator McGovern thinks your vote is in the bag. President Nixon doesn't believe it—look at his record." The ad then listed all of Nixon's legislative accomplishments that had putatively helped African Americans, including the boast that the thirty-seventh president "has made possible more loans to black businesses than any President before him." See Cohen, *A Consumer's Republic*, 340.

71. For more on Nixon's courting of white voters, see Kevin P. Phillips's *Emerging Republican Majority* (New Rochelle, NY: Arlington House, 1969).

72. Kotlowski, "Black Power—Nixon Style," 421. The memo was written to Maurice Stans.

73. This notion that "black capitalism" was preferable to welfare can be seen even after Nixon left office. Records from the agency that resulted from Nixon's pledge to promote black capitalism, the Office of Minority Business Enterprise (OMBE), stated, "When a significant number of citizens cannot participate fully in the economic system, tax revenues are reduced at all levels of Government, public expenditures are likely to increase, and vital human resources are wasted" (no specific author listed). See Summary Statement, OMBE FY 1973 Program Memorandum, Archives II (National Archives, College Park, Maryland), General Records of the Department of Commerce, Record Group 40, Box 244 ("Executive Secretariat's Subject File, 1953–74"), Folder: "MBE/Jenkins."

74. Weems, *Business in Black and White*, 6; Gerald S. Strober and Deborah H. Strober, *Nixon: An Oral History of His Presidency* (New York: HarperCollins, 1994), 112.

75. Kotlowski, "Black Power—Nixon Style," 412.

76. Bruce J. Schulman, *The Seventies: The Great Shift in American Culture, Society, and Politics*, (Cambridge, MA: Da Capo Press, 2002), see chapter 1 ("'Down to the Nut-Cutting': The Nixon Presidency and American Public Life"). Dov Weinryb Grohsgal has similarly argued that when Nixon and his advisers determined that they had little choice but to back liberal policies, they devised ways to place those policies within conservative frameworks. See Grohsgal, "Southern Strategies."

77. Weems, *Business in Black and White*, 115.

78. Ibid., 118.

79. Kotlowski, "Black Power—Nixon Style," 417.

80. Ibid., 415.

81. "Nixon Urges 'Black Ownership' to Help Solve Racial Problems," *New York Times*, April 26, 1968, 27.

82. Ibid.

83. Kotlowski, "Black Power—Nixon Style," 418.

84. Robert D. Hershey, Jr., "'Black Capitalism' Idea Assailed by a Negro Member of Reserve," *New York Times*, December 30, 1969, 49.

85. Irwin F. Gellman, *The President and the Apprentice: Eisenhower and Nixon*,

1952–1961 (New Haven: Yale University Press, 2015), 372–73. Gellman also notes that Nixon "acted as the Eisenhower administration's principal civil rights spokesman" (372). Similarly, historian David A. Nichols points out that in the 1960 presidential election, Nixon pressured the Republican National Convention to adopt a more aggressive civil rights platform. See David A. Nichols, *A Matter of Justice: Eisenhower and the Beginning of the Civil Rights Revolution* (New York: Simon and Schuster, 2007), 257.

86. The consensus among Nixon biographers seems to be that he was foremost a political animal rather than a right-wing ideologue on race. See, for example, David Greenberg, *Nixon's Shadow: The History of an Image* (New York: W. W. Norton & Company, 2003), 306, 313, 314.

87. Rob Stein, "New Nixon Tapes Reveal Anti-Semitic, Racist Remarks," *Washington Post*, December 12, 2010, accessed December 12, 2015, http://www.washingtonpost.com/wp-dyn/content/article/2010/12/11/AR2010121102890.html.

88. "Nixon, Richard Milhous," *King Encyclopedia*, Martin Luther King Jr. Research and Education Institute, Stanford University, accessed April 3, 2015, http://mlk-kpp01.stanford.edu/kingweb/about_king/encyclopedia/nixon_richard.html; Grohsgal, "Southern Strategies."

89. Leah Wright Rigueur, *The Loneliness of the Black Republican: Pragmatic Politics and the Pursuit of Power* (Princeton: Princeton University Press, 2014), 37–38; "Election Polls—Vote by Groups, 1960–1964," Gallup, accessed July 19, 2015, http://www.gallup.com/poll/9454/election-polls-vote-groups-19601964.aspx. Nixon biographer Irwin F. Gellman believes that scholars have overstated the 1960 electoral consequences of Nixon's decision not to reach out to King after the civil rights leader's jail sentence. See Nichols, *A Matter of Justice*, 332n65.

90. "Black Capitalism: A Disappointing Start," *Time*, August 15, 1969, accessed December 12, 2015, http://content.time.com/time/magazine/article/0,9171,901274,00.html.

91. Maurice H. Stans, "Memorandum for the President," Subject: Budget for Office of Minority Business Enterprise, July 21, 1971 (National Archives, College Park, Maryland), General Records of the Department of Commerce, Record Group 40, Box 244 (Executive Secretariat's Subject File, 1953–74), Folder: "MBE/Jenkins." Regarding the OMBE's focus on "technical and managerial training," contemporaneous Nixon critics Arthur I. Blaustein and Geoffrey Faux lamented that "the bureaucracy Nixon created to assist minority businesses cost more than the minority businessmen needed to start up the businesses." See Blaustein and Faux, *The Star-Spangled Hustle*, 206.

92. "Minority Enterprise Message March 18, 1972," Fact Sheet, Office of the White House Press Secretary, Archives II (National Archives, College Park, Maryland), General Records of the Department of Commerce, Record Group 40, Box 274 (Executive Secretariat's Subject File, 1953–74), Folder: "Minority Busi-

ness Enterprise (OMBE) Mar.–Apr., Office of the White House Press Secretary, March 18, 1972, from Nixon to Congress"; Luix Overbea, "Black Capitalism Seen as U.S. Reality," *Christian Science Monitor*, date unknown, Archives II (National Archives, College Park, Maryland), Records of the Office of Minority Business Enterprise, Record Group 40, Box 366 (Office of Secretary, Executive Secretariat, Subject File, 1953–74), Folder: "MBE/Jenkins"; Cottin, "Staff Problems, Mistrust, Delay Nixon Minority Enterprise Plan," 1319.

93. "Minority Enterprise Message March 18, 1972."

94. Cottin, "Staff Problems, Mistrust, Delay Nixon Minority Enterprise Plan," 1319.

95. Ibid., 1324; Bean, *Big Government and Affirmative Action*, 67; Kotlowski, "Black Power—Nixon Style," 420. That the agency, especially in its first years, was beleaguered with bureaucratic squabbling and lack of public support did not help.

96. "Black Capitalism: A Disappointing Start."

97. Figures from John L. Jenkins, Abstract of Secretarial Correspondence, August 23, 1971, Archives II (National Archives, College Park, Maryland), General Records of the Department of Commerce, Record Group 40, Box 244 (Executive Secretariat's Subject File, 1953–1974), Folder: "MBE/Jenkins." It should be noted that African-American entrepreneurs could, however, also seek support through non-racially based government programs intended to assist "economically disadvantaged" small businesses—programs such as the SBA's 8(a) Business Development Program.

98. Maurice H. Stans, "Memorandum for the President" (Subject: "Budget for Office of Minority Business Enterprise"), July 21, 1971, Archives II (National Archives, College Park, Maryland), General Records of the Department of Commerce, Record Group 40, Box 244 (Executive Secretariat's Subject File, 1953–1974), Folder: "MBE/Jenkins."

99. Ibid.

100. "Nixon Asks $100 Million More for OMBE," *Chicago South Suburban News*, October 30, 1971, Archives II (National Archives, College Park, Maryland), General Records of the Department of Commerce, Record Group 40, Box 244 (Executive Secretariat's Subject File, 1953–1974), Folder: "Minority Business Enterprise Reports." In his July 20, 1971, message to Congress, Nixon declared: "I shall submit to the Congress within the next few weeks a program calling for $325 million in grant funds over a three year period ($65 million for fiscal year 1972, $130 million each for fiscal years 1973 and 1974) to be administered by the Department of Commerce for the provision of such managerial services and technical assistance to minority businesses." See Nixon's Message to Congress (p. 10), July 20, 1971, Archives II (National Archives, College Park, Maryland), General Records of the Department of Commerce, Record Group 40, Box 244 (Executive Secretariat's Subject File, 1953–1974), Folder: "MBE/Jenkins."

101. Nixon's Message to Congress (pp. 7–8), July 20, 1971.

102. Ibid., 7.

103. John L. Jenkins to Secretary and Undersecretary of the Commerce Department, Abstract of Secretarial Correspondence, Archives II (National Archives, College Park, Maryland), General Records of the Department of Commerce, Record Group 40, Box 366 (Office of Secretary, Executive Secretariat's Subject File, 1953–74), Folder: "Minority Business Enterprise, Office of, Jan.–June 1973."

104. It is unclear if the OMBE would have been just as satisfied with 10,000 minority-owned franchises.

105. Yancy, *Federal Government Policy and Black Business Enterprise*, 79.

106. Weems, *Business in Black and White*, 143.

107. Blaustein and Faux, *The Star-Spangled Hustle*, 199.

108. Keys was the first African-American Kentucky Fried Chicken franchisee. He subsequently acquired additional Kentucky Fried Chicken and Burger King outlets, in addition to starting his own chain of fried chicken restaurants, "All-Pro Chicken." See "I Recommend Blacks Go into Business via the Franchise Route" (interview with Brady Keys), 30; Latrina M. Patrick, *The Brady Keys, Jr. Story: Overcoming Adversity by Staying within the Blessing* (Albany, GA: Keys Group, 1999).

109. Jay I. Leanse to John L. Jenkins (Subject: "Meetings with Brady Keys, Jr., All-Pro Enterprises, Inc."), January 15, 1971, Abstract of Secretarial Correspondence, Archives II (National Archives, College Park, Maryland), General Records of the Department of Commerce, Record Group 40, Box 244 (Executive Secretariat; Subject Files, 1953–1974), Folder: "MBE/Jenkins."

110. "I Recommend Blacks Go into Business via the Franchise Route (nterview with Brady Keys)," 30.

111. Ibid.; Keys Group Company, accessed July 4, 2011, http://www.keysgroup .com/milestones.html.

112. "Newsletter" section, *Black Enterprise*, June 1973, 24.

113. Keys Group Company; Patrick, *The Brady Keys, Jr. Story*, 97–98.

114. Patrick, *The Brady Keys, Jr. Story*, 98.

115. Weems, *Business in Black and White*, 83.

116. Leah Michele Wright, "The Loneliness of the Black Conservative: Black Republicans and the Grand Old Party, 1964–1980" (Ph.D. diss., Princeton University, 2009), 211.

117. Ibid.

118. Kotlowski, "Black Power—Nixon Style," 419. Regarding Chamberlain's endorsement of Nixon, some sources note that the basketball legend supported Nixon's presidential bids in both 1968 and 1972, while other sources only reference the 1968 campaign.

119. Ralph Novak, "Wilt Chamberlain: As an Actor, or Anything Else, His

Ambition Is Fit for a Giant," *People*, July 30, 1984, accessed March 23, 2015, http://www.people.com/people/archive/article/0,,20088351,00.html; "President Nixon Meets Football Player Jim Brown of the Cleveland Browns in the Oval Office," Oliver F. Atkins Photograph Collection, accessed March 23, 2015, http://images.gmu.edu/luna/servlet/detail/GMUDPSdps~15~15~28969~101381:President-Nixon-meets-football-play?sort=Title%2CDate%2CCreator%2CSubject.

120. For more on Nixon's support among a few African-American celebrities, see Grohsgal, "Southern Strategies"; Leah Wright-Rigueur, *The Loneliness of the Black Republican: Pragmatic Politics and the Pursuit of Power* (Princeton: Princeton University Press, 2014).

121. Jones, *Standing Up and Standing Out*, 202. Jones notes that Embry worked with a business partner.

122. "Hank Aaron Opens Food Chain," *Philadelphia Tribune*, April 18, 1989, 9-C; Tanisha A. Sykes, "Power Hitter: Legendary MLB Player Hank Aaron a Hit in Business Field," *Black Enterprise*, April 10, 2013, accessed December 21, 2015, http://www.blackenterprise.com/lifestyle/sportsbiz/hank-aaron-businesses-entrepreneur/.

123. "Surprising Facts about Your Favorite Fast Food Chain," CBS News (slideshow, 2015, no date listed), accessed December 2, 2015, http://www.cbsnews.com/pictures/things-you-didnt-know-about-your-favorite-fast-food-chains/.

124. Karie Meltzer, "Star Athletes' National Franchises," *ThePostGame.Com*, accessed August 7, 2014, http://m.thepostgame.com/blog/list/201207/star-athletes-national-franchises?page=2#sT; "The All-Franchising Team: Top Pro Athletes Who Own Franchises," *Franchise Help* blog, accessed August 7, 2014, http://www.franchisehelp.com/blog/top-professional-athletes-who-own-franchises.

125. "Small Business Anxiety," Investigative Reporters and Editors, accessed August 10, 2013, http://www.ire.org/resource-center/stories/16986/. The U.S. Census determined the African-American population to be 12.9 percent of the total in 2000. See "The Black Population: 2000," United States Census Bureau, accessed August 23, 2014, http://www.census.gov/prod/2001pubs/c2kbr01-5.pdf.

126. Bean, *Big Government and Affirmative Action*, 52.

127. Christopher Shawn McKeehan, telephone interview with author, November 18, 2010. McKeehan was a program manager with the SBA at the time of the telephone interview.

128. Kevin L. Yuill, *Richard Nixon and the Rise of Affirmative Action* (Lantham, MD: Rowman and Littlefield, 2006), 164; Bean, *Big Government and Affirmative Action*, 67.

129. Yancy, *Federal Government Policy and Black Business Enterprise*, 72–73. Economist Tom Larson also points out that at the SBA, many loans for minority

entrepreneurship were "for refinancing older loans, many were to established firms, and some loans were never actually disbursed." See Tom Larson, "The Impact of Local-Government Affirmative Action Programs for Minority- and Women-Owned Businesses in California," in *The Impact of Affirmative Action on Public-Sector Employment and Contracting in California* (California Policy Seminar, University of California, Berkeley, 1997), 125.

130. John L. Jenkins to Secretary and Undersecretary of the Commerce Department, August 26, 1971, Archives II (National Archives, College Park, Maryland), General Records of the Department of Commerce, Record Group 40, Box 366 (Office of Secretary, Executive Secretariat's Subject File, 1953–1974), Folder: "MBE/Jenkins."

131. Alex Poinsett, "SBA Scandals: Whites Bilk Black 'Fronts,'" *Ebony* (Oct. 1977), 78.

132. Ibid.

133. Jones, *Standing Up and Standing Out*, 123.

134. Ibid., 170

135. Nancy Dooley, "Watergate Panel Joins California SBA Probe," *San Francisco Examiner*, December 2, 1973, accessed August 20, 2014, http://jfk.hood.edu/Collection/White%20%20Files/Watergate/Watergate%20Items%2009122%20to%2009440/Watergate%2009155.pdf.

136. Ibid.; Boas and Chain, *Big Mac*, 189.

137. Dooley, "Watergate Panel Joins California SBA Probe." Blaustein and Faux also charged that the Nixon administration provided "twenty-five hundred to three thousand" jobs to OMBE bureaucrats with the expectation that they would back Nixon's reelection campaign and "neutraliz[e] politically hostile areas" in minority communities. See Blaustein and Faux, *The Star-Spangled Hustle*, 207.

138. Yancy, *Federal Government Policy and Black Business Enterprise*, 83.

139. Maurice H. Stans, "Memorandum for the President" (Subject: "Budget for Office of Minority Business Enterprise"), July 21, 1971.

140. According to the 1970 U.S. Census, African Americans were 11.1 percent of the U.S. population in 1970, while all minorities made up less than 15 percent of the total. See "1970 Census of Population," accessed July 31, 2012, http://www.census.gov/prod/www/abs/decennial/1970cenpop_pcs1.html.

141. John L. Jenkins to Secretary and Undersecretary of the Commerce Department, August 26, 1971.

142. "Newsletter" section, *Black Enterprise*, June 1973, 24.

143. Yancy, *Federal Government Policy and Black Business Enterprise*, 82; Weems, *Business in Black and White*, 170.

144. John L. Jenkins to Secretary and Undersecretary of the Commerce Department, August 26, 1971.

145. Jones, *Standing Up and Standing Out*, 271.

146. Trutko et al., "Franchising's Growing Role in the U.S. Economy," 5–16. (Even though this report was published in 1993, it included prognostications to 2000.) Growth rates ebbed to the single digits in the in the 1980s. Between 1981 and 1982, for instance, the number of minority franchises climbed 7.3 percent. See "Franchising: New Opportunities for Black Business," *Ebony*, October 1984, 118.

147. See Mitchell J. Shields, "Wendy's Courts Minority Markets; The Move to Town Brings New Clientele," *Adweek*, October 21, 1985; Tamar Lewin, "McDonald's Is Battling with Black Franchisee," *New York Times*, March 12, 1984, 1D. According to *Black Enterprise* magazine, in 1988 McDonald's counted 418 minorities out of 4,900 franchisees, or 8.5 percent of the total. See "Franchise 50," *Black Enterprise*, September 1989, 63; Buck Brown, "Minority Franchisees Allege Redlining by the Big Chains," *Wall Street Journal*, October 26, 1988, 1.

148. Trutko et al., "Franchising's Growing Role in the U.S. Economy," ES-9.

149. James Trutko, John Trutko, and Andrew Kostecka, "Franchising's Growing Role in the U.S. Economy, 1975–2000," Research summary, RS Number 136, Completed Under Award No. SBA-66430A-91, May 1993), accessed July 4, 2011, www.sba.gov/advo/research/rs136.html. It is unclear from this source whether the "5 percent" refers to all racial minorities, or just African Americans. Regarding figures on minority ownership, in 1988 the U.S. Commerce Department noted that about 3 percent of 312,000 American franchises were minority-owned. See Buck Brown, "Minority Franchisees Allege Redlining by the Big Chains," 1.

150. "Franchise 50," *Black Enterprise*, September 1989, 63.

151. Ibid.; Matthew C. Sonfield, "Black-Owned Franchise Units," Small Business Institute Director's Association Annual Conference paper, accessed July 13, 2012, http://www.sbaer.uca.edu/research/sbida/1990/PDF/32.pdf.

152. "Franchise 50," *Black Enterprise*, September 1989, 63.

153. Ibid.

154. The political historian Hugh Davis Graham points out that Asian immigrants entering the United States after passage of the Immigration and Nationality Act of 1965 also benefited from affirmative action programs. See Hugh Davis Graham, *Collision Course: The Strange Convergence of Affirmative Action and Immigration Policy in America* (New York and Oxford: Oxford University Press, 2002).

155. Jane Seaberry, "Minority Ownership of Franchises Soaring," *Washington Post*, June 19, 1979, D11.

156. Trutko et al. (not online version), "Franchising's Growing Role in the U.S. Economy," 5–16.

157. *Franchised Business Ownership: By Minority and Gender Groups*, Report for the International Franchise Association Educational Foundation, accessed August 24, 2014, http://emarket.franchise.org/MinorityReport2011.pdf; "Fran-

chises a Draw for Minority Entrepreneurs," *Minority Business Development Agency*, U.S. Department of Commerce, accessed August 24, 2014, http://www .mbda.gov/node/1217. Note that the International Franchise Association refers to the fast food industry as the "quick services restaurant sector."

158. *Franchised Business Ownership*, 5–7.

159. Ibid., "Franchises a Draw for Minority Entrepreneurs."

160. "Inclusion & Diversity," *McDonald's*, accessed August 24, 2014, http:// www.aboutmcdonalds.com/mcd/our_company/inclusion_and_diversity .html; Emily Bryson York, "In Speech, McDonald's Thompson Puts Focus on Diversity," *Chicago Tribune*, May 2, 2012, accessed April 28, 2016, http:// articles.chicagotribune.com/2012-05-02/business/chi-in-speech-mcdonalds -thompson-puts-focus-on-diversity-20120502_1_diversity-women-and -minority-owned-businesses-mcbites.

161. Love, *McDonald's*, 372.

162. Wiley E. Woodard, "Beyond Fast Food," *Black Enterprise*, September 1990, 48–49.

163. The name International Franchise Association may imply that the IFA represents franchisees and franchisors alike. Recent events, however, suggest that the IFA serves to protect the interests of fast food companies above individual franchisees. In 2014, the organization objected to the National Labor Relations Board (NLRB) ruling that McDonald's Corporation is jointly responsible for labor violations and wage standards at franchised outlets. (Previously, McDonald's passed the buck to individual franchisees on issues concerning wages and working conditions, insisting that franchisees had full autonomy on these matters.) See Steven Greenhouse, "Ruling Says McDonald's Is Liable for Workers," *New York Times*, July 30, 2014, B1.

164. Woodard, "Beyond Fast Food," 48–49.

CHAPTER 4

1. Kroc, *Grinding It Out*, 158.

2. Inclusion & Diversity," *McDonald's*, accessed August 24, 2014, http:// www.aboutmcdonalds.com/mcd/our_company/inclusion_and_diversity.html; York, "In Speech, McDonald's Thompson Puts Focus on Diversity." It is unclear whether McDonald's is double-counting its minority and women franchisees in generating its 45 percent minority and women franchisee figure.

3. Jones, *Standing Up and Standing Out*, 102.

4. John A. Jakle and Keith A. Sculle, *Fast Food: Roadside Restaurants in the Automobile Age* (Baltimore: Johns Hopkins University Press, 1999), 22.

5. Phil W. Petrie, "Fast Food and Quick Bucks," *Black Enterprise*, April 1978, 28.

6. Love, *McDonald's*, 371.

7. Trutko et al., "Franchising's Growing Role in the U.S. Economy, 1975–2000," 4–5 (not online version). Trutko et al. also noted that franchise owner

households reported (via the polling firm Gallup) an annual gross income of $124,570 in 1991—more than three times the national average of $39,939.

8. Ibid., 100; figures for 2014 from Hayley Peterson, "Here's How Much It Costs to Open a Fast Food Franchise," *Business Insider Australia*, November 5, 2014, accessed December 12, 2014, http://www.businessinsider.com.au/cost-of -fast-food-franchise-2014-11 (Peterson obtained her figures from Franchise Direct, www.franchisedirect.com, "America's #1 Franchise Directory"). See also Don Daszkowski, "Most Popular Food Franchises and How Much They Cost," no date listed, About.com, accessed July 10, 2012. Regarding the number of Subway and McDonald's outlets, respectively (as of 2016), see "About Us," Subway, accessed April 13, 2016, https://www.subway.com.au/About; "Our Story," McDonald's, accessed April 13, 2016, http://www.mcdonalds.com/content/us/en /our_story.html.

9. Peterson, "Here's How Much It Costs to Open a Fast Food Franchise"; Paul Sullivan, "Franchise Success Means Doing Things the Franchiser's Way," *New York Times*, May 19, 2012, B6.

10. Peterson, "Here's How Much It Costs to Open a Fast Food Franchise"; Naa Oyo A. Kwate, Chun-Yip Yau, Ji-Meng Loh, and Donya Williams, "Inequality in Obesigenic Environments: Fast Food Density in New York City," *Health and Place* 15 (2009): 365. Although *obesigenic* is correct, the usual preferred spelling is *obesogenic.*

11. Jakle and Sculle, *Fast Food*, 22.

12. Robert A. Mittelstaedt and Manferd O. Peterson, "Franchising and the Financing of Small Business," in *Small Business Finance: Sources of Financing for Small Business* (Greenwich, CT: JAI Press, 1984), 179; Charles L. Vaughn, *Franchising* (Lexington, MA: Lexington Books, 1979); Peterson, "Here's How Much It Costs to Open a Fast Food Franchise."

13. Schlosser, *Fast Food Nation*, 100; Luxenberg, *Roadside Empires*, 22; Daszkowski, "Most Popular Food Franchises and How Much They Cost."

14. Mittelstaedt and Peterson, "Franchising and the Financing of Small Business," 179. In 2014, Subway's advertising fee was 4.5 percent of gross sales, and Wendy's was 4 percent. See Peterson, "Here's How Much It Costs to Open a Fast Food Franchise."

15. Luxenberg, *Roadside Empires*, 23.

16. Depending on the franchising corporation, franchisees could either: (1) buy a building outright; (2) agree to a "business facilities lease" in which they leased a building from the franchisor for a specified amount of time with the option to purchase the building; or (3) lease from the franchisor indefinitely. See "Franchising: New Opportunities for Black Business," *Ebony*, October 1984, 122.

17. For more on Ray Kroc and the origins of the leasing component to the McDonald's enterprise model, see Love, *McDonald's.*

18. Mittelstaedt and Peterson, "Franchising and the Financing of Small Business," 179.

19. Love, *McDonald's*, 159. In their book, *Big Mac: The Unauthorized Story of McDonald's*, Max Boas and Steve Chain report that, as of 1973, income from real estate accounted for "more than half" of McDonald's revenue. See Boas and Chain, *Big Mac*, 57. I emailed McDonald's to inquire about its current property ownership and received the following reply from its Customer Response Center: "The information you are specifically requesting is considered proprietary business information. I'm sorry I cannot answer your specific questions." Jennifer, email message to author (reference number 10136453), July 4, 2013.

20. Petrie, "Fast Food and Quick Bucks," 30.

21. Sullivan, "Franchise Success Means Doing Things the Franchiser's Way," B6.

22. Luxenberg, *Roadside Empires*, 22.

23. "About Us," *Black Enterprise*, accessed December 12, 2014, http://www.blackenterprise.com/about-us/; "Content Channels," *Black Enterprise*, accessed December 12, 2014, http://www.blackenterprise.com/mediakit/content-channels/.

24. *Black Enterprise*, April 1978, 36.

25. Chapman, "Black Franchises under the McDonald's Arches," 19.

26. Keys was not the only celebrated African-American athlete-turned-franchisee. For more on African-American athletes who became fast food entrepreneurs, see chapter 3 of this book, and "Black Capitalism: Into the Big Leagues," *Time*, July 25, 1969, accessed July 4, 2011, http://www.time.com/time/magazine/article/0,9171,901148,00.html.

27. Ibid.,116; Keys Group Company, accessed July 4, 2011, http://www.keysgroup.com/read_the_history.html; "I Recommend Blacks Go into Business via the Franchise Route," 27.

28. "Franchising: New Opportunities for Black Business," 116; Daniel Boorstin, *The Americans: The Democratic Experience* (New York: Vintage, 1973), 428. Original emphasis in quote from "Franchising: New Opportunities for Black Business," article.

29. "I Recommend Blacks Go into Business via the Franchise Route," 31.

30. "Franchising: New Opportunities for Black Business," 118.

31. Ibid., 120. Portion in quotes attributed to *Ebony* writer (unnamed), not Beavers.

32. Ibid. Quote from Beavers.

33. *Black Enterprise*, June 1996, 337.

34. Ibid., 338.

35. Terrian Barnes-Bryant, "Franchisors Promote Minority Business Development," *Franchising World*, November/December 1992, 13–14. The Inter-

national Franchise Association's Minorities and Franchising Committee conducted the survey.

36. Gupta, "Franchising Fever," 114.

37. U. B. Ozanne and S. D. Hunt, *The Economic Effects of Franchising*, U.S. Senate, Select Committee on Small Business, Committee Print, 92nd Congress, 1 Session (Washington, DC: U.S. Government Printing Office, 1971), cited in Mittelstaedt and Peterson, "Franchising and the Financing of Small Business," 185.

38. *Black Enterprise*, June 1996, 336.

39. For rates of African-American fast food patronage, see Gupta, "Franchising Fever," 112, 114.

40. See Jones, *Standing Up and Standing Out*, 76, for more on black anger toward white-owned restaurants in Washington in the aftermath of the Martin Luther King, Jr., assassination. Regarding the profitability of inner-city restaurants, Boas and Chain report that, as early as the 1970s, "a disproportionate number of ghetto stands belong to Hamburger Central's [McDonald's] 'million-dollar club,' the restaurants which do over a million dollars a year in business." See Boas and Chain, *Big Mac*, 190.

41. "I Recommend Blacks Go into Business via the Franchise Route," 30.

42. Jones, *Standing Up and Standing Out*, 94.

43. Ibid., 272.

44. Boas and Chain, *Big Mac*, 68.

45. Lewin, "McDonald's Is Battling with Black Franchisee," 1D.

46. Ibid.

47. Christian, "Business; A Mode Partnership for Inner-City Renewal, Derailed."

48. Ibid.

49. For more on philosophies of diet among Nation of Islam spokespersons, see Opie, *Hog and Hominy*, chapter 9, and Jennifer Jensen Wallach, "How to Eat to Live: Black Nationalism and the Post-1965 Culinary Turn," *Study of the South*, July 2, 2014, accessed November 5, 2015, http://southernstudies.olemiss.edu/study-the-south/how-to-eat-to-live/.

50. For more on this, see Cheryl Lynn Greenberg, *Or Does It Explode? Black Harlem in the Great Depression* (New York: Oxford University Press, 1997), chapter 5.

51. Boas and Chain, *Big Mac*, 190.

52. Nishani Frazier, "A McDonald's That Reflects the Soul of a People: Hough Area Development Corporation and Community Development in Cleveland," in *The Business of Black Power: Community Development, Capitalism, and Corporate Responsibility in Postwar America*, eds. Laura Warren Hill and Julia Rabig (Rochester: University of Rochester Press, 2012), 74. Regarding the number of black-owned McDonald's restaurants in 1969, see Jones, *Standing Up and Standing Out*, 122. It should be noted that Boas and Chain have a slightly different figure on

African-American franchisees at McDonald's. They write that the chain pur-
portedly only counted a total of five African-American owner-operators nationwide as of 1969, and all were located in Chicago. See Boas and Chain, *Big
Mac*, 189.

53. Frazier, "A McDonald's That Reflects the Soul of a People," 74. Phrases
in quotations are Frazier's, not Bood's. The OBU had also called on future Mc-
Donald's franchise owners in Cleveland to contribute financially to the organization's own community programs. Bood was infuriated and charged the OBU
with extortion.

54. Emanuel Hughley, Jr., "Shrimpboats in Cleveland," *Black Enterprise*,
March 1980, 19; Frazier, "A McDonald's That Reflects the Soul of a People," 73, 75–
76. Regarding the number of Cleveland restaurants that transferred ownership
in the aftermath of the boycotts, McDonald's own authorized historian John F.
Love writes that six previously white-owned outlets on the city's east side were
replaced with African-American franchises in 1969. See Love, *McDonald's*, 362.

55. Frazier, "A McDonald's That Reflects the Soul of a People," 69, 71–72, 76,
80. According to Frazier, one of the HADC's newly acquired McDonald's restaurants was the largest in Cleveland.

56. It is unclear precisely why the HADC McDonald's restaurants were unprofitable, but Frazier offers some possibilities: "It is possible that the OBU boycott drove away some of the customer base . . . McDonald's Corporation also
displayed a tendency to sell off those restaurants most in need of repair and
to inflate the value of a franchise. There were various overhead problems: employees appropriating food, sporadic incidents of petty theft that added up, high
employee turnover, inefficient workforce scheduling, turnover of general managers, funding Black managers to support their partial ownership, the costs of
repurchasing from managing partners who backed out, and the perception that
McDonald's failed to provide parking at the sit-down restaurant." See Frazier,
"A McDonald's That Reflects the Soul of a People," 84–85.

57. Ibid., 89.

58. Love, *McDonald's*, 371.

59. Jones, *Standing Up and Standing Out*, 122; emphasis in original.

60. Frazier, "A McDonald's That Reflects the Soul of a People," 85.

61. Love, *McDonald's*, 373. Boas and Chain, whose book appeared ten years
before Love's, also note that "within two years [of the Cleveland boycott] fifty
[McDonald's burger] stands were black-owned, while a dozen more applicants
were on the waiting list." See Boas and Chain, *Big Mac*, 190.

62. Hughley, "Shrimpboats in Cleveland," 19.

63. Love, *McDonald's*, 373.

64. Boas and Chain, *Big Mac*, 83; Jones, *Standing Up and Standing Out*, 182, 185.

65. Boas and Chain, *Big Mac*, 83; phrases in quotation marks are from Boas
and Chain.

66. Jones, *Standing Up and Standing Out*, 185.

67. Boas and Chain, *Big Mac*, 83, 185.

68. For more on redlining in the context of housing, see Arnold Hirsch, *Making the Second Ghetto: Race and Housing in Chicago, 1940–1960* (Chicago: University of Chicago Press, 1998); Douglas S. Massey and Nancy A. Denton, *American Apartheid: Segregation and the Making of the Underclass* (Cambridge, MA: Harvard University Press, 1998); Thomas J. Sugrue, *The Origins of the Urban Crisis: Race and Inequality in Postwar Detroit* (Princeton: Princeton University Press, 1996).

69. Griffis maintained that the Popeyes franchises belonged to his wife. McDonald's, meanwhile, insisted that Griffis's wife's ownership of the Popeyes restaurants was nominal, and that Griffis was actually operating the Popeyes franchises and diverting resources from his McDonald's restaurants to his Popeyes stores. McDonald's also sued Griffis for not paying advertising dues. Griffis acknowledged this charge, but brushed it aside, countering that McDonald's failed to "cater to [his] inner-city customers." See Lewin, "McDonald's Is Battling with Black Franchisee," 1D.

70. McDonald's General Counsel Shelby Yastrow was quoted as saying: "We paid this money to buy back Mr. Griffis's four restaurants . . . We didn't give [Griffis] 15 cents for those bogus racial discrimination claims." See Tamar Lewin, "McDonald's Dispute on Coast," *New York Times*, November 9, 1984, accessed June 30, 2013, https://www.nytimes.com/1984/11/09/business/mcdonald-s-dispute-on-coast.html.

71. Lewin, "McDonald's Is Battling with Black Franchisee," 1D.

72. Jones, *Standing Up and Standing Out*, 182.

73. Ibid., 183.

74. Lewin, "McDonald's Is Battling with Black Franchisee," 1D. "Recycled" is quoted from Lewin, not Jackson.

75. Ibid. John T. McDonald reported that the NAACP was also investigating potential redlining nationwide.

76. Jube Shiver Jr., "Blacks Feel Door Shut on Fast Food," *Los Angeles Times*, August 12, 1984, E3.

77. Penny Spar, "NAACP Ends Boycott of the McDonalds [sic] Chain," *Baltimore Afro-American*, April 21, 1984, 1.

78. Kevin D. Thompson, "Franchising Grows Up; The B.E. Franchise 50," *Black Enterprise*, September 1991, 60; Malcolm Gladwell and Paul Farhi, "Black Franchise Owners Sue Burger King Chain; Company Accused of Site, Price Deceptions," *Washington Post*, October 18, 1988, accessed December 12, 2015, https://www.highbeam.com/doc/1P2-1285104.html.

79. Brown, "Minority Franchisees Allege Redlining by the Big Chains," 1.

80. Shiver, "Blacks Feel Door Shut on Fast Food," E3; Michael King, "Finding the Franchise Formula for Success," *Black Enterprise*, September 1987, 50.

CHAPTER 5

1. Jones, *Standing Up and Standing Out*, 53. Jones does not specify the year in which he came across this Birmingham McDonald's.

2. Ibid. Jones does not indicate whether African-American customers could dine inside the McDonalds; the implication is that they could not.

3. See Chin Jou, "Neither Welcomed, Nor Refused: Race and Restaurants in Postwar New York City," *Journal of Urban History* 40.2 (March 2014): 232–51.

4. Historians Lizabeth Cohen and Tracey Deutsch have written about how chain stores were known for offering a more standardized customer experience, and were thus seen as less likely to discriminate than so-called mom-and-pop stores. See Lizabeth Cohen, *Making a New Deal: Industrial Workers in Chicago, 1919–1939* (Cambridge: Cambridge University Press, 1990), 152–53; Deutsch, *Building a Housewife's Paradise*, 52–53.

5. For more on this point, see Allen Shelton, "Writing McDonald's, Eating the Past: McDonald's as a Postmodern Space," in *Studies in Symbolic Interaction* 15 (1993): 103–18.

6. Freeman, "Fast Food," 2231; Austin, "Bad for Business," 228.

7. This is not to suggest, however, that African-American diners have been entirely shielded from discriminatory customer service at fast food restaurants. As both Freeman and legal scholar Regina Austin have noted, African Americans have sued Domino's Pizza for its refusal to make pizza deliveries in predominantly minority neighborhoods. (The pizza chain maintained that safety concerns, not racism, informed such policies.) See Freeman, "Fast Food," 2231; Austin, "Bad for Business," 239–40.

8. Barboza, "How Fast Food Companies 'Super Size' African Americans."

9. "Franchising: New Opportunities for Black Business," *Ebony*, October 1984, 116.

10. "The Gibson Report," D. Parke Gibson International, May 1974, in Archives II (National Archives, College Park, Maryland), Records of the Minority Business Development Agency, Record Group 427, Box 3 of 5, Accession No. 427-82-005, Folder: "The Gibson Report." And according to a 1971 marketing guide to African-American consumers, "the Negro population rose from 13 million in 1940 to approximately 21 million today—an increase of over 60 percent. See Charles E. Van Tassel, "The Negro as a Consumer—What We Know and What We Need to Know," in *The Black Consumer: Dimensions of Behavior and Strategy*, ed. George Joyce and Norman A. P. Govoni (New York: Random House, 1971), 359.

11. Leonard Evans, Jr., "Ghetto Marketing: What Now?" in *The Black Consumer: Dimensions of Behavior and Strategy*, 350.

12. Kotlowski, "Black Power—Nixon Style," 445.

13. "America's Rising Black Middle Class," *Time*, June 17, 1974, Archives II (National Archives, College Park, Maryland), Records of the Minority Business

Development Agency), Record Group 42, Box 3 of 5, Accession No. 427-82-005, Folder: "The Gibson Report."

14. "America's Rising Black Middle Class," 3–4. Twelve percent of African Americans reported an income of at least $15,000 annually in 1971.

15. Faltermayer, "More Dollars and More Diplomas," 141, 222.

16. "America's Rising Black Middle Class," 4.

17. Faltermayer, "More Dollars and More Diplomas," 140.

18. For more on this in the context of the automotive industry in Detroit, see Sugrue, *The Origins of the Urban Crisis*.

19. "America's Rising Black Middle Class," 12.

20. Weems, *Desegregating the Dollar*, 102; David Rohde, "White House: The American Middle Class Is Shrinking," Reuters, January 13, 2012, accessed June 3, 2012, http://blogs.reuters.com/david-rohde/2012/01/13/white-house-the -american-middle-class-is-shrinking/.

21. Weems, *Desegregating the Dollar*, 102.

22. See Sugrue, *The Origins of the Urban Crisis*, for more on the effects of the deindustrialization of the auto industry in Detroit.

23. See Wilson, *The Truly Disadvantaged*. It should be noted, however, that more affluent African Americans who moved out of declining inner-city neighborhoods did not necessarily move to racially mixed neighborhoods. See Douglas S. Massey, "Racial Segregation Directly Itself Remains a Corrosive Force: Blacks Held Back by Isolation within Cities," *Los Angeles Times*, August 13, 1989, accessed June 17, 2015, http://articles.latimes.com/1989-08-13/opinion/op-607 _1_racial-segregation.

24. Wilson, *The Truly Disadvantaged*.

25. "America's Rising Black Middle Class," 4.

26. Anthony J. Cortese, *Provacateur: Images of Women and Minorities in Advertising* (Lanham, MD: Rowman and Littlefield, 1999), 106; Lenika Cruz, "'Dinner-timin' and 'No Tippin': How Advertisers Targeted Black Consumers in the 1970s," *The Atlantic*, June 7, 2015, accessed August 21, 2015, http://www.theatlantic.com /entertainment/archive/2015/06/casual-racism-and-greater-diversity-in-70s -advertising/394958/.

27. Cruz, "'Dinnertimin' and 'No Tippin.'" Cosby's now severely tarnished reputation stems from the accusations, going back to the 1960s, from dozens of women that he drugged and raped them. See Noreen Malone and Amanda Demme, "I'm No Longer Afraid: 35 Women Tell Their Stories about Being Sexually Assaulted by Bill Cosby, and the Culture That Wouldn't Listen," *New York* (magazine), July 26, 2015, accessed August 23, 2015, http://nymag.com/thecut /2015/07/bill-cosbys-accusers-speak-out.html.

28. "America's Rising Black Middle Class," 4. According to this *Time* article, African Americans purchased 23 percent of shoes and 25 percent of music cassette tapes sold in the United States.

29. Faltermayer, "More Dollars and More Diplomas," 140.

30. D. Parke Gibson, "Why There Is a Negro Market," in *The Black Consumer*, ed. Joyce and Govoni, 39.

31. Ibid.; "America's Rising Black Middle Class," 4.

32. Freedman, "Fast-Food Chains Play Central Role in Diet of the Inner-City Poor," A1; Edward Lucas, "Junk Food: A 'Prison' Diet for the Poor; People in US Inner-City Communities Are Fat Yet Undernourished Because of Too Much Fast Food," *Independent*, December 28, 1990, 9.

33. Barboza, "How Fast Food Companies 'Super Size' African Americans."

34. Roberto A. Ferdman, "The Disturbing Ways That Fast Food Chains Disproportionately Target Black Kids," *Washington Post*, November 12, 2014, accessed January 11, 2015, http://www.washingtonpost.com/blogs/wonkblog/wp/2014/11/12/the-disturbing-ways-that-fast-food-chains-disproportionately-target-black-kids/; Punam Ohri-Vachaspati, Zeynep Isgor, Leah Rimkus, Lisa M. Powell, Dianne C. Barker, and Frank J. Chaloupka, "Child-Directed Marketing Inside and on the Exterior of Fast Food Restaurants," *American Journal of Preventive Medicine* 48.1 (2015): 22–30. Regarding advertising to children in the form of kids' meals displays, Ohri-Vachaspati et al. report that "restaurants in majority black neighborhoods had almost two times the odds of displaying kids' meal toys compared to those in white neighborhoods; both of these differences were statistically significant" (25–26).

35. Sonya A. Grier and Shiriki K. Kumanyika, "The Context for Choice: Health Implications of Targeted Food and Beverage Marketing to African Americans," *American Journal of Public Health* 98.9 (September 2008): 1617.

36. See Hirsch, *Making the Second Ghetto*; Massey and Denton, *American Apartheid*; Sugrue, *The Origins of the Urban Crisis*; and Kevin M. Kruse, *White Flight: Atlanta and the Making of Modern Conservatism* (Princeton: Princeton University Press, 2005).

37. For more on the history of African-American suburbanization, see Andrew Wiese, *Places of Their Own: African American Suburbanization in the Twentieth Century* (Chicago: University of Chicago Press, 2004). For more on the more recent exodus of African Americans from U.S. city centers, see Alex Kellogg, "D.C., Long 'Chocolate City,' Becoming More Vanilla," National Public Radio, February 15, 2011, accessed April 6, 2015, http://www.npr.org/2011/02/15/133754531/d-c-long-chocolate-city-becoming-more-vanilla; Sabrina Tavernise and Robert Gebeloff, "Many U.S. Blacks Moving South, Reversing Trend," *New York Times*, March 25, 2011, A1.

38. Van Tassel, "The Negro as a Consumer," 359.

39. Gibson, "Why There Is a Negro Market," 41; D. Parke Gibson, *$70 Billion in the Black: America's Black Consumers* (New York: Macmillan, 1978), 4.

40. Gibson, "Why There Is a Negro Market," 41; Gibson, *$70 Billion in the Black*, 4; Grier and Kumanyika, "The Context for Choice," 1617.

41. John Reynolds and Polly Larson, "Presenting IFA's Award Winners—Free Enterprise: McDonald's Corporation," *Franchising World*, January/February 1993, 13–14.

42. The Gibson Report" ("Minority Marketing/Communications Publication"), published by D. Parke Gibson International, Inc., May 1974, Archives II (National Archives, College Park, Maryland), Records of the Minority Business Development Agency), Record Group 427, Box 3 of 5, Accession No. 427-82-005, Folder: "The Gibson Report," (no page number). The Burger Chef chain, which would later be purchased by Hardee's, became defunct in 1996. It is unclear whether Chicken Unlimited outlets are still in operation.

43. Shields, "Wendy's Courts Minority Markets; The Move to Town Brings New Clientele"; "Episode 628: This Ad's for You."

44. Ken Smikle, "Golden Nuggets," *Black Enterprise*, October 1986, 26.

45. Dina Bunn, "McDonald's Ads to Focus on Minorities," *Rocky Mountain News*, December 28, 1997, 5G.

46. Freedman, "Fast-Food Chains Play Central Role in Diet of the Inner-City Poor," A1.

47. "Really Cookin'" (McDonald's ad, 1988), YouTube, accessed December 13, 2013, https://www.youtube.com/watch?v=IHlEjp1SqP4.

48. Cruz, "'Dinnertimin' and 'No Tippin': How Advertisers Targeted Black Consumers in the 1970s."

49. Ibid. Whether printed news reports of Obama's speech should have also g-dropped in transcriptions of his words was the subject of some controversy. Some commentators claimed that to do so was racist, while defenders of the practice maintained g-dropping was necessary to provide readers with the most faithful transcriptions of Obama's speech. It should also be noted that white politicians such as George W. Bush, Rick Perry, and Sarah Palin have also employed "g-dropping" in their speeches to appeal to conservative white voters and to sound more Southern, rural, and populist. See "AP Obama Transcript Sparks 'Complainin',"' *Politico*, September 26, 2011, accessed August 22, 2015, http://www.politico.com/blogs/onmedia/0911/AP_Obama_transcript_sparks _complainin.html.

50. Jennifer Jacobs Henderson and Gerald J. Baldasty, "Race, Advertising, and Prime-Time Television," *Howard Journal of Communications* 14.2 (2003): 97–112.

51. Burt Helm, "McDonald's Draws Ethnic Flavor into Menus, Ads to Draw Sales," *Bloomberg Businessweek Magazine*, July 8, 2010, accessed January 13, 2014, http://www.bloomberg.com/news/2010-07-08/mcdonald-s-draws-ethnic -flavor-into-menus-ads-to-drive-sales.html.

52. Ibid.

53. Henderson and Baldasty, "Race, Advertising, and Prime-Time Television," 103.

54. Grier and Kumanyika, "The Context for Choice," 1619; Manasi A. Tirod-

kar and Anjali Jain, "Food Messages on African American Television Shows," *American Journal of Public Health* 93.3 (March 2003): 439–41; Vani R. Henderson and Bridget Kelly, "Food Advertising in the Age of Obesity: Content Analysis of Food Advertising on General Market and African American Television," *Journal of Nutrition Education and Behavior* 37.4 (2005): 191–96.

55. Henderson and Kelly, "Food Advertising in the Age of Obesity," 193.

56. Tirodkhar and Jain, "Food Messages on African American Television Shows," 440. The authors also note that 17 percent of actors in commercials airing during African-American programming were overweight, compared to 4 percent of actors on shows for general audiences.

57. Henderson and Kelly, "Food Advertising in the Age of Obesity," 191, 193.

58. For more on the founding of the NBMOA, see Jones, *Standing Up and Standing Out*.

59. Boas and Chain, *Big Mac*, 191.

60. Jakle and Sculle, *Fast Food*, 22.

61. Boas and Chain, *Big Mac*, 191.

62. Ibid. There were other ways in which urban African Americans resisted fast food during the 1970s. In Las Vegas, Ruby Duncan, a community activist and founder of an antipoverty program called Operation Life, enjoined members of her organization to "open and support local food businesses instead of giving all our money to fast food chains whose central offices are located out of state." In 1979, Duncan's organization established a food cooperative and community garden in the Westside neighborhood of Las Vegas in part to provide affordable, healthy, fresh food, and to reduce the community's dependence on fast food. See Annelise Orleck, *Storming Caesars Palace: How Black Mothers Fought Their Own War on Poverty* (Boston: Beacon Press, 2005), 263.

63. Leon E. Wynter, "Business & Race," *Wall Street Journal*, December 6, 1993, B1.

64. Michael Dresser, "'Neighborhood KFC' Targets Black Locales," *Baltimore Sun*, April 17, 1993, accessed December 16, 2013, http://articles.baltimoresun.com/1993-04-17/business/1993107054_1_kfc-abc-box-fink.

65. Ibid.

66. Wynter, "Business & Race," B1.

67. Matt Michalec, "KFC's Pride 360 to Sponsor NSU-FAMU Homecoming Game," Norfolk State University Press Release, September 23, 2008, accessed December 29, 2013, http://www.nsuspartans.com/news/2008/9/23/GEN_0923081112.aspx. Kentucky Fried Chicken has since retired Pride 360°.

68. Vincent Thompson, "McDonald's Goes Afrocentric," *Philadelphia Tribune*, April 5, 1994, 1B.

69. Ibid.

70. Bunn, "McDonald's Ads to Focus on Minorities."

71. See Love, *McDonald's*.

72. See *Golden Arches East*. These changes occurred alongside broader modifications McDonald's implemented starting in the late-1980s, when competition from other fast food chains such as Wendy's and Taco Bell bit into McDonald's profits. To remain competitive and burnish its reputation for fast service, the company updated its menu, hired more employees, and made technology upgrades to its drive-through service. See Robert Charette, "Reinventing McDonald's, Again," *CutterBlog* (Cutter Consortium), February 18, 2009, accessed January 15, 2014, http://blog.cutter.com/2009/02/18/reinventing-mcdonalds -again/.

73. See *Golden Arches East*.

74. Warner, "Salads or No, Cheap Burgers Revive McDonald's." Figures originally reported by Nielsen Monitor-Plus, an advertising tracking service.

75. Freeman, "Fast Food," 2238; Austin, "Bad for Business," 229; Maureen Minehan, "Going Public with Diversity," *HR Magazine*, March 1999, 159.

76. Freeman, "Fast Food," 2238; Helm, "McDonald's Draws Ethnic Flavor into Menus, Ads to Draw Sales."

77. Guadalupe X. Ayala, Kristin Mueller, Eva Lopez-Madurga, Nadia R. Campbell, and John P. Elder, "Restaurant and Food Shopping Selections Among Latino Women in Southern California," *Journal of the American Dietetic Association* 105.1 (January 2005): 38–45.

78. Bunn, "McDonald's Ads to Focus on Minorities."

79. For more on the McLawsuit, see Marc Santora, "Teenagers' Suit Said McDonald's Made Them Obese," *New York Times*, November 21, 2002, B1; Michelle M. Mello, Eric B. Rimm, and David M. Studdert, "The McLawsuit: The Fast Food Industry and Legal Accountability for Obesity," *Health Affairs* 22.6 (November/December 2003): 207–16.

80. See Brownell, *Food Fight*; Rachel Gordon, "SF Fast-food Toy Ban Gets Supervisors' First OK," *San Francisco Chronicle*, November 3, 2010, accessed December 23, 2013, http://www.sfgate.com/health/article/SF-Fast-food-toy-ban-gets -supervisors-first-OK-3167850.php.

81. See, for example, Kelly D. Brownell and Kenneth E. Warner, "The Perils of Ignoring History: Big Tobacco Played Dirty and Millions Died. How Similar Is Big Food?" *Milbank Quarterly* 87.1 (March 2009): 259–94; Mello et al., "The McLawsuit."

82. As noted in the introduction to this book, the rate of obesity among African-American women is 41.2 percent, compared to 24.5 percent for white women.

83. *Fast Food FACTS 2013: Measuring Progress in Nutrition and Marketing to Children and Teens* (Yale Rudd Center for Food Policy & Obesity: November 2013), 66, 105. The Rudd Center report obtained its data from Nielsen Media Research.

84. Ibid., viii.

85. *Fast Food FACTS 2013: Measuring Progress in Nutrition and Marketing to Children and Teens*, 71, 77.

86. Ibid., 70.

87. Jennifer A. Emond, Amy M. Bernhardt, Diane Gilbert-Dimong, Zhigang Li, and James D. Sargent, "Commercial Television Exposure, Fast Food Toy Collecting, and Family Visits to Fast Food Restaurants among Families Living in Rural Communities," *Journal of Pediatrics*, October 20, 2015 (article in press), accessed November 5, 2015, http://www.jpeds.com/pb/assets/raw/Health %20Advance/journals/ympd/Emond.pdf.

88. Ibid.

89. Kathy L. Peiss, "American Women and the Making of Modern Consumer Culture," Phi Alpha Theta Lecture, University of Albany, State University of New York, March 26, 1998.

90. Grier and Kumanyika, "The Context for Choice," 1617.

91. Peiss, "American Women and the Making of Modern Consumer Culture."

92. For more on the history of the American candy industry, see April Merleaux, *Sugar and Civilization: American Empire and the Cultural Politics of Sweetness* (Chapel Hill: University of North Carolina Press, 2015); Wendy Woloson, *Refined Tastes: Sugar, Confectionery and Consumers in Nineteenth Century America* (Baltimore: Johns Hopkins University Press, 2002); Tim Richardson, *Sweets: A History of Candy* (New York: Bloomsbury, 2002).

93. Nina Martyris, "Tainted Treats: Racism and the Rise of Big Candy," The Salt, National Public Radio, October 30, 2015, accessed November 5, 2015, http://www.npr.org/sections/thesalt/2015/10/30/453210765/tainted-treats-racism -and-the-rise-of-big-candy.

94. Allan M. Brandt, *The Cigarette Century: The Rise, Fall, and Deadly Persistence of the Product That Defined America* (New York: Basic, 2007), 310.

95. Ibid. Like McDonald's, Philip Morris touted its own African-American executives as examples of the company's diversity on both the consumer and sales ends.

96. "Avoice Heritage Celebration," Avoice (African American Voices in Congress), accessed November 5, 2015, http://www.avoiceonline.org/news/heritage _awards.html. McDonald's has also advertised its relationship with the Congressional Black Caucus. In publicizing the company's sponsorship of the Annual Legislative Conference of the Congressional Black Caucus in 2014, the National Black McDonald's Operators Association posted the following headline on its website: "McDonald's Deeply Rooted with the Congressional Black Caucus." See "McDonald's Deeply Rooted with the Congressional Black Caucus," National Black McDonald's Operators Association (NBMOA), October 9, 2014, accessed November 5, 2015, http://nbmoa.org/2014/10/mcdonalds-deeply-rooted-with -the-congressional-black-caucus/

97. Ibid., 311. In some African-American communities in the 1980s and 1990s, cigarette billboards were four or five times as prevalent as in white neighborhoods. See Cortese, *Provocateur*, 131.

98. Anthony Ramirez, "A Cigarette Campaign under Fire," *New York Times*, January 12, 1990, http://www.nytimes.com/1990/01/12/business/a-cigarette -campaign-under-fire.html, accessed July 27, 2015; Claudia Morain, "Blacks and the Tobacco Industry," *Fort Worth Star-Telegram*, April 5, 1994, http://academic .udayton.edu/health/NAATPN/tobacco.htm, accessed July 27, 2015. After the tobacco industry discovered that African-American smokers preferred menthol cigarettes, they were particularly aggressive in promoting menthols in their advertising to African Americans.

99. Ramirez, "A Cigarette Campaign under Fire"; Brandt, *The Cigarette Century*, 311, 313; Cortese, *Provocateur*, 131. The retraction of the Uptown brand in 1990 could not undo the effects of decades of tobacco industry marketing to African Americans. According to market research from 1990, the smoking rate among African-American adults was 44 percent—7 percent higher than for whites. African-American men, moreover, had significantly higher rates of lung cancer diagnosis and mortality than white men, although a host of factors (e.g. health care access, later-stage diagnosis, workplace exposures, and even possibly genetics) may have contributed to these disparities.

100. Marion Nestle, "When Soda Companies Target Minorities, Is It Exploitation?" *Washington Post*, October 10, 2015, accessed November 20, 2015, https://www.washingtonpost.com/lifestyle/food/when-soda-companies -target-minorities-is-it-exploitation/2015/10/10/28df5870-6c63-11e5-aa5b -f78a98956699_story.html. For the book from which this *Washington Post* article was excerpted, see Nestle, *Soda Politics*.

101. *Fast Food FACTS 2013: Measuring Progress in Nutrition and Marketing to Children and Teens*, 68.

102. Ibid. See also Sonya A. Grier and Anne M. Brumbaugh, "Noticing Cultural Differences: Ad Meanings Created by Target and Non-Target Markets," *Journal of Advertising* 28.2 (Spring 1999): 79–93; Sonya A. Grier and Rohit Deshpande, "Social Dimensions of Consumer Distinctiveness: The Influence of Social Status on Group Identity and Advertising Persuasion," *Journal of Marketing Research* 38.2 (May 2001): 214–24; Jerome D. Williams and Marye C. Tharp, "African Americans: Ethnic Roots, Cultural Diversity," in *Marketing and Consumer Identity in Multicultural America*, ed. Marye C. Tharp (Thousand Oaks, CA: Sage, 1992): 75–85.

103. Cohen, *A Consumer's Republic*, 323. For example, the November 1959 issue of *Ebony* featured the prominent African-American actor Frederick O'Neal testifying to the "great taste" of Lucky Strikes cigarettes. (See page 10 of magazine issue.)

CHAPTER 6

1. "Small Business Administration Franchise Loans: Risk of Loss Can Be Reduced and Program Effectiveness Improved," *Report by the Comptroller General of the United States*, April 11, 1980, i.

2. Ibid., i, 2; "SBA 7a and 504 Gross Loan Approval Volume," e-mailed report from C. Shawn McKeehan, Special Assistant to the Director/OFA, SBA, to author, November, 24, 2010. The $1 billion figure appears to be in 1981 dollars.

3. "Small Business Administration Franchise Loans," 13; Luxenberg, *Roadside Empires*, 259.

4. "Small Business Administration Franchise Loans," 37.

5. Petrie, "Fast Food and Quick Bucks," 28.

6. Hodge, "For Big Franchisers, Money to Go; Is the SBA Dispensing Corporate Welfare?"

7. "10 Most Popular Franchises," CNNMoney.com, accessed July 4, 2011, http://money.cnn.com/galleries/2010/smallbusiness/1004/gallery.Franchise_failure_rates/index.html. This source did not indicate the percentage of all new Subways between 2000 and 2009 that were financed by SBA loan guarantees.

8. "Small Business Administration Franchise Loans," ii, 35–36, 58.

9. Ibid., 58; Luxenberg, *Roadside Empires*, 257.

10. "Small Business Administration Franchise Loans," i, 13.

11. Hodge, "For Big Franchisers, Money to Go; Is the SBA Dispensing Corporate Welfare?"

12. Mittelstaedt and Peterson, "Franchising and the Financing of Small Business," 191.

13. Hodge, "For Big Franchisers, Money to Go; Is the SBA Dispensing Corporate Welfare?"

14. Refer to chapter 3, n24.

15. Mittelstaedt and Peterson, "Franchising and the Financing of Small Business," 191.

16. "Small Business Administration Franchise Loans," 35.

17. "Burger King Launches Largest Minority Venture in History," *New Journal and Guide*, March 6, 1996, 5; Lara Wozniak, "Burger King Targeting Inner Cities," *St. Petersburg Times* (Florida), February 23, 1996, 1E.

18. Administration for Children and Families, U.S. Department of Health and Human Services, accessed August 1, 2012, http://www.acf.hhs.gov/programs/ocs/ez-ec/aboutus/factsheets.htm.

19. Wozniak, "Burger King Targeting Inner Cities," 1E.

20. Will Lester (Associated Press), "Burger King Launches Effort to Build in Depressed Communities," *New Pittsburgh Courier*, March 26, 1996, 6.

21. Wozniak, "Burger King Targeting Inner Cities," 1E. Clinton also explicitly thanked Hawkins and Lowes in a speech at the event, stating that, he wished

to acknowledge: "Members of Congress from empowered zones; Mayors from Empowerment and Enterprise Cities; current and future partners in our empowerment strategy who have come here today; in particular, Robert Lowes, CEO of Burger King and La-Van Hawkins, CEO of Urban City Foods." See "President William J. Clinton Prepared Remarks Empowerment Zones Conference February 22, 1996, Folder Title: "EZ/EC Conf. Edinburg, TX 5/29/99—EZ Conference Past POTUS Remarks," Clinton Presidential Records, Subgroup/Office of Origins: Speechwriting, Series/Staff member: Jeff Shesol; OA/ID Number: 19945, FOIA Number: 2006-0467-F," accessed November 7, 2015, clinton .presidentiallibraries.us/items/show/12101.

22. Christian, "Business; A Model Partnership for Inner-City Renewal, Derailed."

23. Wozniak, "Burger King Targeting Inner Cities," 1E.

24. Christian, "Business; A Model Partnership for Inner-City Renewal, Derailed."

25. Ibid.; Michael O'Connor, "Al Sharpton Plans Burger King Boycott," *ABC News*, October 10, 2000, accessed January 13, 2015, http://abcnews.go.com/US /story?id=95439. A number of other sources note that Hawkins had planned to eventually open 125 Burger Kings rather than the 225 O'Connor reports.

26. Christian, "Business; A Model Partnership for Inner-City Renewal, Derailed."

27. "Sharpton Threatens Boycott of Burger King," Associated Press, September 11, 2000, accessed February 16, 2015, http://staugustine.com/stories/091100 /sta_20000911.018.shtml.

28. Christian, "Business; A Model Partnership for Inner-City Renewal, Derailed"; O'Connor, "Al Sharpton Plans Burger King Boycott." Burger King asserted that 1,173 of its franchises as of October 2000, were minority-owned. As O'Connor states, however, "It was not clear how many of the minority owners were black."

29. O'Connor, "Al Sharpton Plans Burger King Boycott." Media reports of what Burger King claimed Hawkins owed vary. O'Connor reports that Burger King claimed that Hawkins owed $8 million in "back fees," while O'Connor places the figure at $6.5 million. Burger King's countersuit also sought to bar Hawkins from using the Burger King trademark at his restaurants, and to reclaim franchises that Hawkins leased from the company; the company noted that reclaimed franchises would be relocated to other "qualified" minority franchise owners.

30. Taylor, "La-Van Hawkins Returns to Detroit."

31. Susan Levine, *School Lunch Politics: The Surprising History of America's Favorite Welfare Program* (Princeton: Princeton University Press, 2008), 182.

32. Lesley Alderman, "Putting Nutrition at the Head of the School Lunch Line," *New York Times*, November 6, 2010, B6.

33. Levine, *School Lunch Politics*, 183.

34. Ashlesha Datar and Nancy Nicosia, "Junk Food in Schools and Childhood Obesity," *Journal of Policy Management and Analysis* 31.2 (Spring 2012): 312–37.

35. See Nestle, *Food Politics*; Nicholas Confessore, "How School Lunch Became the Latest Political Battleground," *New York Times Magazine*, October 7, 2014, accessed January 18, 2015, http://www.nytimes.com/2014/10/12/magazine /how-school-lunch-became-the-latest-political-battleground.html.

36. Levine, *School Lunch Politics*, 187.

37. Ibid.

38. Nat Ives, "Fast Food and the Obesity Problem," *New York Times*, December 4, 2002, accessed January 19, 2015, http://www.nytimes.com/2002/12/04 /business/media/04ADCO.html?pagewanted=all.

39. Michael Moss, "The Domino's Smart Slice Goes to School," *New York Times*, June 10, 2014, accessed January 19, 2015, http://www.nytimes.com/2014 /06/11/dining/the-dominos-smart-slice-goes-to-school.html.

40. "U.S. Approves Cheeseburger Bill," *BBC News*, March 12, 2004, accessed May 29, 2012, http://news.bbc.co.uk/2/hi/americas/3500388.stm. For a list of Keller's campaign donors in 2004, see the Center for Responsive Politics, accessed May 29, 2012, http://www.opensecrets.org/politicians/summary.php ?cycle=2004&type=I&cid=N00009614&newMem=N.

41. "'Cheeseburger Bill' Puts Bite on Lawsuits," CNN.com, October 20, 2005, accessed May 29, 2012, http://articles.cnn.com/2005-10-20/politics /cheeseburger.bill_1_cheeseburger-bill-fast-food-chains-food-industry?_s= PM:POLITICS.

42. "Minnesota's 'Cheeseburger Bill' Seeks to Block Obesity Suits," *Fair Warning*, February 11, 2011, accessed July 2, 2013, http://www.fairwarning.org/2011/02 /cheeseburger-bill-moves-minnesota-closer-to-ban-on-obesity-suits/; Jennifer Pomeranz and Lainie Rutkow, "Efforts to Immunize Food Manufacturers from Obesity-Related Lawsuits: A Challenge for Public Health," *Corporations & Health Watch*, August 17, 2011, accessed January 25, 2015, http://corporationsandhealth .org/2011/08/17/efforts-to-immunize-food-manufacturers-from-obesity -related-lawsuits-a-challenge-for-public-health/.

43. Food industry critic Marion Nestle, for example, declared to the *New York Times* that the FDA's proposed trans fats ban indicated that "the F.D.A. is back." See Sabrina Tavernise, "F.D.A. Seeking Near Total Ban on Trans Fats," *New York Times*, November 8, 2013, A1.

44. The particulars of the FDA's calorie-labeling rules may not have been known before the agency announced them in November 2014, however.

45. Sabrina Tavernise and Stephanie Strom, "U.S. to Require Calorie Count, Even at Movies," *New York Times*, November 25, 2014, A1.

46. Ibid. According to Taverise and Strom, among food industry interests, only pizza restaurants and movie theaters pitched a fight against calorie label-

ing. The pizza chains lobbied for calorie posting on pizza slices rather than on entire pizza pies; their efforts were ultimately successful.

47. Frank Bruni, "Don't Count on Calorie Counts," *New York Times*, June 23, 2013, SR3; Aaron E. Carroll, "The Surprising Failure of Calorie Counts on Menus," *New York Times*, November 30, 2015, accessed December 1, 2015, http://www.nytimes.com/2015/12/01/upshot/more-menus-have-calorie-labeling-but -obesity-rate-remains-high.html?_r=0; Pooja S. Tandon, Chuan Zhou, Nadine L. Chan, Paula Lozano, Sarah C. Couch, Karen Glanz, James Krieger, and Brian E. Saelens, "The Impact of Menu Labeling on Fast-Food Purchases for Children and Parents," *American Journal of Preventive Medicine* 41.1 (October 2011): 434–38; Michael W. Long, Deirdre K. Tobias, Angie L. Cradock, Holly Batchelder, and Steven L. Gortmaker, "Systematic Review and Meta-analysis of the Impact of Restaurant Menu Calorie Labeling," *American Journal of Public Health* 105.5 (May 2015): e11–e24. In some instances, menu labeling has also coincided with diners consuming slightly *more* calories. See Julie S. Downs, Jessica Wisdom, Brian Wansink, and George Loewenstein, "Supplementing Menu Labeling with Calorie Recommendations to Test for Facilitation Effects," *American Journal of Public Health* 103.9 (September 2013): 1604–9. Additionally, it may even be the case that some calorie counts on menus are inaccurate. See Lorien E. Urban, Megan A. McCrory, Gerard E. Dallal, Sai Krupa Das, Edward Saltzman, Judith L. Weber, and Susan B. Roberts, "Accuracy of Stated Energy Contents of Restaurant Foods," *Journal of the American Medical Association* 306.3 (2011): 287–93.

48. Bruni, "Don't Count on Calorie Counts."

49. Darlene Superville, "First Lady on Obesity in America: 'Fast Food Has Become the Every Day Meal,'" *Huffington Post*, February 28, 2011, accessed April 19, 2011, http://www.huffingtonpost.com/2011/02/09/first-lady-on-obesity-in-_n _820612.html. Mrs. Obama, however, also revealed that she had a personal weakness for french fries. See Amie Parnes, "Michelle Obama: I Love French Fries," *Politico*, September 13, 2010, accessed July 4, 2011, http://www.politico .com/click/stories/1009/first_lady_i_love_french_fries.html. Barack Obama made a similar comment while campaigning for the Democratic presidential nomination in 2007. During a candidates' forum on health care in Las Vegas on March 24 of that year, Obama offered the following response to a voter who asked about health care for racial minorities in the United States: "Obesity and diabetes in minority communities are more severe, so I think we need targeted programs, particularly to children in those communities, to make sure that they've got sound nutrition, that they have access to fruits and vegetables and not just Popeyes, and that they have decent spaces to play in instead of being cooped up in the house all day." See Larissa MacFarquhar, "The Conciliator," *New Yorker*, May 7, 2007, accessed November 5, 2015, http://www.newyorker .com/magazine/2007/05/07/the-conciliator; Robert Pear, "Candidates Outline

Ideas for Universal Health Care," *New York Times*, March 25, 2007, accessed November 5, 2015, http://www.nytimes.com/2007/03/25/us/politics/25dems.html.

50. Lynn Elber, "Michelle Obama, Gabby Douglas 'Tonight Show' Appearance: First Lady Teases Olympic Champion about McDonald's," August 13, 2012, *Huffington Post*, accessed January 19, 2015, http://www.huffingtonpost.com/2012/08/13/michelle-obama-gabby-douglas-tonight-show_n_1774171.html.

51. Statista, accessed June 18, 2015, http://www.statista.com/topics/863/fast-food/. The industry revenue figure is from 2013.

52. The documentary film *Fed Up*, for example, has been critical of partnerships between the food industry and "Let's Move." See *Fed Up*, directed by Stephanie Soechtig (Santa Monica, CA: Atlas Films, 2014).

53. Katie Kindelan, "McDonald's Wins First Lady's Approval with Happy Meal Makeover," *ABC News*, July 26, 2011, accessed January 25, 2015, http://abcnews.go.com/Health/mcdonalds-puts-fruit-veggies-happy-meals/story?id=14159121.

54. "First Lady Michelle Obama Announces Commitment by Subway® Restaurants to Promote Healthier Choices to Kids," White House, Office of the First Lady Press Release, January 23, 2014, accessed January 27, 2015, http://www.whitehouse.gov/the-press-office/2014/01/23/first-lady-michelle-obama-announces-commitment-subway-restaurants-promot.

55. Incredibly, Fogel's defense included the ludicrous claim that his criminal behavior was induced by his dramatic weight loss. The disgraced Subway pitchman's defense included the testimony of a forensic psychiatrist named John Braford, who testified that "once [Fogel] lost weight, it seemed as though in a short time he had hypersexuality." See Joanna Rothkopf, "Jared Fogel's Defense Connects His 'Mild Pedophilia' to a Diet of Subway Sandwiches," *Jezebel*, November 19, 2015, accessed November 20, 2015, http://jezebel.com/jared-fogles-defense-connects-his-mild-pedophilia-to-a-1743542424.

56. Rheana Murray, "Subway Commercial Spokesman Jared Fogel Marks 15 Years of Turkey Subs and Keeping the Weight Off," *New York Daily News*, June 9, 2013, accessed January 27, 2015, http://www.nydailynews.com/life-style/health/jared-subway-guy-marks-15-years-turkey-subs-article-1.1365511.

57. Steven Greenhouse, "$15 Wage in Fast Food Stirs Debate on Effects," *New York Times*, December 5, 2013, B1.

58. Robert Pollin and Jeannette Wicks-Lim, "A $15 U.S. Minimum Wage: How the Fast-Food Industry Could Adjust Without Shedding Jobs," University of Massachusetts, Amherst Department of Economics and Political Economy Research Institute (PERI) Working Paper Series 373 (January 2015): 1–33, accessed February 15, 2015, http://www.peri.umass.edu/fileadmin/pdf/working_papers/working_papers_351-400/WP373.pdf. Pollin and Wicks-Lim assert that since all companies would be affected by minimum wage legislation, "the likelihood

is that all affected firms within a given area will raise their prices at about the same time and no individual company would be disadvantaged" (11).

59. Melanie Trottman, "Groups Ask Obama to Boost Contractors' Minimum Wage to $15," *Wall Street Journal* ("Washington Wire"), November 10, 2014, accessed January 27, 2015, http://blogs.wsj.com/washwire/2014/11/10/groups-ask -obama-to-boost-u-s-contractors-minimum-wage-to-15/; Jim Tankersley and Ylan Q. Mui, "It's Hillary Clinton and Barack Obama Versus Liberals on the Minimum Wage," *Washington Post*, August 17, 2015, accessed December 26, 2015, https://www.washingtonpost.com/news/wonk/wp/2015/08/17/its-hillary -clinton-and-barack-obama-versus-liberals-on-the-minimum-wage/.

60. Patrick McGeehan, "New York State to Mandate $15 Minimum Pay," *New York Times*, July 23, 2015, A1.

CHAPTER 7

1. "Potatoes," Economic Research Service, United States Department of Agriculture, accessed July 1, 2013, http://www.ers.usda.gov/topics/crops/vegetables -pulses/potatoes.aspx#.UdNyzZwto3w.

2. Alexis C. Madrigal, "A Journey into Our Food System's Refrigerated-Warehouse Archipelago," *The Atlantic*, July 15, 2013, accessed July 16, 2013, http:// www.theatlantic.com/technology/archive/2013/07/a-journey-into-our-food -systems-refrigerated-warehouse-archipelago/277790/.

3. Luxenberg, *Roadside Empires*, 118; Jakle and Sculle, *Fast Food*, 22; Scott Mowbray, "You Really Can't Eat Just One. And Here's the Reason," *New York Times*, March 18, 2013, C4. Like french fries, per capita hard cheese consumption has also soared. With pizzas piled high with shredded mozzarella, and slices of American and cheddar hugging hamburgers, Americans currently polish off an average of 33 pounds of cheese and cheese products per person, up from 8.3 pounds in 1960 and 15.9 pounds in 1976. These increases no doubt have something to do with greater overall restaurant patronage and grocery sales of cheese. But it is impossible to discount the role that fast food burger, pizza, and taco outlets have had in promoting the consumption of America's favorite dairy product.

4. "Fast Food," Palo Alto Medical Foundation, accessed July 13, 2013, http:// www.pamf.org/teen/health/nutrition/fastfood.html; Steven Greenhouse, "The Rise and Rise of Big Mac," *New York Times*, June 8, 1986, accessed January 8, 2013. http://www.nytimes.com/1986/06/08/business/the-rise-and-rise-of-big-mac .html.

5. N. R. Kleinfield, "Fast Food's Changing Landscape,' *New York Times*, April 14, 1985, accessed December 13, 2013, http://www.nytimes.com/1985/04 /14/business/fast-food-s-changing-landscape.html.

6. See Michelle Fay Cortez, "McDonald's in Hospitals Targeted by Group Seeking Fast Food End," *Bloomberg News*, April 11, 2012, accessed July 16, 2013,

http://www.businessweek.com/news/2012-04-11/mcdonald-s-in-hospitals
-targeted-by-group-seeking-fast-food-end; Greenhouse, "The Rise and Rise of
Big Mac"; Freeman, "Fast Food," 2224.

7. At least seven other McDonald's restaurants in hospitals have closed
since 2009 due to criticisms of hospitals hosting the fast food chain. See Allison Aubrey, "So Long, Big Mac: Cleveland Clinic Outs McDonald's from Cafeteria," The Salt, National Public Radio, August 19, 2015, accessed August 20, 2015,
http://www.npr.org/sections/thesalt/2015/08/19/432885995/so-long-big-mac
-cleveland-clinic-ousts-mcdonalds-from-cafeteria.

8. See Sam Oches, "The QSR 50," QSR (Quick Service Restaurant) Magazine, August 2012, accessed July 16, 2013, http://www.qsrmagazine.com/reports
/qsr50-2012-top-50-chart?sort=total_units&dir=desc.

9. Specter, "Freedom from Fries."

10. For at least four decades, critics have commented on the homogenizing
effects of Big Fast Food and its potential to efface smaller, local, independent
competitors. See Jim Hightower, Eat Your Heart Out: Food Profiteering in America
(New York: Crown, 1975). Similarly, in 1993, the sociologist George Ritzer first
observed an even broader homogenizing effect of Big Fast Food in which American society more broadly had become "McDonaldized." Ritzer defined "McDonaldization" as "the process by which the principles of the fast food restaurant
[efficiency, calculability, predictability, and control] are coming to dominate
more and more sectors of American society as well as the rest of the world." See
Ritzer, The McDonaldization of Society, 1.

11. Specter, "Freedom from Fries."

12. "McDonald's Looks to Address Its 'Millennial Problem,'" Forbes, April 3,
2013, accessed February 19, 2015, http://www.forbes.com/sites/brandindex
/2013/04/03/mcdonalds-looks-to-address-its-millennial-problem/.

13. Ashley Lutz, "Chipotle Has Unseated Subway as America's Healthy Fast
Food of Choice," July 27, 2015, accessed July 31, 2015, http://www.businessinsider
.com.au/americas-favorite-healthy-food-is-chipotle-2015-7. Incidentally, Mc-
Donald's Corporation once owned a majority equity stake in Chipotle, although
in 2006 McDonald's divested entirely from the burrito chain.

14. Specter, "Freedom from Fries."

15. Freeman, "Fast Food," 2224.

16. For more on the price points of healthy fast casual dining, seeing Mark
Bittman, "Fast, Good and Good For You," New York Times Magazine, April 7, 2013,
MM26.

17. Specter, "Freedom from Fries."

18. Legal scholar Regina Austin writes: "Blacks, along with Hispanics whose
sales totaled $279 million, accounted for 25 cents of every $1 spent at McDonald's. Sales to blacks and Hispanics represented 30% of Burger King's total." See
Austin, "Bad for Business," 230. Austin's source is "Targeted Promotions/Adver-

tising: Fast Food: Minority Consumers Mean Major Revenues," *Minority Markets Alert*, May 1, 1998. See also Critser, *Fat Land*, 112; Freedman, "Fast-Food Chains Play Central Role in Diet of the Inner-City Poor," A1; Lucas, "Junk Food," 9.

19. For more on the "reverse Great Migration," see Tavernise and Gebeloff, "Many U.S. Blacks Moving South, Reversing Trend." For more on the history of African-American suburbanization, see Wiese, *Places of Their Own*. McDonald's defines "heavy users" as those who patronize the restaurant chain at least once a week. See *Super Size Me*, directed by Morgan Spurlock (New York: The Con, 2004), DVD.

20. Jones, *Standing Up and Standing Out*, 271.

21. Bunn, "McDonald's Ads to Focus on Minorities."

22. Warner, "Salads or No, Cheap Burgers Revive McDonald's."

23. Luxenberg, *Roadside Empires*, 118. The survey was conducted by *Newspaper Advertising*.

24. Cheryl D. Fryar and R. Bethene Ervin, "Caloric Intake from Fast Food among Adults: United States, 2007–2010," *National Center for Health Statistics Data Brief* 114 (February 2013), 1–8; Mike Stobbe, "Adults Get 11 Percent of Calories from Fast Food," Associated Press, February 21, 2013, accessed December 13, 2015, http://news.yahoo.com/adults-11-percent-calories-fast-134848483.html#. The CDC's figure for Hispanics seemed to be slightly at odds with the *New York Times*'s claim that Hispanics made up 17 percent of McDonald's sales. See Melanie Warner, "Salads or No, Cheap Burgers Revive McDonald's."

25. Stobbe, "Adults Get 11 Percent of Calories from Fast Food."

26. DaeHwan Kim and J. Paul Leigh, "Are Meals at Full-Service and Fast-Food Restaurants 'Normal' or 'Inferior'?" *Population Health Management* 14.6 (December 2011): 307, 312–13, 315.

27. See, for example, Kwate, "Fried Chicken and Fresh Apples," 36; H. L. Burdette and R. C. Whittaker, "Neighborhood Playgrounds, Fast Food Restaurants, and Crime: Relationships to Overweight in Low-Income Preschool Children," *Preventive Medicine* 38 (2004): 57–63; R. W. Jeffrey and S. French, "Epidemic Obesity in the United States: Are Fast Foods and Television Viewing Contributing?" *American Journal of Public Health* 88.2 (February 1998): 277–80; S. A. French, L. Harnack, and R. W. Jeffrey, "Fast Food Restaurant Use among Women in the Pound of Prevention Study: Dietary, Behavioral, and Demographic Correlates," *International Journal of Obesity and Metabolic Disorders* 24.10 (October 2000): 1354–59. Fast food may be even more economical than fresh produce and other grocery items at home, although some food writers, like the Mark Bittman, have strenuously objected to the notion that fast food and junk food are cheaper than home cooking. See Mark Bittman, "Is Junk Food Really Cheaper?" *New York Times*, September 24, 2011, accessed March 21, 2012, http://www.nytimes.com/2011/09/25/opinion/sunday/is-junk-food-really-cheaper.html?pagewanted=all.

28. Warner, "Salads or No, Cheap Burgers Revive McDonald's."

29. Melanie Hicken, "This Interactive Map Shows Exactly How Many Fast Food Restaurants There Are in Every State," *Business Insider*, January 28, 2012, accessed December 13, 2015, http://www.businessinsider.com.au/this-interactive-map-shows-exactly-how-many-fast-food-restaurants-there-are-in-every-state-2012-1. With the exception of the District of Columbia and Rhode Island, these states are relatively sparsely populated, which may account for their relatively high number of per capita fast food outlets.

30. Ibid.

31. Sarah Kliff, "Who Eats Fast Food? Not Who You'd Expect," *Washington Post*, November 15, 2011, accessed July 16, 2013, http://www.washingtonpost.com/blogs/wonkblog/post/who-eats-fast-food-not-who-youd-expect/2011/11/15/gIQAFrxeON_blog.html.

32. Brennan Davis and Christopher Carpenter, "Proximity of Fast-Food Restaurants to Schools and Adolescent Obesity," *American Journal of Public Health* 99.3 (March 2009): 505–10.

33. David Just and Brian Wansink, "Fast Food, Soft Drink, and Candy Intake Is Unrelated to Body Mass Index for 95% of Adults," *Obesity Science and Practice*, November 15, 2015, advance paper accessed November 13, 2015, http://foodpsychology.cornell.edu/OP/fast_food_science; Maria Godoy, "Are Junk Food Habits Driving Obesity? A Tale of Two Studies," The Salt, National Public Radio, November 12, 2015, accessed November 13, 2015, http://www.npr.org/sections/thesalt/2015/11/12/455074815/are-junk-food-habits-driving-obesity-a-tale-of-two-studies.

34. Faye Flam, "The False Claim That Soda and Junk Food Don't Matter in Obesity," *Forbes*, November 13, 2015, accessed November 19, 2015, http://www.forbes.com/sites/fayeflam/2015/11/13/the-false-claim-that-sugar-junk-food-dont-matter-in-obesity/.

35. Roland Sturm and Deborah Cohen, "Zoning for Health? The Year-Old Ban on New Fast-Food Restaurants in South LA: The Ordinance Isn't a Promising Approach to Attacking Obesity," *Health Affairs* 28.6 (2009): 1088–97. South Los Angeles had 19 fast food chain restaurants per 100,000 residents and a 26 percent obesity rate; West Los Angeles, by contrast, had 30 fast food chains per 100,000 residents and an 18 percent obesity rate. A follow-up study published by RAND researchers six years later, however, found negligible evidence linking Los Angeles County residents' BMI to the proximity of either fast food restaurants, smaller grocery stores, supermarkets, or convenience stores in neighborhoods. See Nelly Mejia, Amy S. Lightstone, Ricardo Basurto-Davila, Douglas M. Morales, and Roland Sturm, "Neighborhood Food Environment, Diet, and Obesity Among Los Angeles County Adults, 2011," *Preventing Chronic Disease* 12 (September 3, 2015), accessed November 5, 2015, http://dx.doi.org/10.5888/pcd12.150078.

36. Roland Sturm and Aiko Hattori, "Diet and Obesity in Los Angeles County,

2007–2012: Is There a Measurable Effect of the 2008 'Fast Food Ban'?" *Social Science & Medicine* 133 (May 2015): 205–11, accessed March 23, 2015, http://dx.doi.org /10.1016/j.socscimed.2015.03.004.

37. Dan Charles, "Why Los Angeles' Fast Food Ban Did Nothing to Check Obesity," The Salt, National Public Radio, March 20, 2015, accessed March 23, 2015, http://www.npr.org/blogs/thesalt/2015/03/20/393943031/why-los-angeles-fast -food-ban-did-nothing-to-check-obesity.

38. Ruopeng An, "Fast-Food and Full-Service Restaurant Consumption and Daily Energy and Nutrient Intakes in U.S. Adults," *European Journal of Clinical Nutrition* (1 July 2015, advance online publication): 1–7, accessed July 31, 2015, http://www.nature.com/ejcn/journal/vaop/ncurrent/full/ejcn2015104a.html. The NHANES data were from 2003 to 2010.

39. See Ruopeng An and Roland Sturm, "School and Residential Neighborhood Food Environment and Diet among California Youth," *American Journal of Preventive Medicine* 42.2 (2012): 129–35; Mejia et al., "Neighborhood Food Environment, Diet, and Obesity among Los Angeles County Adults, 2011."

40. An and Sturm, "School and Residential Neighborhood Food Environment and Diet among California Youth," 131. This study examined data from the California Health Interview Survey between 2005 and 2007.

41. Researchers whose findings cast doubt on the relationship between food environments and BMI have offered such a suggestion. For example, Mejia et al. write: "Little evidence was found for associations between proximity of respondents' homes to food outlets and dietary intake or BMI among adults in Los Angeles County. A possible explanation for the null finding is that shopping patterns are weakly related to neighborhoods in Los Angeles County because of motorized transportation." See Mejia et al., "Neighborhood Food Environment, Diet, and Obesity Among Los Angeles County Adults.

42. For more on the biological mechanisms that affect appetite and weight, see Ellen Ruppel Shell, *The Hungry Gene: The Inside Story of the Obesity Industry* (New York: Grove, 2003); Gina Kolata, *Rethinking Thin: The New Science of Weight Loss—and the Myths and Realities of Dieting* (New York: Farrar, Straus and Giroux, 2007).

43. Lucas, "Junk Food," 9.

44. Warner, "Salads or No, Cheap Burgers Revive McDonald's."

45. Mayer did allow for occasional fast food indulgences, however, telling *Time* magazine that McDonald's fare was all right as a "weekend treat." Boas and Chain, *Big Mac*, 84.

46. Ibid., 84–95.

47. For a history of the counterculture's critique of the food industry and of the food industry's subsequent attempt to co-opt that critique, see Warren James Belasco, *Appetite for Change: How the Counterculture Took on the Food In-*

dustry, 1966–1988 (New York, Pantheon, 1989). For more on the food movement from the 1970s to 2010, see Michael Pollan, "The Food Movement, Rising," *New York Review of Books,* June 10, 2010, accessed December 4, 2015, http://www.nybooks.com/articles/2010/06/10/food-movement-rising/.

48. Sheraton, "The Burger That's Eating New York," 33.

49. See, for example, P. W. Siri-Tarino, Q. Sun, F. B. Hu, and R. M. Krauss, "Meta-analysis of Prospective Cohort Studies Evaluating the Association of Saturated Fat with Cardiovascular Disease," *American Journal of Clinical Nutrition* 91.3 (March 2010): 535–46. Regarding how dietary fat became maligned in the first place, see Ann F. LaBerge, "How the Ideology of Low Fat Conquered America," *Journal of the History of Medicine and Allied Sciences* 63.2 (April 2008): 139–77.

50. "Are You Eating Right?" *US News & World Report,* November 28, 1977, 39; Marian Burros, "Dietary Goals—Becoming a Matter of National Policy," *Washington Post,* October 4, 1979, E1. Both articles found in Box 617, George S. McGovern Papers, Mudd Manuscript Library, Princeton University, Princeton, New Jersey.

51. "Excerpts," *Dietary Goals for the United States,* George S. McGovern Papers, Mudd Manuscript Library, Princeton University, Princeton, New Jersey.

52. "Are You Eating Right?"; "Excerpts"; "McGovern Releases Second Edition of Dietary Goals for the United States."

53. "McGovern Releases Second Edition of Dietary Goals for the United States."

54. "McGovern Presenting a Summary of Hearings on Diet and Disease," July 26–27, 1976, 1, Box 628, George S. McGovern Papers, Mudd Manuscript Library, Princeton University, Princeton, New Jersey.

55. Shanthy A. Bowman and Bryan T. Vinyard, "Fast-Food Consumption of U.S. Adults: Impact on Energy and Nutrient Intakes and Overweight Status," *Journal of the American College of Nutrition* 23.2 (April 2004): 163–68; O. M. Thompson, "Food Purchased Away from Home as a Predictor of Change in BMI Z-score among Girls," *International Journal of Obesity* 28 (2004): 282–89; K. N. Boutelle, "Fast Food for Family Meals: Relationships with Parent and Adolescent Food Intake, Home Food Availability and Weight Status," *Public Health Nutrition* 10 (2007), 16–23; J. Kruger, H. M. Blanck, and C. Gillespie, "Dietary Practices, Dining Out Behavior and Physical Activity Correlates of Weight Loss Maintenance," *Preventing Chronic Disease: Public Health Research, Practice, and Policy* 5 (2008), 1–14; Heather M. Niemeier Hollie, Elizabeth E. Raynor, Lloyd-Richardson, Michelle L. Rogers, and Rena R. Wing, "Fast-Food Consumption and Breakfast Skipping: Predictors of Weight Gain from Adolescence to Adulthood in a Nationally Representative Sample," *Journal of Adolescent Health* 39 (2006): 842–49; Kiyah J. Duffey, Penny Gordon-Larsen, David R. Jacobs, O. Dale Williams, and Barry M. Popkin, "Differential Associations of Fast-Food and Restaurant

Food Consumption with 3-y Change in Body Mass Index: The Coronary Artery Risk Development in Young Adults (CARDIA) Study," *American Journal of Clinical Nutrition* 85.1 (2007): 201–8.

56. Cynthia Ogden, Margaret D. Carroll, Brian K. Kit, and Katherine M. Flegal, "Prevalence of Obesity in the United States, 2009–2010," National Center for Health Statistics Data Brief, No. 82 (January 2012): 1–8.

57. Block et al., "Fast Food, Race/Ethnicity, and Income," 211.

58. Jekanowski et al., "Convenience, Accessibility, and the Demand for Fast Food," 58.

59. Schlosser, *Fast Food Nation*, 3.

60. Chou et al., "An Economic Analysis of Adult Obesity," 568.

61. Ibid., 582.

62. Jekanowski et al., "Convenience, Accessibility, and the Demand for Fast Food," 58.

63. University of Wisconsin Population Health Institute, County Health Rankings & Roadmaps, accessed April 5, 2012, www.countyhealthrankings.org.

64. Boone-Heinonen et al., "Fast Food Restaurants and Food Stores," 1162–70.

65. Bowman and Vinyard, "Fast-Food Consumption of U.S. Adults," 166.

66. Brennan Davis and Christopher Carpenter, "Proximity of Fast-Food Restaurants to Schools and Adolescent Obesity," *American Journal of Public Health* 99.3 (March 2009): 505. The authors controlled for "student demographic characteristics, school characteristics, and . . . for the type of community in which the school was located" (508). To be sure, other considerations, such as these students' socioeconomic status, may have informed whether or not they were obese. Nevertheless, it would be telling if the neighborhoods of poorer students were more likely to be surrounded by fast food restaurants. On African-American and urban schoolchildren, see 508–9. The study's link between fast food and obesity was not observed among other racial and ethnic minorities.

67. Researchers in New Zealand, for example, have not found a clear relationship between geographic access to fast food restaurants and weight, or to fast food access and fruit and vegetable consumption. See Jamie Pearce, Rosemary Hisock, Tony Blakely, and Karen Whitten, "A National Study of the Association between Neighbourhood Access to Fast Food Outlets and the Diet and Weight of Local Residents," *Health & Place* 15 (2009): 193–97.

68. Thomas Burgoine, Nita G. Forouhi, Simon J. Griffin, Nichoas J. Wareham, and Pablo Monsivais, "Associations between Exposure to Takeaway Food Outlets, Takeaway Food Consumption, and Body Weight in Cambridgeshire, UK: Population Based, Cross Sectional Study," *British Medical Journal* 13 (March 2014), open access, PDF pages 1, 2, and 4 of 10, accessed 24 February 2015, http://www.bmj.com/content/348/bmj.g1464.full.pdf+html.

69. Daniel J. Kruger, Emily Greenberg, Jillian B. Murphy, Lindsay A. DiFazio, and Kathryn R. Youra, "Local Concentration of Fast-Food Outlets Is Associated

with Poor Nutrition and Obesity," *American Journal of Health Promotion* 28.5 (May/June 2014): 342.

70. Boone-Heinonen et al., "Fast Food Restaurants and Food Stores," 1162.

71. Fryar and Ervin, "Caloric Intake from Fast Food among Adults," 4; Stobbe, "Adults Get 11 Percent of Calories from Fast Food."

72. Kim and Leigh, "Are Meals at Full-Service and Fast-Food Restaurants 'Normal' or 'Inferior'?" 312.

73. Ibid.; Block et al., "Fast Food, Race/Ethnicity, and Income," 214.

74. University of Wisconsin Population Health Institute, County Health Rankings & Roadmaps; "Bronx County, New York Obesity Rates and Fast Food Consumption," FindTheData, accessed April 7, 2012, http://county-food .findthedata.org/l/1828/Bronx.

75. "Bronx County, New York Obesity Rates and Fast Food Consumption."

76. For more on the combined effects of poverty and deficient health care in urban America, see Laurie Abraham, *Mama Might Be Better Off Dead: The Failure of Health Care in Urban America* (Chicago: University of Chicago Press, 1993). Not all neighborhoods in the Bronx are impoverished. The Riverdale neighborhood, for instance, is affluent.

77. University of Wisconsin Population Health Institute, County Health Rankings & Roadmaps; Sabrina Tavernise, "Longevity Up in U.S., but Education Creates Disparity, Study Says," *New York Times*, April 3, 2012, A14. "Premature death" refers to death by preventable causes, and death before 75 years of age. For more on how the Bronx compares to other New York City boroughs, see Sewell Chan, "Data Show Manhattan Is Svelte, and Bronx Is Chubby, Chubby," *New York Times*, July 22, 2009, A18.

78. "U.S. Blacks Still Lag Whites in Life Expectancy," *MedlinePlus*, July 18, 2013, U.S. National Library of Medicine, National Institutes of Health, accessed July 29, 2013, https://www.nlm.nih.gov/medlineplus/news/fullstory_138840 .html.

CONCLUSION

1. See Sturm and Hattori, "Diet and Obesity in Los Angeles County, 2007–2012."

2. See Nestle, *Soda Politics.*

3. "McDonald's Pledges Healthier Promotions," United Press International, September 27, 2013, accessed November 17, 2015, http://www.upi.com /Business_News/2013/09/27/McDonalds-pledges-healthier-promotions /68001380292635/.

4. For a sense of how salad orders stack up to burgers at McDonald's, see Warner, "Salads or No, Cheap Burgers Revive McDonald's."

5. See Moss, *Salt Sugar Fat*; Kessler, *The End of Overeating.*

6. "Food Retail Expansion to Support Health," Official Website of the City of

New York, accessed November 17, 2015, http://www.nyc.gov/html/misc/html /2009/fresh.shtml.

7. David Bornstein, "Conquering Food Deserts with Green Carts," *New York Times* (Opinionator), April 18, 2012, accessed November 21, 2015, http:// opinionator.blogs.nytimes.com/2012/04/18/conquering-food-deserts-with -green-carts/.

8. Ridgeway, "Segregated Food at the Supermarket." As noted earlier, poor urbanites have long suspected that their neighborhood grocery stores are stocked with food inventory deemed no longer fit to sell at grocery stores in better-served communities.

9. For an account of the Healthy Corner Store Initiative in Philadelphia, see Mark Bittman, "Go Philly!" *New York Times* (Opinionator), April 5, 2011, accessed November 21, 2015, http://opinionator.blogs.nytimes.com/2011/04/05/go -philly/.

10. Hamida Kinge, "Pass the Peas: Making a Food Desert Bloom in the South Bronx," *Next City*, July 30, 2012, accessed November 17, 2015, https://nextcity.org /features/view/pass-the-peas.

11. Richard Casey Sadler, "Strengthening the Core, Improving Access: Bringing Healthy Food Downtown via a Farmers' Market Move," *Applied Geography* 67 (February 2016): 119–28.

12. Tracie McMillan, "In Flint, Mich., Moving the Farmer's Market Drew More Poor Shoppers," National Public Radio, February 19, 2016, http://www .npr.org/sections/thesalt/2016/02/19/467368993/in-flint-mich-moving-the -farmers-market-drew-more-poor-shoppers, accessed February 21, 2016.

13. Michele Ver Ploeg, Lisa Mancino, Jessica E. Todd, Dawn Marie Clay, and Benjamin Scharadin, "Where Do Americans Usually Shop for Food and How Do They Travel to Get There? Initial Findings from the National Household Food Acquisition and Purchase Survey," U.S. Department of Agriculture Economic Research Service *Economic Information Bulletin* 138 (March 2015): 13. This study indicates that in addition to cost, the quality and selection of food also influence where consumers obtain their groceries.

14. See Michael Pollan, "Farmer in Chief," *New York Times Magazine*, October 12, 2008, accessed November 19, 2015, http://michaelpollan.com/articles -archive/farmer-in-chief/.

15. Guthman, *Weighing In*, 122.

16. "USDA Awards $31 Million in Grants to Help SNAP Participants Afford Healthy Food," U.S. Department of Agriculture Press Release, March 31, 2015, accessed November 19, 2015, http://nifa.usda.gov/resource/usda-awards-31 -million-grants-help-snap-participants-afford-healthy-foods. The USDA pilot grants were awarded through the Food Insecurity Nutrition Incentive (FINI) grants in the 2014 Farm Bill.

17. For more on the success of a program in Philadelphia raising SNAP par-

ticipants' purchasing power on fruits and vegetables by 40 percent, see Bittman, "Go Philly!"

18. McWhorter, "The Food Desert Myth."

19. "About Us," Food Corps, accessed November 24, 2015, https://foodcorps .org/about. The figure for the number of school districts in the United States is from the U.S. Census Bureau. See "School Districts," United States Census Bureau, accessed November 24, 2015, https://www.census.gov/did/www /schooldistricts/.

20. The living allowance is current as of November 2015. In addition to the living allowance, service members may receive possible loan forbearance, health insurance, partial childcare subsidies, and a $5,730 "education award" that can be applied toward educational expenses and loans. See "Benefits," FoodCorps, accessed November 24, 2015, https://foodcorps.org/become-a-service-member /benefits.

21. For examples of food commentators who have proposed instituting home economics or cooking instruction under a different name, see Helen Zoe Veit, "Time to Revive Home Ec," *New York Times*, September 6, 2011, A27; Mark Bittman, "A Food Manifesto for the Future," *New York Times* (Opinionator), accessed November 24, 2015, http://opinionator.blogs.nytimes.com/2011/02/01/a-food -manifesto-for-the-future/.

22. Vivian Yee, "No Appetite for Good-for-You School Lunches," *New York Times*, October 6, 2012, A1.

23. Ariana Eunjung Cha, "Why the Healthy School Lunch Program Is in Trouble. Before/After Photos of What Students Ate," *Washington Post*, August 26, 2015, accessed November 25, 2015, https://www.washingtonpost.com /news/to-your-health/wp/2015/08/26/schoolchildren-are-tossing-an-average -of-more-than-a-third-cup-of-fruits-and-veggies-in-the-trash-each-lunch/.

24. Allison Aubrey, "Lunch Ladies Want Healthy Hunger-Free Kids Act to Lighten Up," National Public Radio, September 10, 2015, accessed November 25, 2015, http://www.npr.org/2015/09/08/438473608/lunch-ladies-want-healthy -hunger-free-kids-act-to-lighten-up.

25. Alison Leigh Cowan, "A Dining Hall Where Students Sneak In," *New York Times*, May 10, 2005, accessed November 25, 2015, http://www.nytimes.com /2005/05/10/nyregion/a-dining-hall-where-students-sneak-in.html.

26. Aubrey, "Lunch Ladies Want Healthy Hunger-Free Kids Act to Lighten Up."

27. *An Evaluation of the School Lunch Initiative: A Report by the Robert C. and Veronica Atkins Center for Weight and Health, University of California at Berkeley* (Berkeley: Chez Panisse Foundation, 2010), 1, accessed November 26, 2015, http:// www.schoollunchinitiative.org/downloads/sli_eval_full_report_2010.pdf.

28. Ibid.; Sarah Henry, "Berkeley's New School Food Study: A Victory for Alice Waters," *The Atlantic*, September 23, 2010, accessed November 25, 2015,

http://www.theatlantic.com/health/archive/2010/09/berkeleys-new-school
-food-study-a-victory-for-alice-waters/63465/.

29. Journalist Hamida Kinge describes a sixth-grader in the South Bronx
named Emely Liz who became a "proselytizer for healthier eating" after participating in an antiobesity initiative sponsored by the city of New York. See
Kinge, "Pass the Peas."

30. For the U.S. government's own figures on the costs of obesity and related
conditions to employers, see "Workplace Health Promotion," Centers for Disease Control and Prevention, last updated October 23, 2013, accessed November 26, 2015, http://www.cdc.gov/workplacehealthpromotion/businesscase
/reasons/productivity.html.

31. Guthman, *Weighing In*, 87.

32. Chin Jou, "The Biology and Genetics of Obesity—A Century of Inquiries,"
New England Journal of Medicine 370.20 (2014): 1874–77.

33. Guthman, *Weighing In*, 186.

34. For more on how poverty can affect people's diets, see Chin Jou, "Cutting
Food Stamps Will Cost Everyone," *The Atlantic*, June 17, 2013, accessed December 9, 2015, http://www.theatlantic.com/health/archive/2013/06/cutting-food
-stamps-will-cost-everyone/276905/.

35. Jou, "Fighting Obesity Requires a War on Poverty."

INDEX